A HISTORY
OF THE
UNDEAD

A HISTORY OF THE UNDEAD

MUMMIES, VAMPIRES AND ZOMBIES

CHARLOTTE BOOTH

PEN & SWORD
HISTORY

AN IMPRINT OF PEN & SWORD BOOKS LTD.
YORKSHIRE – PHILADELPHIA

First published in Great Britain in 2021 by
PEN AND SWORD HISTORY
An imprint of
Pen & Sword Books Ltd
Yorkshire – Philadelphia

ISBN 978 1 52676 906 0

Typeset in Times New Roman 11.5/14 by
SJmagic DESIGN SERVICES, India.
Printed and bound in the UK by TJ Books Ltd.

Pen & Sword Books Limited incorporates the imprints of Atlas, Archaeology,
Aviation, Discovery, Family History, Fiction, History, Maritime, Military, Military
Classics, Politics, Select, Transport, True Crime, Air World, Frontline Publishing,
Leo Cooper, Remember When, Seaforth Publishing, The Praetorian Press,
Wharncliffe Local History, Wharncliffe Transport, Wharncliffe True Crime and
White Owl.

For a complete list of Pen & Sword titles please contact
PEN & SWORD BOOKS LIMITED
47 Church Street, Barnsley, South Yorkshire, S70 2AS, England
E-mail: enquiries@pen-and-sword.co.uk
Website: www.pen-and-sword.co.uk

Or
PEN AND SWORD BOOKS
1950 Lawrence Rd, Havertown, PA 19083, USA
E-mail: Uspen-and-sword@casematepublishers.com
Website: www.penandswordbooks.com

Contents

Illustrations

Mummies

Fig 1 – Coffin for modern mummification. Copyright Summum. Used by Permission. All Rights Reserved.

Fig 2 – Mummy plant pot. Canada, Halloween 2019. Photograph Courtesy of David Valentine.

Fig 3 – The Jeremy Bentham auto-icon in a meeting at UCL. Photograph Courtesy of UCL Museums.

Fig 4 – Lord Carnarvon's grave on Beacon Hill at Highclere. Photograph by the author.

Zombies

Fig 5 – Halloween zombies, Canada 2019. Photograph courtesy of David Valentine.

Fig 6 – Mariachi Band at the Toronto Zombie Walk, 2011. Photograph by Stacie DaPonte. Wikimedia Commons.

Fig 7 – Decontamination suits at the Toronto Zombie Walk, 2011. Photograph by Stacie DaPonte. Wikimedia Commons.

Fig 8 – Zombie Island Massacre (1985) film poster. There is only one zombie in this film, which is part of a voodoo ritual. Courtesy of Free Classic Images https://freeclassicimages.com/Film_Posters.html

Vampires

Fig 9   – Whitby Abbey, Yorkshire. Photograph by the author.

Fig 10 – The Circle of Lebanon, Highgate Cemetery, where the Charles Fisher Wace Mausoleum is located. Picture by Michael Reeve, Wikimedia Commons.

Fig 11 – Bran Castle, Romania. Photograph by the author.

Fig 12 – Dracula's House, Sighisoara, Romania. Photograph courtesy of BKB Photography.

Fig 13 – The Dracula Experience at Dracula's House, Sighisoara, Romania. Photograph courtesy of BKB Photography.

Fig 14 – Vampire make-up kits, Halloween 2019. UK. Photograph by the author.

Introduction

In the modern West we are fascinated by reanimated corpses in the form of mummies, zombies and vampires, making them a popular addition to the media. In the following pages we will discuss all the ways in which the reanimated corpse is a fundamental part of literature, movies and popular culture and how this has changed over the past century. Why contemporary society is fascinated and entertained by the undead is not easy to pinpoint, but as a society we seem to revel in being scared by tales of things that go bump in the night.

This fascination with the reanimated dead, however, is not a modern phenomenon and has existed around the world for thousands of years. This ancient fascination was born out of superstition and a genuine fear of the dead returning rather than as macabre entertainment. This book will discuss in depth how these ancient origins have influenced the modern representation of the reanimated corpse. In a volume of this size it would be impossible to include every instance of the undead in world folklore so I have had to choose only those aspects that are relevant to the modern representation of mummies, zombies and vampires in the West. In much of the folklore the boundaries are blurred between the creatures, with the addition of werewolves and witches thrown into the mix. Unless they can clearly be identified as one of the three under discussion they have been omitted.

In pre-modern Fiji, for example, the fear of the dead was incorporated into a coming-of-age ceremony for young boys:

> 'Beginning with puberty, boys were taken at night to an area where the adult men had placed a group of bloody supposedly dead and decaying bodies covered with intestines. The boys were forced to crawl through the "dead" bodies which suddenly "came to life". Boys who showed fear were denied manhood.'[1]

Introduction

While a fascinating introduction to gender politics, superstition and a blatant disregard for hygiene, this case cannot be directly connect to common myths of vampires or zombies and therefore has been omitted from the discussion.

My own fascination with the undead came from my career as an Egyptologist and, therefore, a passion for mummies. I have even written about 'The Curse of the Mummy' in two publications (*The Curse of the Mummy* (Oneworld) and *The Myth of Ancient Egypt* (Amberley)) but wanted to explore mummies further as well as extend the research process to other reanimated corpses. However, the myth of the reanimated mummy is remarkably different from the myths of vampires and zombies. I found this extremely disappointing as the difference is such that it could almost be argued that they should not be included in this book. This is because the myth of the reanimated mummy is a modern Western construct taken from literature and adapted by the movies, whereas vampires and zombies have a far longer folkloric history. There is, therefore, less distinction between the Western media's reanimated mummy (Chapter 1) and the origin story (Chapter 2). Everything is connected to the curse mythology devised from literature and perpetuated by the archaeologists themselves. There are in fact more people today who believe in the curse of the mummy and the perceived danger than a century ago when the myth was created; which in itself is a fascinating social observation.

For many years I have been an avid fan of horror movies and books and so it seemed a natural progression to combine my love of horror with my love of research and write a book about it. It is a great feeling to declare watching B-movie zombie flicks as 'research' and be able to state 'I'm working' while watching *True Blood*. I have learned, though, while writing this book that the undead genre is bigger than I anticipated and each section could be developed further into a book of its own. This book, therefore, could be considered an introduction to the history of the undead.

It is laid out in three sections: Mummies, Zombies and Vampires. Each section is divided into two chapters: the first outlining how the reanimated corpse in question is presented in the modern West in movies, literature and other media where appropriate; the second then investigates the history behind the modern representations, looking at folklore, mythology, religion and archaeology. Wherever possible, first-hand accounts and primary sources are used, but when dealing with folklore and superstition a lot of the evidence is hearsay.

The section on vampires also has an additional chapter. Chapter 6 investigates the modern vampire. Unlike the genre of zombies and mummies, vampires have inspired a sub-culture of society who choose to lead a vampire lifestyle. This extends to drinking blood, being nocturnal and having fangs created.

The objective of this book is to offer a deeper insight into the world of the undead. Hopefully it will offer information previously unknown, inspire questions and introduce new movies or literature to whet your appetite. The reanimated corpse is, strangely, a part of everyday life, included in our day-to-day language with easily recognisable imagery and characteristics known by all generations. How have such corpses in the form of zombies, mummies and vampires entered the twenty-first century; one that is governed by technology and science? Read on to find out.

Chapter 1

Mummies in the West

Introduction

Mummies are a relatively new introduction to Western media; only really making an appearance in the early twentieth century. They are inevitably associated with the mummified human remains from ancient Egypt and were therefore more prolific once Egyptology as a discipline became more mainstream at the end of the nineteenth century.

So what is a 'traditional' mummy in Western media? Essentially, mummies presented in literature, movies and television series are reanimated corpses wrapped in bandages. As Dendle commented in 2001, 'a mummy is just a zombie with bandages,'[1] which to a certain extent is true.

Unlike zombies, how mummies are reanimated is not always considered that important to the plot. A typical trope in both movies and literature is that reanimation is often due to a curse cast upon the person by ancient Egyptian necromancers, making them victims rather than perpetrators.

It is an interesting twist to the mummy 'history' that the British were once thought to be such necromancers, as Egyptologist, Arthur Mace, wrote in his journal (February 6, 1900):

> 'The Arabs have a very curious notion as to the reason why
> we take so many skeletons. They think that in England we
> are very short of men, and so being very great magicians we
> can take these bones and bring them to life again.'[2]

In literature and movies, however, Western necromancers are rarely the ones who bring mummies back to life, despite the Egyptians'

1

superstitions to the contrary. The necromancers are always represented as being Egyptian; often descendants of the ancients.

Although mummies are the product of such necromancers, when reanimated they are considered 'evil' and intent on causing harm even though they are under control of their masters. This adds fuel to the further popular theme of the 'curse of the mummy,' which is visited upon its unfortunate victims. This will be discussed further in the following chapter.

Mummy Medicine

Mummies, unlike zombies and vampires, have been embraced in an entirely different way in the West; possibly because they are 'real' and can be viewed in museums. They have also been used in a practical way due to their very tangible and real nature.

One of the most bizarre practical applications of mummies is as a medicament. For hundreds of years in the West people knowingly ingested ground-up corpse – known as *mummia* – for their health. *Mummia* has been recorded as a medicine since the tenth century and one of the earliest records is of a Persian physician called Avicenna (980–1037 CE), who claimed *mummia* was used for treating abscesses, eruptions, fractures, concussions, paralysis, epilepsy, vertigo, blood from the lungs, throat, coughs, nausea and disorders of the liver and spleen. It was mixed with herbs before being taken internally.[3]

Whether this early *mummia* had any connection to mummies is unlikely as the name *mummia* was closely associated with a type of bitumen that flowed from a mountain in Persia. When mixed with water it gave off an odour considered beneficial when inhaled. However, the practice of mummification in the later years of Egyptian history included coating the body in a layer of bitumen as an aid to preservation. It is therefore likely that as the name *mummia* was so similar it was soon to be considered as the same. The earlier records of *mummia* as medicine probably referred to bitumen whereas by the sixteenth century *mummia* was made with ground mummies.

Records of *mummia* being ingested by the rich and influential of Western society for their health become more prevalent in the sixteenth century. In 1549 André Thevat, chaplain to Catherine de Medici, queen of France between 1547 and 1559, is recorded as travelling on expedition to search for mummies for medicine in Saqqara.[4]

It is also recorded that the physician John Hall (1575–1635), Shakespeare's son-in-law, used *mummia* to treat a case of epilepsy. He added it to a mixture of black pitch, benzoic resin and juice of rue and had his patient inhale the smoke when it was burned,[5] perhaps closer to the original use of *mummia* bitumen.

Royalty were known to take *mummia*, with François I of France (1515–1547) mixing it with rhubarb to treat all manner of ailments from headaches to broken bones.[6] Even Britain's Queen Victoria was recorded as using it when the King of Persia sent her some from the mummy mountain in Persia.[7] This was, however, more likely to be bitumen than powdered mummy.

Once the popularity of the medicine became apparent among the wealthy, there was a prolific trade in human and animal mummies from Egypt to Europe to meet demand. Thomas Pettigrew in his *History of Egyptian Mummies* (1834) said: 'No sooner was it credited that mummy constituted an article of value in the practice of medicine than many speculators embarked in the trade; the tombs were sacked, and as many mummies as could be obtained were broken into pieces for the purpose of sale.'[8]

People were buying mummies in bulk for medicines and it is recorded that in 1564 Guy de la Fontaine, the physician of the king of Navarre (a Basque-based kingdom bear the Pyrenees), purchased a bulk order of mummies for this purpose. However, he was horrified to note they were not the genuine article and were, in fact, no older than four years.

The supply and demand disparity started the trade in unclaimed bodies of criminals and the poor. De la Fontaine investigated the trade and discovered that such 'unclaimed wretches were treated with bitumen and then aged in the sun, producing a rather good likeness of ancient mummified flesh.'[9] Pettigrew further added that one particular merchant stated: 'he cared not when they came, whether they were old or young, male or female, or of what disease they had died, so long as he could obtain them … when embalmed no one could tell.'[10]

Indeed, even fake mummies were put together with so-called children's mummies, being made of ibises or even the flesh of camels moulded into the right shape.[11] Such fakes had been in circulation from about 1200 CE onwards,[12] and there are numerous tales of people purchasing fake mummies believing them to be the genuine article.

However, they were not always the bodies of the poor and criminal classes. W.M.F. Petrie, the eminent Egyptologist, was told of a tourist who had bought a mummy from Aswan, which was eventually identified as the body of an English engineer who had died there.

This entrepreneurial idea was later adopted in Anne Rice's novel *The Mummy*, where Henry Stratford, the well-born, gambling drunk was murdered and ended up 'floating in the bitumen,'[13] turning him into a lovely mummy for tourists to buy.

The practice, while a common one, was generally condemned, and as early as 1645 an apothecary admonished his staff for selling 'arm or a leg of a decaying or hanged leper or of some whorehopper suffering from syphilis' as genuine mummy.[14]

The threat of purchasing a fake, however, did not deter people from purchasing such a souvenir from their trip to Egypt. Many ended up as *mummia* until as recently as 1908 when it was still being sold as a cure-all medicine. It was advised that it should be applied to the affected area or ingested in water. It was not only in the West either that *mummia* was considered useful. In Egypt at this time it was mixed with butter as a cure for bruises.[15]

Surprisingly, using *mummia* in medicine was not considered quackery, and there were some distinguished members of Western society who advocated its use. Francis Bacon (1561–1626), for example, believed it 'hath great force in staunching of blood',[16] and the Irish philosopher, chemist and physicist Robert Boyle (1627–1691) recommended it for falls and bruises,[17] following the native Egyptian use of it.

It is likely that using *mummia* fell out of popularity, not due to the horror of consuming dead human flesh, but the growth in scientific thinking, as well as the rumour that it may have been instrumental in spreading the plague.[18] Although the demand plummeted, as recently as 1973 a New York store sold powdered mummy as a witches' supply,[19] although whether it was the 'genuine article' has not been confirmed.

Art Materials

Medicine was not the only dubious use of crushed corpses. Artists were also prolific users of ground-up mummies in the paint colour known as 'Mummy Brown', *caput mortuum* or Egyptian Brown. This colour was popular from the early 1700s but by the 1960s it was falling out of fashion as the supply of mummies came to an end.

The paint was produced by London manufacturer, C. Roberson who stocked and sold 'Mummy Brown' throughout the 1920s and 1930s. By the 1960s, sales were declining and in 1964 the managing director said: 'We might have a few odd limbs lying around somewhere, but not enough to make any more paint.'[20]

It is recorded that one Egyptian mummy provided enough material to produce paint to satisfy their artists for two decades.[21] To produce the paint, crushed mummy was mixed with white pitch and myrrh producing a rich colour which by the mid-nineteenth century was very popular. 'The pigment itself wasn't easily imitated. It wasn't just made of regular long-dried out corpses. The mummification process involved asphaltum or bitumen, often in place of the removed organs. Whole mummies were then ground for commercial and just plain wrong use. Mummy Brown was a fugitive colour, meaning it faded easily.'[22]

However, despite the name not everyone was aware of the grisly ingredients. Once these became common knowledge it contributed to the decline in popularity.

There is one well-known tale of the funeral of a tube of Mummy Brown, which is recounted by the widow of Pre-Raphaelite artist Edward Burne-Jones, Georgina. She recalls how Lawrence Alma-Tadema and his family were visiting them: 'We were sitting together after lunch ... the men talking about different colours that they used, when Mr Tadema startled us by saying he had lately been invited to go and see a mummy that was in his colourman's workshop before it was ground down into paint.' The artists did not believe the paint was made with real mummy, stating it must simply be a clever name. 'When assured that it was actually compounded of real mummy, he left us at once, hastened to the studio, and returning with the only tube he had, insisted on our giving it decent burial there and then. So a hole was bored in the green grass at our feet, and we all watched it put safely in, and the spot was marked by one of the girls planting a daisy root above it.'[23]

At the height of the use of Mummy Brown paint Isaac Augustus Stanwood, an American paper manufacturer, was also using mummy wrappings to make brown paper. This was then sold to butchers and grocers to wrap food for sale. When there was an outbreak of cholera the paper was no longer made or used, though whether the outbreak was due to the paper was never proved.[24]

Although mummies were used as a commodity for both medicine and paint for centuries there were people who objected to the practice. As early as 1658, the philosopher Sir Thomas Browne stated: 'The Egyptian mummies, which Cambyses or time hath spared, avarice now consumeth. Mummie is become Merchandise, Mizraim cures wounds, and Pharaoh is sold for Balsoms[25] ... surely such diet is dismal vampirism; and exceeds in horror the black banquet of Domitan, not to be paralleled expect in those Arabian feasts, wherein Ghoules feed horribly.'[26]

Mummies for Entertainment

The nineteenth century was the height of archaeological practice in Egypt and there was, therefore, a large supply of mummies which, as discussed, were used in medicine and paint production. They were also often the centre of an entertaining evening, disguised as education, in the form of 'mummy unrollings.'

These were essentially upper-class soirées where the main entertainment of the night was the unrolling of a mummy, revealing the corpse within. These unrollings were not carried out by trained doctors or even Egyptologists but were instead carried out by the wealthy owners of the townhouse where the entertainment was being held, or the tourist who bought the mummy.

The earliest recorded unrolling was in September 1698 when Benoit de Maillet (1656–1738), the consul in Cairo of Louis XIV, unwrapped a mummy for a group of French travellers. He did not record anything other than a few of the amulets that were discovered on the body.[27] Trinkets such as these were considered one of the most important aspects of the unrollings.

In 1715 Christopher Hertzog, apothecary to the Duke of Saxe-Gotha, unwrapped a mummy and recorded some of his findings in his book *Mummiographia*, before he ground it down to be sold as medicine.[28]

Such public unrollings became so popular that one held by Thomas Pettigrew (1791–1865) in Charing Cross in April 1833 was so crowded with antiquarians, excavators, Egyptologists, Members of Parliament, artists, authors, peers, princesses, military officers, statesmen and diplomats, that when the Archbishop of Canterbury showed up he was turned away. However, he was given a private showing at a later date.[29]

At this period in history mummies were being unrolled regularly, which did little to expand knowledge of mummification and destroyed a lot of archaeological evidence.

A mummy has not been unwrapped since the unwrapping of 'mummy 1770' in 1975 at Manchester University Museum. This mummy was chosen to be investigated as it was unimpressive with no elaborate wrappings and was not in good enough condition for display in the museum. Despite the wrappings there was a gilded cartonnage funerary mask with inlaid eyes and eyebrows as well as gilded slippers over her feet. This scientific unwrapping and investigation of the body took two weeks to complete and everything was meticulously recorded.[30]

Unlike the nineteenth-century unrollings, mummy 1770's unwrapping was carried out scientifically and all pathology of the mummy was studied and recorded. Once unwrapped, the mummy was then x-rayed, identifying that the lower parts of both of her legs had been amputated. The left just below the knee and the right just above the knee. Bony growths at the end of the legs were minimal and suggest this amputation happened a couple of weeks before death. The embalmers had made prosthetics out of wood, which were splinted to the remainder of the limbs, and covered with a moulded layer of mud.

Upon completion of the unwrapping, the face of mummy 1770 was reconstructed using the numerous pieces of the broken skull. This was problematic as each piece had to be separately cast in methacrylate (a form of cold curing casting plastic) before attempting to rebuild the skull. When completed they discovered that large pieces of it were missing. These gaps were then modelled from wax and a cast was made of the completed skull in order to create a facial reconstruction.[31]

Reanimated Body Parts

As the sale of mummies became popular in the nineteenth century, so too did the sale of individual body parts: a mummified hand or foot for example. Mummy parts were cheaper to buy than a whole mummy, easier to export back from Egypt, and more widely available. They were considered interesting curiosities. Since 1968 *Ripley's Believe it or Not* in San Francisco has had a mummy hand on display, and they created an interesting backstory to make it more appealing. They claimed it once

7

wore a cursed golden disc causing the death of Walter Ingram, who acquired it.[32]

> WALTER INGRAM of London, England, brought back from Egypt in 1884 the mummified hand of an ancient Egyptian princess, which was found to be clutching a gold plaque inscribed:
>
> "Whoever takes me away to a foreign country will die a violent death and his bones will never be found!"
>
> 4 years later Ingram was trampled to death by a rogue elephant near Berbera, Somaliland, and his remains were buried in the dry bed of a river but an exhibition sent to recover his body found a flood had washed it away.[33]

It is believed that *Ripley's Believe it or Not* have a number of mummified hands, always displayed alongside this particular story.

A mummified body part also became a useful tool for horror writers and tellers of tall tales as they could become reanimated and cause havoc. One such tale concerns the mummified hand of Meketaten, a daughter of Akhenaten. This hand was owned by a psychic called Cheiro who apparently warned Lord Carnarvon that he would die if he took anything from the tomb of Tutankhamun during the excavation (see Chapter 2).

This hand apparently became reanimated and oozed fresh blood. In an attempt to staunch the bleeding Cheiro soaked it in pitch and shellac although this only worked as a temporary fix. The hand was used by the psychic as a paperweight, and the day before the tomb of Tutankhamun was discovered he cremated it. It was after the cremation that Meketaten visited the psychic twice to warn him of the curse that would befall Carnarvon at the violation of the tomb of Tutankhamun.[34] Ironically, no curse fell upon Cheiro who had violated a corpse by using the hand as a paperweight.

The account Cheiro gives of the mummy's hand is remarkably similar to Theophile Gautier's short story *The Mummy's Foot* written in 1840. The narrator goes into an old curiosity shop to purchase something to use as a paperweight. He chooses the mummified foot of princess Hermonthis, which at first he thought was bronze:

> I was surprised at its lightness. It was not a foot of metal but in sooth a foot of flesh, an embalmed foot, a mummy's foot.

On examining it still more closely the very grain of the skin, and the almost imperceptible lines impressed upon it by the texture of the bandages, became perceptible. The toes were slender and delicate, and terminate by perfectly formed nails, pure and transparent as agates. The great toe, slightly separated from the rest, afforded a happy contrast, in the antique style, to the position of the other toes, and lent it an aerial lightness – the grace of a bird's foot. The sole, scarcely streaked by a few almost imperceptible cross lines afforded evidence that it had never touched the bare ground, and had only come in contact with the finest matting of Nile rushes and the softest carpets of panther skin.

In this story the foot reanimates one evening while he is asleep amid a wonderful waft of perfume. '[It] contracted itself, and leaped over the papers like a startled frog. One would have imagined that it had suddenly been brought into contact with a galvanic battery ... I became rather discontented with my acquisition, inasmuch as I wished my paper-weights to be of a sedentary disposition.'

Princess Hermonthis then appeared in order to reclaim her foot, and there is a rather bizarre exchange between the princess and her foot. The narrator gives her the foot back and she repays him with a trip to visit her father and other mummified ancestors to show that she has once more reacquainted with her extremity. When meeting her father the narrator then asks for her hand in marriage. Certain elements of this story make it clear that it was meant to be a light-hearted romantic comedy rather than a horror story.

Modern Mummification

Egyptian mummies are such a focus of interest that many wealthy people in the West, from the nineteenth century through to the modern day, have requested mummification after death.

Alexander, tenth Duke of Hamilton (1757–1852), for example, asked Thomas Pettigrew to mummify him upon his death. His wishes were carried out and he was placed in a Ptolemaic sarcophagus, which he had purchased at auction in 1836, inside the Hamilton Mausoleum in the grounds of Hamilton Palace. The tomb was found to be structurally unsound due to being undermined by coal mining, and in 1921 a number of Dukes of Hamilton were moved to the Bent cemetery, Hamilton.[35] It is thought he still rests here in his sarcophagus.

Even in 2020, at the time of writing, it was possible to be mummified after death. Summum, based in Salt Lake City, Utah USA will perform a mummification for $67,000 (see fig. 1):

> A very thorough, detailed, yet gentle process that allows one to be memorialised for eternity, Mummification is the only form of Permanent Preservation. The rites of Mummification of Transference allow you to leave this life in as beautiful a manner as possible.
>
> Our in depth research, experience, and knowledge in realms of both science and esoterica has resulted in Modern Mummification® – a synthesis of medical technology, modern chemistry, and esoteric art. Still, our process of Mummification includes traditional wrappings in fine cloth (embroidered, representing your personal philosophy or religion).[36]

For an additional cost, Summum's clients can opt for a bespoke mummiform coffin, made to individual specifications out of bronze or steel. If mummifying loved ones is out of your price range, Summum will also mummify pets, costing between $4,000 and $28,000 depending on the animal's size, and if a mummiform coffin is also required an additional $5,000 to more than $100,000 will be required.

Mummies in Literature

One of the earliest references to mummies in literature is in Shakespeare, who mentions *mummia* in both *Othello* and *The Merry Wives of Windsor*. In *Othello* it refers to using mummified virgins' hearts as a dye, which may have been a forerunner of the paint colour that was to prove popular in the nineteenth century:

> The worms were hallow'd that did breed the silk;
> And it was dyed in mummy which the skilful
> Conserved of maidens' hearts. (Act III, scene 4)

The reference in *The Merry Wives of Windsor* is more obscure and refers to dying and swelling up to resemble a mummified corpse:

> 'I had been drowned, but that the shore was shelvy and shallow, a death that I abhor; for the water swells a man; and what a thing should I have been when I had been swelled! I should have been a mountain of mummy.' (Act III, scene v).

It should be noted that while in the modern world Shakespeare is considered a highbrow form of literature, at the time it was written it was popular theatre for the commoners. This means that despite the cultural disparity and geographical distance, references to mummy would have been well-known enough even by hearsay by the common people for them to be understood.

In the nineteenth century at the height of mummy unrollings the knowledge they provided leaked into the literature of the time: no doubt because the literati were among the guests. In early literature one of the key reasons for reanimating mummies was for them to speak and provide information. For example, in *Jerry Todd and the Whispering Mummy*[37] the mummy was forced to speak,[38] and in Edgar Allan Poe's *Some Words with a Mummy* the mummy and narrator, in a rather civilised manner, discuss the benefits of the modern era. Poe was heavily influenced by Shelley's *Frankenstein* as electricity is fundamental in reanimating the corpse: 'The application of electricity to a mummy some three or four thousand years old at the least, was an idea, if not very sage, still sufficiently original, and we all caught it at once. About one tenth in earnest and nine tenths in jest, we arranged a battery in the Doctor's study, and conveyed thither the Egyptian.'

Gradually, the knowledge mummies could provide was overtaken by the grotesqueness of their appearance and they were then adopted into the horror genre. In Louisa May Alcott's *Lost in a Pyramid* (1869) she describes the mummy as: '[a] shrivelled specimen, perched like a hobgoblin on the little shelves where the dead used to be stowed for ages.'

In Mary Shelley's *Frankenstein* the description of the monster prior to reanimation is very similar to a mummy, indicating that mummies were well-known images in Victorian society and suitably gruesome for gothic horror: 'His limbs were in proportion, and I had selected his features as beautiful. Beautiful! Great God! His yellow skin scarcely covered the work of muscles and arteries beneath; his hair was of a lustrous black, and flowing; his teeth of a pearly whiteness; but these luxuriances only formed a more horrid contrast with his watery eyes, that seemed almost of the same colour as the dun-white sockets in which they were set, his shrivelled complexion and straight black lips.'[39]

Indeed, *Frankenstein* and the earliest *The Mummy* movie, produced in 1911 by Thanhouse Company, had some crossovers. In *The Mummy* Jack Thornton purchased a mummy and reanimated it by using electricity. The body that emerged from the coffin was one of a beautiful Egyptian princess. When Jack refuses her advances the princess turns him into a mummy and he is placed in the coffin in her stead. She changes her mind just in the nick of time as Professor Dix is about to cut into the 'mummy', and saves him.

One of the earliest cursed mummy stories is a children's book from 1827, written by twenty-five-year-old English author Jane Loudon Webb. She bases her story in England in 2126. Her protagonist, Edric, wishes to reanimate a corpse but knows that the only way to identify a true corpse is through putrefaction. He asks: 'But where shall I find a body, which has been dead a sufficient time to prevent the possibility of its being only in a trance, and which yet has not begun to decompose?' Obviously a mummy is the only answer as the process of mummification prevents putrefaction.

Loudon Webb was inspired by watching a mummy unrolling carried out by Giovanni Belzoni, an explorer who discovered the tomb of Sety I.[40] In her tale *The Mummy; a tale of the 22nd century* the mummy was reanimated only to strangle the hero, following the style of Shelley's *Frankenstein* with a man-made monster. This was to become a common trope throughout much of the mummy fiction that was to follow.

An anonymous story from 1862, *The Mummy's Soul*, sees an archaeologist unwrapping a female mummy which then crumbles away. He gathers some of the dust from the mummy along with an ancient fly. He uses a scarab, which claims the mummy will reanimate after 3,000 years, to reanimate the fly, which then drains the blood of the archaeologist's wife so she 'resembles the mummy in the tomb'. The archaeologist is then bitten by the insect, but he puts up a fight and kills it by hitting it with the vase containing the mummy's ashes. These intermingle with his blood and the mummy is once more reanimated. The narrator runs from his house in terror.[41]

Jane Austen also wrote a story about a mummy in 1868, called *After Three Thousand Years*. The main character, Millard Vance, takes a scarab with diamond eyes and green enamel wings from a princess's mummy for his sweetheart. The scarab is inscribed with a curse and she initially refuses to wear it. She is eventually persuaded to put it on and is later found dead after the scarab pierces her neck with its claws and kills her.[42] Millard Vance laments: 'I never have quite forgiven myself for stealing [the mummy's treasure], or for burning her.'[43]

Louisa M. Alcott's 1869 story, *Lost in a Pyramid*, or *The Mummy's Curse,* follows a similar theme. The main character, Forsyth, steals some seeds from a female mummy he discovers in a pyramid. In order to escape from the labyrinth of corridors Forsyth and his companion, Niles, build a fire, burning the coffin and the mummy. Within the box holding the seeds was a small piece of parchment stating the mummy was a very powerful sorceress.

Forsyth burns the seeds to prevent Evelyn from planting them, but one of them escapes the flames and Forsyth gets Niles to secretly plant it. It grows into a serpent-headed flower that saps the life out of Niles and Evelyn: 'Alas for the young wife! The superstitious fear at which she had smiled had proved true: the curse that had bided its time for ages was fulfilled at last, and her own hand had wrecked her happiness for ever. Death in life was her doom, and for years Forsyth secluded himself to tend with pathetic devotion the pale ghost, who never, by word or look, could thank him for the love that outlived even such a fate as this.'

Sir Arthur Conan Doyle was an avid believer in the curse theory[44] and this leaked into his writing. In 1892 he wrote *Lot No. 249* which was about a mummy purchased at an auction and reanimated by an Oxford student. The student then used the mummy as a weapon. Conan Doyle was the first author to use a live mummy to act violently on the behalf of another.[45]

He then wrote the novel *The Ring of Thoth*, which followed the popular theme of lovers across the millennia. The story tells of Sosra, an attendant at the Louvre Egyptian department. He was an ancient Egyptian priest of Osiris from Avaris who possessed an immortality potion. He had intended to drink it with his lover but she had died before she was able to. Parmes, his colleague, had been working on an antidote to the potion, which would allow Sosra to die and be with the woman he loves. Sosra then found out that a tomb had been discovered in Avaris with the body of a young woman inside. He manages to get into the tomb, open the coffin and finally look into the face of his lost love. He then takes the potion and dies in her arms.

Theophile Gautier's short story, *The Mummy's Foot* (1840) and book, *The Romance of the Mummy* (1857), explores themes of eroticism and death. In the book, archaeologists discover the body of Queen Tahoser, who was the daughter of a high priest during the Exodus. The body was perfectly preserved and it was the first example in a novel of the living falling in love with the dead:[46] 'As for Lord Evandale, he has never cared to marry, although he is lord of his race. The young ladies cannot understand his coldness towards the fair sex, but would they in all likelihood ever imagine that Lord Evandale is in love retrospectively with Tahoser, a daughter of the high-priest Pelamounoph, who died three thousand five hundred years ago?'[47]

Another book that follows this theme of the living falling in love with the dead is that of Anne Rice's *The Mummy*, or *Ramses the Damned*. An expedition to Egypt uncovers the tomb of Ramses II, but they are confused by the Greek and Latin inscriptions in the tomb and the references to Cleopatra who lived 1,000 years after his death.

It was discovered that Ramses had used an elixir of life that kept him alive. He refused to give it to Antony, resulting in Cleopatra taking her own life to be with him. Ramses was distraught and ordered that he be buried alive.

Following discovery, the contents of his tomb, including his mummy, are returned to London: 'Rice's mummy is a benevolent, handsome devil who adapts to modern times as Reginald Ramsey.'[48] Trouble starts when Ramsey spots an unknown mummy in the British Museum and recognises her immediately as Cleopatra. He administers the elixir but she had been left too long and was damaged beyond redemption.

Throughout the book he is helped by Julie, the daughter of the archaeologist who discovered the tomb, and a romance develops between them. A perfect example of the 'human falling in love with the mummy' plot.

Rice was clearly influenced in her writing by H. Rider Haggard and his book *She* (1887), which tells the story of an immortal queen from the late period of Egyptian history. Although she is not a mummy, she is immortal, like Reginald Ramsey. The only mention of mummies in the novel is in their use as torches: 'I stared and stared again – he was perfectly right – the torches that were to light our entertainment were human mummies from the caves.'[49]

Moving away from the elixir of life plots and inter-millennia romance, in 1911 *The Eye of Osiris*, first published as *The Vanishing Man* and written by R. Austin Freeman, introduces the mummy detective story. The detective, Dr Thorndyke, is investigating the disappearance of John Bellingham, an Egyptologist. The body has not been found and it is suspected that he has been murdered. Two years later body parts are discovered which could belong to Bellingham. However, it soon transpires that he had in fact been mummified and placed on display in the museum. This harkens back to the nineteenth-century mummy trade where fake mummies were created using the bodies of criminals, or in this case, a murder victim.

Another take on the mummy detective genre is that of *The Judgement of the Mummy* (2008)[50] in which Professor Higgins, a top British detective, and his sidekick, Lady Suzanna, are investigating the murder of three men with embalming hooks: an elderly lord, a pathologist and a priest. All three had demanded the destruction of a beautifully preserved mummy that Giovanni Belzoni had displayed in London. The mummy had been discovered with a papyrus that stated:

> 'Living one, who pass by my house of eternity, make a libation on my behalf, for I am master of the secret. My head is fixed to my neck, my limbs are put back together and my bones knitted, and my body will not decay. I was asleep and I have awakened. The great god will judge profaners. Anyone who assaults a mummy, anyone who attacks it, will not be welcomed into the Western goddess's bosom. Criminals will suffer the second death, and the Soul Eater will destroy them.'[51]

The mummy also conveniently disappeared on the night the three men were brutally murdered. The novel ends with the mummy lying on a table in the middle of the courtroom in order to stand trial for 'four murders and reducing six people to a state of living death'.[52] Here we also learn that Lady Suzanna is a reincarnation of the mummy's lover,[53] just touching on the inter-millennia romance plot line.

Elizabeth Peters, in her Amelia Peabody books, brings the detective genre a new lease of life and makes great use of mummies. In *The Curse of the Pharaohs* (1981),[54] at the moment the archaeologists are about to enter the tomb an anonymous voice from the crowd shouts: 'Desecration! Desecration! May the curse of the gods fall on him who disturbs the king's eternal rest.'[55] Later in the story an imam further emphasises the danger the archaeologists are in by stating ominously: 'I bring no blessing but a warning. Will you risk the curse of the Almighty? Will you profane the dead?'[56]

From the beginning of the novel the main character, Egyptologist Amelia Peabody, makes it clear she does not believe in the curse, and ascertains that someone is in fact using the superstitions of the locals to cover a murder. This is a common plot tool in the mummy genre: the archaeologists are warned about the 'curse' or impending danger before entering a tomb, which they all ignore. This will be discussed further below.

Terry Pratchett, in his fantasy Disc World series, introduces the concept of a dour, humanised mummy, which is a theme adopted by most children's literature. In his *Pyramids* (1989) we follow the story of Pteppic, the son of a king who was training in the Assassin's Guild in Ankh Morpork. While training, his father dies and he inherits the throne of the desert kingdom of Djelibeybi.

The mummy of the king, however, is not, according to tradition, tatty and terrifying. Instead he is dour and glib. When his coffin is heaved open by Dios the immortal high priest, who pretty much had ruled the kingdom for centuries, does not react well: 'Don't bother to knock,' the king grumbles. 'It's not as if I'm going anywhere.'[57] When Pteppic re-enters the kingdom of Djelibeybi he wants to destroy the great pyramid, and with the help of 'resurrected ancestors', or mummies, he does so.

The power of the priests, like Dios in Pratchett's book, is commonly used throughout the mummy genre, including in Lumley's horror novel, *Khai of Ancient Khem* (1980). The High Priest, Anulep, had the ability to reanimate the dead and control them: '"Dead, eh, boy? Dead and falling into decay, returning to dust. Ah, but they have known the touch of the Dark Seven! They are not incorruptible, no – but neither are they wholly dead – not yet. Look!" And from a pocket he took a tiny golden whistle which he put to his lips. He blew a single note and eerie, undulating note … and at once the air was full of a leathery creaking, the suffocating stink of death and motion!'[58]

Not all reanimated mummy demonstrations are so gruesome, however, and are often included in comedies and cartoons. For example, in the Egyptian special of the afternoon UK television chat show, *The New Paul*

O'Grady Show[59] a reanimated mummy was the main 'gag'. It lay calmly on the couch while the Egyptologist (the author) explained the mummification process, only to sit up and attack the host of the show (Paul O'Grady).

Mummies also feature heavily in children's literature, either as creative fiction or 'true stories', albeit it with a horror twist. For example, in *True Horror Stories* by Terry Deary there is a chapter on *The Mummy's Curse* which tells the story of the mummy of the princess Amen-Ra who had been stabbed to death by a lover. The mummy was purchased in Luxor by tourists, who subsequently all died in unusual circumstances. The mummy then found her way into the British Museum where she started causing more havoc with one workman breaking a leg and another, who had flicked the mummy with a duster, suffering the death of his child through measles. The museum decided to sell the mummy on, and inadvertently sold it to an American archaeologist who transported it to the US on the ill-fated Titanic.[60] This is one of the many curse conspiracy stories that will be discussed in the next chapter.

A young adult offering by Justin Richards introduces a juxtaposition between mummies and vampires. The novel, set in London in 1886, starts with the unrolling of an Egyptian mummy called Orabis in the British Museum. During the unrolling, the mummy is revived as Professor Brinson, who was performing the task, cut his wrist accidentally and: 'a cascade falling into the open mouth of the wrapped figure ... steam was rising from the point where the blood had dripped, drifting away in a faint mist to reveal the weathered, parchment-like skin beneath.'[61]

This mummy is in fact a vampire, as is proved when the scholars at the museum develop the photographs of the mummy before it was unrolled, only to show an empty casket. Vampires clearly cannot be photographed. This is discussed further in Chapter 5.

Although a vampire, Orabis, Lord of the Dead, was a true mummy and had been embalmed: 'They embalmed him according to ancient lore. They prepared canopic jars, as is the custom. But as well as the lungs and the liver and the intestine and the stomach being placed in jars fashioned after the sons of Horus, a fifth jar was prepared. And this was in the form of Nehebkau the Scorpion, Guardian of the gates to the Underworld. And into this jar was placed the heart of Orabis, removed from his chest by Heba, daughter of Pharaoh even as it still beat and pumped lifeblood.'[62]

Jackson and Livingstone take a completely different approach to their children's book, *The Curse of the Mummy*,[63] which is a game and a book all in one. The basic premise of the story is that the reader will be helping an archaeologist who discovers a tomb in the Desert of Skulls that belongs to Akharis. Some unscrupulous fellows are attempting to bring this ancient king back to life and it is up to the reader to save the day.

Throughout the book the reader has to make a number of decisions such as: 'Answer, apologizing for trespassing? Answer, demanding that the owner of the voice show himself? Say nothing and approach the doorway? Leave the Theatre of the Gods and continue your quest?'[64] Each decision will lead the reader to a different section meaning that each decision leads to a different experience for each reader. To add an extra element to the book, there are another series of questions following some sections of the story that are determined by the throw of the dice.

Following the tradition of evil mummies, those in *The Curse of the Mummy* are no different. The guardian of the tomb, the vizier Amentut, who was buried alive with his master, was described as 'the corpse of an old man, clothed in scarlet and gold robes, but there is not a single drop of moisture left within it! Sunken eyes stare at you from a face dried tight over the man's skull. In places the desiccated skin has torn so that yellowed bone is visible, making the undead horror appear even more dreadful.'[65] It may be a rather complex approach to reading, but it is one that is likely to keep the reader in the world of *The Curse of the Mummy* for a long time, with a different outcome every time.

Common Tropes

Since the mummy genre started there have been a number of common tropes that are repeatedly used in both literature and moving image. Some of these have been introduced above. Quite often, for example, the mummy is violent, killing those who pillaged their tomb or the tomb of a beloved princess. Alternatively the mummy is violent while pursuing a modern woman who is the reincarnation of his dead love.[66]

An alternative plot is that a tomb is despoiled by archaeologists or treasure hunters, thus invoking the curse of the mummy. A mummy is then reanimated, generally due to ancient magic, and goes on the rampage murdering all in his path before being destroyed.[67] Universal's *The Mummy's Tomb* (1942), with Lon Chaney as the mummy, follows this plot line with the mummy killing the descendants of the archaeologists who discovered his tomb.

There is often a clairvoyant, medium or psychic, who, just prior to them making an important discovery, warns archaeologists of the danger they are in should they continue with their excavations. This was demonstrated clearly, as discussed above in Peters' *The Curse of the Pharaohs* (1981).

If there is no room in the narrative for such a character, the warning will be written prominently in the tomb as a curse, or on a papyrus or scarab on or near the mummy, which of course is ignored with wanton disregard by the archaeologists. In the movie *The Mummy's Shroud* (1967) the premonition is given via a crystal ball, and in many of the earlier Hammer Horror offerings the premonitions are often taken as a sign of madness and fall on deaf ears.[68] Most of those in official positions, such as archaeologists, museum curators, scientists and police, are therefore presented as fools in their disregard for these premonitions.[69]

Another trope commonly used in curse fiction is also demonstrated in Peter's *The Curse of the Pharaohs*. This is the 'ominous and portentous last word' scenario. Following an attack, Arthur Baskerville, while regaining consciousness, murmurs weakly: 'The beautiful one has come … Sweet of hands, beautiful of face; at hearing her voice one rejoices.' Radcliffe Emerson, Amelia's husband, points out these were the titles of Nefertiti,[70] the wife of Akhenaten, and therefore an Amarnan queen. In fiction as in Egyptology the Amarna period features heavily, not because this period was prolific in curses but because in the nineteenth century the period was instantly recognisable to the public.

It is also popular to base a plot around a cursed mummy or coffin in a museum. This plot makes an appearance in *The Deeds of the Disturber* (2001) in which Amelia Peabody and her husband, Radcliffe Emerson, investigate a suspicious death in the British Museum in the mummy room: 'Going to his post in the Egyptian Room one morning, a guard had discovered the body of one Albert Gore, a night watchman, sprawled on the floor in front of one of the exhibits. The poor fellow had apparently suffered a stroke or a heart attack, and if he had collapsed by a black-figured vase or a medieval manuscript, his passing would have attracted no interest.'[71]

The press commented that two other people connected with the mummy had died: one by catching a disease and another in a hunting accident. However, there were some odd bits of evidence near the body: 'broken bits of glass, scraps of paper and cloth, dried splashes of some dark liquid substance and – most peculiar of all – a few crushed, withered flowers.'[72] All of these artefacts are designed to guide the reader to believe this death was caused by a mummy.

Another plot line, as was seen in Anne Rice's *The Mummy,* or Conan Doyle's *The Ring of Thoth*, has the theme of immortality as central, with the living trying to obtain a secret elixir that will give them immortality,[73] or, in the case of Conan Doyle, trying to find an antidote for it. The most common plot line, however, is that of a reanimated mummy that causes harm to other people. This has remained a constant in literature, movies and television shows, thus marking the mummy as a terrifying thing.

Mummies in the Movies

These tropes have formed common plot lines in mummy movies since the first one in 1899. This movie, *Robbing Cleopatra's Tomb*, sees a magician dismembering a mummy with the intention of creating a Frankenstein's monster type of creature.[74]

Between 1899 and 1924 just shy of thirty[75] mummy films were produced including the 1909 film *The Mummy of the King Ramses*, followed in 1911 by three films called *The Mummy* which have all subsequently been lost.[76] These mummies were hopeless romantics coming back from the dead in order to rekindle relationships with their reincarnated sweethearts.

However, it is the six mummy movies made between 1932 and 1955 that establish mummies as a horror genre in the mind of film-makers and film-goers alike. Mummies were predominantly in the horror genre in the adult movie market, evolving into family comedies by the end of the twentieth century. However, regardless of the genre the idea of the mummy as something evil is prevalent in nearly every representation. For example, unlike vampires, in the early mummy movies the mummy did not speak, which accentuated the monstrous status.[77] In the later movies of the twentieth century and early twenty-first century they often speak in their native tongue, which in some ways can be even more menacing as it shows that they are in fact sentient, ancient beings.

One of the most iconic movies is *The Mummy*, directed by Karl Freund in 1932 with Boris Karloff in the title role. It was originally called *Cagliostro* and then changed to *Im-ho-tep* before being released as *The Mummy*.[78] It was the first movie with an 'ambulatory' mummy rather than the curse being manifest in invisible forces.[79] It combined the idea of the reanimated corpse and reincarnation, which has formed a staple in the mummy genre.

In this movie the ancient princess Ankhesenamen dies and is buried by her father the king. Her lover and high priest, Imhotep, tries to revive her with the Scroll of Thoth, but is caught before it is complete and is buried alive. When his grave is discovered by the archaeologists Imhotep is reanimated as they read the scroll aloud.

It is not unusual for the soul of a long-dead Egyptian to enter into the body of a contemporary involved in the reanimation of the mummy, therefore re-enacting a love-story across the millennia. Cut scenes of this movie show that Ankhesenamen was intended to be reincarnated as Helen Grosvenor. This was by far the most popular of the mummy films due to the humanity of the mummy who shows an array of emotions[80] that are not displayed in mummies in other movies.

Universal Studios then made a series of mummy films, although they were not considered sequels to *The Mummy*. They made *The Mummy's Hand* in 1940 which had the sequels of *The Mummy's Tomb*, (1942) *The Mummy's Ghost* (1944) and *The Mummy's Curse* in 1944. All of these films tell the story of the mummy Kharis who has to take the tana leaf potion in order to maintain his reanimated life.[81]

Hammer Films in the UK were not to be outdone and also produced a series of mummy movies: *The Mummy* (1959), *The Curse of the Mummy's Tomb* (1964), *The Mummy's Shroud* (1967) and *Blood from the Mummy's Tomb* (1971). In *The Mummy* Christopher Lee played the mummy Kharis and Peter Cushing played the archaeologist John Banning. It tells the same story as the 1932 version with the mummy attempting to resurrect his lost princess.

It was common in these early movies for the mummies to be 'dressed' in dirty, torn, aged bandages, with their faces exposed. This trope was still being used in the most recent version of *The Mummy* (2017) with Ahmanet dressed in skin-tight bandages with her tattooed face exposed. The original costume of *The Mummy* played by Boris Karloff is often said to have been inspired by the New Kingdom mummies of Sety I[82] and Ramses III, with a scarf mimicking the bandages of the original being used in the costume.[83]

Even in literature mummies are also presented in this way: 'Strips of ragged bandage hung from the body. A golden ankh hung on a chain round the neck. Long dead eyes started out from wizened features as Orabis surveyed the assembled mass of vampires.'[84]

There are, of course, exceptions, and in *The Mummy's Curse* (1944) when the mummy of Ananka is reanimated she bathes in a swamp and emerges wearing a nightgown, in full make-up and her hair beautifully styled: similar in appearance to the traditional victims of vampires.

The method of mummy reanimation varies from film to film with *The Mummy's Hand* introducing the fictional plant tana, which was subsequently used in all the Universal sequels. Three of the leaves were used to keep the mummy's heart beating and nine gave him movement. However, in all of the Universal sequels the reanimated mummy is little more than a zombie carrying out the will of the High Priest of Karnak.[85] The brains in the operation is the priest, who is in control of the distribution of the tana leaves and directs the mummy to murder at will. This introduces the idea of a cult that has lasted millennia,[86] with the mummy being little more than a pawn in the priest's invariably evil plan.

Such a trope limited the scope and interest of the mummy as a horror character and, unlike zombies and vampires, mummies did not evolve into sentient beings in movies until very recently. Consequently they fell out of fashion until the genre was reanimated in 1999 when a new movie franchise was born with *The Mummy* (1999) and *The Mummy Returns* (2001), both directed by Stephen Sommers and starring Brendan Fraser and Rachel Weisz. These are loosely based on the 1932 movie *The Mummy*. They were a great success: the first movie made $416 million worldwide and the sequel made $433 million.

The plot is a familiar one. A librarian, Evelyn Carnahan (Weisz), adventurer Rick O'Connell (Fraser), and Evelyn's brother start an archaeological excavation at the ancient city of Hamunaptra, without realising that this would awaken the evil mummy Imhotep, a high priest of the pharaoh Sety I, who was buried alive for killing the king. His main objective after millennia in the tomb is to reunite with his lover, Anck-su-namun, who was the mistress of Sety I. Following the traditional movie tropes Evelyn is to be the vessel by which Anck-su-namun will be brought back to life. In the sequel, *The Mummy Returns*, Evelyn, Rick and their son, Alex, are investigating a pyramid in ancient Thebes. They discover a bracelet known as the Bracelet of Anubis, which Alex puts on and is unable to remove. The bracelet reveals directions to the oasis of Ahm Shere. Alex has seven days to reach it or face certain death as on the eighth day the mummy of the pharaoh Scorpion and his army will reanimate. The mummy Imhotep from the first movie then has a fierce battle with the Scorpion king.

The success of these movies inspired a further sequel, *The Mummy; Tomb of the Dragon Emperor* (2008), and prequel, *The Scorpion King* (2002). Both were successful although they did not make as much at the box office as the first two.

The latest Hollywood blockbuster is *The Mummy* (2017), with Tom Cruise playing soldier-cum-black-market antiquity trader, Nick Morton. The movie was directed by Alex Kurtzman and cost an incredible $125 million to make. The main plot is that the reanimated mummy of the Egyptian queen Ahmanet chases the antiquity trader who disturbs her slumber with millennia of pent-up anger and frustration. Unfortunately, the movie was a massive flop, making only $80 million in the US box office, although it did fare better overseas.

In the 2017 film the resting place of Ahmanet is discovered by accident in northern Iraq (ancient Mesopotamia) following an unofficial raid by US soldiers on the village held by insurgents. The removal of the mummy and her coffin has a completely different perspective to earlier movies: it is not tomb raiding or archaeology but instead a rescue from destruction by Islamist insurgents, reflecting the political climate since 9/11. To rejuvenate, Ahmanet sucks the life force out of unsuspecting bystanders who become emaciated mummies under the power of the queen. They look and act like zombies, demonstrating a cross-over between reanimated corpses in the movies.

However, the idea of healthy mortals withering into corpses was also seen in *The Mummy's Ghost* (1967) in which Amina Mansouri, played by Ramsay Ames, is carried by Kharis into a swamp as she slowly loses all her life until she is 'infected by the mummy's antiquity.'[87]

With the 2017 movie, director Kurtzman had been planning to start a dark universe, following in the footsteps of the Marvel universe, with the Invisible Man and Frankenstein's Monster as sequels. He commented that: 'Those films are beautiful because the monsters are broken characters, and we see ourselves in them.'[88] This idea was in fact one of the criticisms of *The Mummy*, in that the monster was the lead in a 'superhero origin story rather than leaning into the tragic horror aspect of the character'.[89] In the film, the reanimated mummy, Ahmanet, was captured by an organisation that collects 'evil' entities headed by Dr Henry Jekyll who needed to inject himself to avoid turning into his alter-ego. It is easy to see how they could have incorporated other monsters into the sequels.

A common but not new theme is that of a mummy falling in love with a modern woman, and *The Curse of the Mummy's Tomb* (1964) adopts this angle. It was directed by Michael Carreras and starred Terence Morgan, Ronald Howard and Jeanne Roland. The plot follows the traditional lines, with an excavation in Egypt in 1900 involving three British Egyptologists and a French professor, Eugene Dubois. They are assisted by Professor Dubois' daughter, Egyptologist Annette, who is engaged to one of the British Egyptologists, John Bray. In order to reanimate the mummy, a special medallion is required, similar to the *Ring of Thoth* in the Conan Doyle story.[90] Once the mummy is reanimated it kills those involved in the excavation, but though it has more than one opportunity to kill Annette, as one of those who pillaged the tomb, it is captivated by her beauty and does not do it, and even protects her against wealthy but deadly arts patron Adam Beauchamp.

The final Hammer film to be released was *Blood from the Mummy's Tomb* (1971), which was based on Bram Stoker's *The Jewel of Seven Stars* (1912). This book was the first to connect the reanimation of the ancient queen with a contemporary woman. The ka (spirit) of the queen inhabits the body of the Egyptologist's daughter and as with *The Ring of Thoth* and *The Curse of the Mummy's Tomb* an object is required for the reanimation, in this instance a ruby set with seven stars. The resurrection scene is very similar to that of Frankenstein and involves electricity, a doctor and a surgical table. *The Jewel of Seven Stars* was made into a series of movies, including Hammer's *Blood from the Mummy's Tomb* (1971) and the final episode of a television series called *Mystery and the Imagination* (1970).

The Awakening (1980), with Charlton Heston playing the Egyptologist, was the third adaptation and, unfortunately, was not successful in the cinema. The plot starts at an excavation in Egypt where Matthew Corbeck (Heston), his pregnant wife, Anne Corbeck, and his assistant, Jane Turner, are discussing how to uncover the tomb of Queen Kara. Above the entrance to the tomb is the warning, 'Do Not Approach the Nameless One Lest Your Soul Be Withered.' Obviously Corbeck ignores this and enters the tomb with his assistant. At the moment they enter Corbeck's wife goes into premature labour and loses the baby. However, when the mummy's sarcophagus is opened, the stillborn baby is brought back to life. Anne and Matthew subsequently get divorced and Matthew marries his assistant. Eighteen years later his daughter, Margaret, travels to England to meet him while he continues to work with the mummy of Queen Kara. Margaret undergoes some personality changes and Corbeck believes that Kara had possessed his daughter when she was born. He endeavours to resurrect the mummy in order to save his daughter. Needless to say the resurrection does not go according to plan, as Kara is now able to take control of Margaret completely. This movie has not stood the test of time and tvguide.com rated it one star out of four, stating: 'Although given a big-budget production with excellent set design, gorgeous cinematography by veteran Jack Cardiff (a Michael Powell fave), and a first-rate musical score, the film is predictable, unrelentingly dull, and padded with tedious Egyptian travelog footage. Heston, in his only horror film, gives a rather ridiculous impersonation of a British scientist.'[91]

By the 1940s adults had become desensitised to horror movies.[92] The genre had become stale with little deviation in the plots:[93] 'it was usually kids and teenagers that went to see this kind of picture.'[94] The behaviour of mummies in movies became predictable and directors rarely deviated from the standard plots,[95] as discussed above, with dull, zombie-like creatures in the title role.

Mummies were consequently relegated to the level of children's matinee shows, demonstrating an element of farce.[96] This has continued in modern movies such as *The Mummy* (1999) and *The Mummy Returns* (2001), which appeal to both adults and children. The Tom Cruise version of *The Mummy* (2017) was one that tried, unsuccessfully, to a certain extent to revitalise the mummy genre as a horror adventure movie.

In 1955 Universal Studios made a spoof of their popular mummy movies with their horror-comedy *Abbot and Costello Meet the Mummy*, starring the mummy Klaris, a play on the name of the original mummy Kharis. In this slapstick comedy the mummies are all based on the mummy of Ramses III, with each limb wrapped separately including extra bandages wrapped around the throat.

Over the past century representation of mummies in literature and movies has evolved from sources of knowledge, to terrifying creatures intent on killing or creatures following a lost love over the centuries. They are generally seen as a 'loathsome and loveless creature,'[97] which to a certain extent could be a reflection of the reluctance of the English-speaking world to address death and the human body after death.

Hidden Agendas

Mummies in the media can have a hidden agenda, often making political or social commentary. However, as they are real ancient artefacts there appears to be one overriding message in many early movies: the ethics of excavation of the dead. Cinema turned the mummy genre from its criticism of grave-robbing into a celebration of it.[98] Regardless of the era of the mummy film, a nostalgic, colonial view of archaeology and archaeologists is presented;[99] all adventure and pith helmets.

In Hammer House of Horror's *The Mummy* (1959), the Egyptian Mehmet Bey and Egyptologist John Banning debate whether excavating the dead is ethical or not, demonstrating that this was an important aspect of the movie's message. Taking into consideration that the mummy's violent behaviour was often in retaliation for the tomb being opened, it sends the less-than-subtle message that the archaeologists should have heeded the psychic's warnings and left the tomb alone.

In 2017's *The Mummy* there was a different take on the idea of removing archaeological artefacts following the politically unstable situation in the Middle East after 9/11. The US soldier Nick Morton removes the mummy from its coffin in order to protect it from Islamist insurgents who have been destroying archaeological sites in the area.

Mummies in the majority of literature and movie appearances are considered to be the opposite of everything good. They are frequently presented with dirty, tatty bandages, in direct contrast to the obsession with cleanliness prevalent in the West at the time.[100] Evil creatures like this must therefore be destroyed.

In *The Mummy's Shroud* (1967) directed by John Gilling the mummy is covered in blood, and in Hammer's *The Mummy* (1959) the mummy is covered in mud, adding to its gruesome appearance. Archaeologically speaking, mummies are never found in such condition and therefore this was simply a tool to emphasise their distastefulness in the horror genre. The appearance of mummies as old and wrinkled and in decaying, dirty bandages created the image of a terrifying creature: essentially a corpse which should not be ambulatory. This is in complete contrast to the suave sophistication of the average vampire, a creature who is equally unnaturally ambulatory.

As with many movies based in fact, there are factual errors throughout mummy movies and literature. The biggest and most common is to state that the mummy was buried alive and yet at the same time was embalmed.[101] In *The Mummy's Tomb* (1942) the resin used in the embalming process is in fact used by scientists to identify that the rampaging murderer was the mummy. However, when the mummy was discovered the archaeologists made it clear he had been buried alive. Clearly the fact that a person buried alive would have no need for embalming – and that the act of embalming would actually kill them – does not resonate with most film-makers.

Children's Mummies

As mummies have become a major inclusion in children's cartoons so the frightening element of them being reanimated corpses is removed or toned down in order to appeal to a younger market. Empathy is a perfect way of appealing to children by making them sympathise with the mummy. This is often done by presenting the mummy as an outsider. A perfect example of this can be found in Tim Burton's poem *Mummy Boy:*[102]

> He wasn't soft and pink with a fat little tummy;
> he was hard and hollow, a little boy mummy.
> "Tell us, please, Doctor, the reason or cause,
> why our bundle of joy is just a bundle of gauze."
> "My diagnosis," he said, "for better or worse, is that your
>   son is the result of an old pharaoh's curse."
> That night they talked of their son's odd condition – they
>   called him "a reject from an archaeological expedition."
> They thought of some complex scientific explanation, but
>   assumed it was simple supernatural reincarnation.

> With the other young tots he only played twice, an ancient
>   game of virgin sacrifice.
> (But the kids ran away, saying, "You aren't very nice.")
> "Look it's a píñata," said one of the boys,
> "Let's crack it wide open and get the candy and toys."
> They took a baseball bat and whacked open his head.
> Mummy Boy fell to the ground; he finally was dead.
> Inside of his head were no candy or prizes,
> just a few stray beetles of various sizes.[103]

This poem appeals to children's sympathies as it focuses on the humanity of the Mummy Boy, presenting him as a child who only wanted to make friends. Using evocative language such as 'reject', making him the victim of a curse and young bullies encourages the reader to change perspectives of this 'terrifying monster' into a young boy. Essentially someone with whom they could empathise.

Other examples of evoking sympathy in the child audience can be seen in the animated *Tutenstein*[104] and *L'il Horrors*. *Tutenstein* (2003) was based on the comic books by Jay Stephens and tells the story of Tutankhensetamun (a combination of Tutankhamun and Frankenstein), who had been reanimated in a museum using the electricity from lightning, rather like Shelley's *Frankenstein*.

When he is first reanimated he can only make an aggressive and terrifying growling sound and is covered in tatty bandages. However, as the cartoon progresses, to reduce the terrifying aspect of the mummy, he is presented as a small boy with a small boy's needs, and indeed the first thing he needs to do is to use the bathroom.

The characterisation for *Tutenstein*, however, is straight from the Bible and Herodotus. The show features an arrogant and pompous ruler[105] who is grumpy and commands people to do his bidding. Even though Tutankhensetamun is an unpleasant character as a small child he is one which the young audience can feel empathy for. Cleo Carter and her cat, Luxor, who were instrumental in bringing him back to life, help him to adjust to the modern world, and help him understand he is no longer a king with a kingdom. He is dressed in mummy bandages with the head exposed. He is wearing a kilt over the top of the bandages and a nemes (funerary headdress in blue and gold).

Li'l Horrors (2001) was an Australian puppet show set in a large mansion, Maug Stone Hall, owned by Morbidda Bates and run as a boarding school. The Li'l Horrors themselves are group of children taken from the horror genres and include a vampire, werewolf and a mummy. The mummy is called Cleo Patra and is a typical ditzy 'high school' character. Her costume follows the traditional mummy costume of bandages with only the face exposed, with the added characteristic of her bunches poking out of each side of her head. She is very spiritual and greets her fellow students with 'are you feeling cosmically balanced'. All of the horror characters in this show are presented in a way that is recognisable to the young audience, thus enabling them to empathise with them.

Empathising with the mummy is also achieved in the book *Magnificent Mummies,*[106] and the subsequent sequels. This is the story of a family of mummies – Daddy, Mummy, Tut and Sis – who befriend a travelling archaeologist, Sir Digby Digger. The mummies, while living in a very human way, are presented in a stereotypical manner, with dirty bandages covered in cobwebs and living inside a pyramid. The family eat at a dining table, but the children are told off by their parents for making a mess, something all children will be able to relate to.

At bedtime the whole Mummy family cross their arms over their chests and step into their coffins, which are displayed vertically against the wall. Mummy coffins are always represented vertically in museums, on television shows, and in movies, leading many people to think this is the normal position for an Egyptian coffin, whereas in the tomb they were laid horizontally in order to protect the human remains within. In museums they are displayed vertically to enable the visitor to see as much of the decoration as possible, while in movies and television the coffins need to be vertical in order to enable to mummy to stumble out of them.

What is particularly interesting in cartoons in particular is when the mummy cases are given the power of movement or speech. Often in movies it is the shifting of the coffin lid which alerts the audience to the presence of the mummy, but in cartoons like *Bananaman*,[107] for example, benevolent coffin cases are, bizarrely, able to talk and laugh with animated facial features. These animated coffins are normally empty and the animation is of the coffin itself rather than a mummy within. The benevolence of the original mummy transfers to the coffin.

Children enjoy the concept of mummies as they go against the realities of their life, and they are attracted to unpleasant things such as dirt and disruption[108] without the fear normally associated with death. Indeed, reanimated mummies are now almost as synonymous with *Scooby Doo* as they are with ancient Egypt. The earliest introduction of a mummy in the cartoon was in 1969 in *Scooby Doo and a Mummy Too*, which focuses on the 'curse of the mummy' which has the power to turn people to stone. The mummy is shown with grey skin reminiscent of bandages, wearing a nemes headdress and a kilt, and is terrifying in appearance.

The mummy in *Scooby Doo and Mummy's the Word* (1980) is not as terrifying and is simply a bandaged human-shaped being. The mummy lives in a pyramid with the door at ground level. The lower levels of the pyramid have a river complete with crocodiles, which the gang use in an attempt to escape. The pyramid is more than a tomb and is in fact the home of the mummy. However, when Scrappy Doo unwraps the mummy it loses its substance, resulting in a pile of bandages, but he is still able to chase them out of the pyramid leaving visible footprints in the sand. It is clear that the mummy in this cartoon is not malevolent, but rather just wants them to leave his home. Once they have gone he goes back inside and slams the door.

The idea that mummies are made simply of bandages is an intriguing one, as most people are aware that there is a more complex process behind mummification (discussed further in Chapter 2). In order to create a mummy in cartoons and movies all one has to do is wrap the person in bandages and to disseminate their power all you have to do is unwrap them.

This is picked up in the Futurama episode, *A Pharaoh to Remember*[109] in which the dead king is simply wrapped in bandages in preparation for burial. The idea that a mummy is constructed simply of bandages makes for comedy unwrapping whereby one bandage can be pulled and the mummy will spin like a top.

This idea of single bandage unwrapping was adapted in 1993 into a mummy sticky-tape dispenser; the mummy was unwrapped as the sticky tape was used. A modern take on this is a recumbent mummy with the sticky tape dispenser in his stomach. Another mummy stationery staple is Mummy Mike rubber band holder, which is in the form of a recumbent mummy with the rubber bands being wrapped around his limbs like bandages.

Mummies in Music

Not surprisingly, mummies have also made their appearance in music. At the end of the nineteenth century and the beginning of the twentieth century piano music with amusing lyrics about mummies became popular. However, these mummies were not the precursors of the mummies of horror movies to come, but generally female and with a romantic air.

An example of such a song, *My Egyptian Mummy* (1913), laments the concept of lost love:

> My Egyptian mummy from the land of the pyramids,
> We were sweethearts years ago.
> That's why I know, though you were turned to stone,
> I almost hear you moan.
> I'm in love with you, I'm in love with you.[110]

In the 1921 *At the Mummies Ball* the mummies are all portrayed as party animals 'dressed in magnificent style.'[111]

A more recent contribution to the music industry is the American garage punk band, The Mummies, who formed in California in 1988. The band's line-up comprised Maz Kattuah on bass guitar, Larry Winther on lead guitar, Trent Ruane on organ and saxophone and Russell Quan on drums. They were known for wearing mummy bandages on stage, which earned them the name 'The Mummies', rather than the other way around. They released a number of albums before they disbanded in 1992. They took part in a comeback tour in 1994 before disbanding again, and another tour in 2003.[112]

Another US-based band is Here Come the Mummies, who formed in 2000 and comprise a series of anonymous band members. Their website claims: 'Cursed after deflowering a great Pharaoh's daughter (or daughters), Here Come The Mummies (HCTM) have been delivering their brand of *Terrifying Funk from Beyond the Grave* since the year 2000 AD.'[113] This whole gimmick of being a band of genuine mummies extends to their online store which claims everything is shipped by mummies when they 'get back from the crypt'.

Whilst not basing their entire image on the mummy, the Backstreet Boys in 1997 produced a music video for *Everybody*[114] with the band members stranded in a haunted house. In the basement they were confronted with werewolves, vampires and mummies, which emerged from an iron-maiden devise instead of a coffin, with yellowing bandages trailing behind.

Cursed Objects

As well as being a popular form of entertainment in the West, mummies make the press headlines during periods of renewed interest in ancient Egypt, often referred to as Egyptomania. There was a spike of interest in the early nineteenth century following Napoleon's expedition to Egypt and the subsequent decipherment of ancient Egyptian hieroglyphs. A renewed Egyptomania phase followed a century later, in 1923, following the discovery of the tomb of Tutankhamun. Egyptian motifs were then used in fashion, advertising, architecture and homeware.

A rather strange Egyptomania phase was then renewed in the 1970s when the *Treasures of Tutankhamun* exhibition toured the world, reaching the British Museum in 1972. It was the first time the mask of the boy king had left Egypt and people in the West were fascinated. One of the common memories of the exhibition in London was the queues to get in. It is said to have attracted more than 1.7 million visitors. Michael Health, a cartoonist who visited the exhibition said: 'The whole country had gone Tutankhamun mad: there were Tutankhamun stamps, Tutankhamun pencil-sharpeners, Tutankhamun vacuum flasks, Tutankhamun cocktails, Tutankhamun slippers. I couldn't see the exhibition, there were eight million other people in the way. We queued for days. Inside, it was packed with thousands of people in overcoats.'

Writer A.N. Wilson said: 'It did knock me for six. I queued with my father, a potter, who'd done a head of Nefertiti for Wedgwood. The objects were incredibly beautiful. We were also confronted by an alien way of life, quite different from the progression from Plato and Aristotle through Christianity to us. But the chief attraction was aesthetic.'[115]

In the 1970s this renewed interest in ancient Egypt was not related to religion, architecture or art, but to pyramid power with revitalised theories of aliens constructing the pyramids and, of course, the curse of the mummy. In 1972 new cases of curse victims were making front-page news and providing added publicity for the Tutankhamun exhibition. Mohammed Mahdy, the head of the Egyptian Antiquities Organisation which signed off on the objects to leave Egypt for the exhibition was hit by a car and killed when he left his office on that day.[116] It was reported that the flight crew who transported the artefacts from Egypt were all cursed with bad luck. For example, one of the crew was playing cards on the case containing the mask when he kicked it and joked, 'Look, I'm kicking the most expensive thing in the world.' Some time later he broke the same leg. Another member of the crew was divorced shortly after the flight and of course the curse was blamed.[117]

A new exhibition, *Tutankhamun: Treasures of the Golden Pharaoh*, was touring the world at the end of 2019, and while it is still attracting the crowds,[118] there has not been the 'cursemania' that followed it in the 1970s. However, *The Sun* newspaper carried such lurid headlines as 'Mystery box from Tutankhamun's "cursed tomb" opened for the first time ever on camera'.[119] Then, in November 2019, they announced that 'Tutankhamun's "cursed" trumpet that causes "deadly conflict" has arrived in the UK.'[120]

If the story is to be believed, the first time this trumpet, discovered in Tutankhamun's tomb, was played the lights went out in Cairo. This is not an unusual occurrence; the lights regularly go out all over Egypt. The second time it was played was shortly before the Second World War started. However, this is not the extent of the theory.

A member of staff at the Egyptian Museum in Egypt reportedly blew into one of the trumpets a week before a revolution broke out.

The same thing is said to have happened before the 1967 Arab–Israeli War and the 1991 Gulf War.

The BBC did record the haunting sound of the bronze trumpet when it was first played in 1939 after nearly 3,000 years. Just five minutes before the recording was about to happen the museum in Cairo was plunged into darkness and the recording had to be made over candlelight.

The silver instrument shattered and injured the musician trying to play it during an earlier attempt to hear the sound of the trumpets.

They failed to mention that the silver trumpet shattered because the musician who played it, Bandsman James Tappern of the 11th Prince

Albert's Own Hussars, inserted a modern trumpet mouth piece into it, which resonated too much through the fragile, 3,000-year-old instrument. This first attempt, which took place in 1939, ended in disaster and it was not played again until 1975 by Philip Jones, which is when the BBC recorded it.[121]

Tutankhamun's belongings are not the only items that have the power to curse, if the curse theorists are to be believed. Over the past century or so cursed coffins have been blamed for all manner of disasters and mishaps. For example, the *Titanic* – which sunk in 1912 after hitting an iceberg – has been reported as having a mummy-board on board. A mummy-board is a piece of wood placed over the top of the mummy, within the coffin, and was highly decorated with funerary prayers as well as a portrait of the deceased.

The mummy-board on the Titanic apparently belonged to a priestess from the eighteenth dynasty, discovered at Amarna, which was being transported by Lord Canterville from England to New York. It was shipped in a wooden crate and stored behind the command bridge. Phillipp Vandenberg, an advocator of the mummy's curse, believes the presence of the mummy turned the captain's mind, causing him to make wrong decisions, which led to the disaster. He claims: 'Many scientists who handled mummies showed clear signs of mental derangement. Did Captain Smith, too, look into those fatal radiant eyes? Could he, too, have been the curse's victim?'[122] According to Vandenberg, the mummy had an amulet of the god of the dead, Osiris behind her head which was inscribed with: 'Awake from the swoon in which you sleep, and with a glance of your eyes will triumph over everything that is done against you.'[123]

This type of curse would be unprecedented on a mummy, which in itself could cast doubt on the scenario. Continuing with a seafaring theme, mummies smuggled out of Egypt were thought by superstitious sailors to cause storms at sea and were often thrown overboard in order to prevent them.[124]

In the modern West, museums now bear the brunt of cursed objects as they are institutions that are seen to objectify and display mummies, coffins and other funerary items. Museums therefore represent the new tombs for the deceased, and many modern displays present funerary assemblages together, creating a faux-tomb environment with which to invoke any so-called curses.

People's imaginations are then sparked by these scenes, as well as literature and movies, to invent cursed objects. For example, in 1927 the British Museum Sculpture Gallery was widely reported to be haunted. One of the glass cases held an empty sarcophagus, but when viewed through another case the reflections and lighting superimposed a reflection of a face from another anthropoid coffin onto it.[125]

While this example was easily explained, one of the most famous haunted coffins, also from the British Museum, was the cursed mummy-board, often referred to as the 'unlucky' mummy (accession number EA22542). This mummy-board is said to have terrified night watchmen by making strange noises, and prior to being donated to the British Museum it was apparently unlucky for anyone who owned it. Once it was in the museum it was only unlucky to those who disrespected it. For example, one lady who was rude to it fell down the stairs and sprained her ankle, and a journalist who wrote about it in jest apparently died a few days later,[126] although what they died of is not stated.

The mummy-board was originally purchased in the 1860s by a group of Englishmen, all of whom were injured or died. One of them, Douglas Murray, shortly after purchasing the mummy-board, lost an arm on a hunting trip when his gun exploded. Further fuel to this story is added when both the cab and the ship that transported the mummy-board were wrecked and the house the mummy-board was originally stored in burned down. According to the *New York Times* in 1923, at the height of the renewed Egyptomania and Carnarvon-induced cursemania, it was stated that any photographs of the face appeared to be contorted with agony. It is also rumoured to be the same mummy-board that was on board the *Titanic*, though since it was purchased it has only left the museum once for a temporary exhibition in 1990, some time after the ship sank. The curator's comments on the British Museum website states unequivocally: 'None of these stories has any basis in fact, but from time to time the strength of the rumours has led to a flood of enquiries.'[127]

As with all good cases of curse victims, the connections between them and the cursed object start getting more and more creative. For instance, a photographer who took pictures of the mummy-board shot himself, and another woman loosely connected to the mummy-board suffered terrible family losses and was almost lost at sea.[128] 'The celebrated clairvoyant Madame Helena Blavatsky is alleged to have detected an evil influence, ultimately traced to the mummy-board. She urged the owner to dispose of it and in consequence it was presented to the British Museum.'[129] The mummy-board has since been 'exorcised', after which, apparently, a green mist left the face and since then nothing bad has happened.

Another example of a so-called cursed object was in the 1930s-1940s when guards patrolling the Field Museum, Chicago, reported hearing screams from the Egyptian department. Although they found no sign of intruders, one of the mummies, which was displayed upright, was now leaning its head against a display case. A conflicting report, however, states it was in fact face down inside its case. Further conflicting reports concern the identity of the mummy. In one report it was identified as Harwa, the naked mummy. However, the only naked mummy in the exhibition was of a child and was clearly not the mummy being referred to. It was a well-known fact at the time that lovers hid in the museum at night because of the reduced security and it is quite likely they bumped into a display case, knocking the mummy over and making a noise before they ran.[130]

Every now and then the press will run a story on so-called cursed objects (see above). One of the most recent cases to get national attention was in 2013, when Manchester University Museum was being plagued by a so-called cursed statue. The 10-in (24-cm) statue of Nebsenyu (1800 BCE) slowly rotated throughout the day in the display case, remaining stationary at night. The statue had entered the museum in 1933, donated by Annie Barlow of Bolton. Dr Campbell Price, curator at Manchester University, said: 'I thought it was strange because it is in a case and I am the only one who has a key. I put it back, but then the next day it had moved again. We set up a time-lapse video and, although the naked eye can't see it, you can clearly see it rotate.'[131]

The time-lapse camera took an image every minute for one week and clearly showed the statue moving. It turned a full 180° causing some people to speculate whether the statue was deliberately showing its back to the visitors as it was inscribed with the *htp di nsw* offering, requesting offerings of bread, beer, oxen and fowl.[132]

Price had speculated that as the statue was carved from steatite and then fired it may have been more susceptible to magnetic forces that were causing its movement. He toyed with the idea of applying museum wax to the base of the statue to prevent it moving but commented, 'what if the statue continued to keep moving? What would our explanation be then?'[133]

Staff at the museum called in an engineer to examine the cases and try to work out what was happening. As with many of these unexplained phenomena there was a rational explanation: the shelf on which the statue was displayed was vibrating due to traffic on a busy road nearby, and the statue had a convex base which made it less stable than others in the case. However, it does not provide an explanation as to why, after decades in the same spot, the statue chose to move at this point in time. Dr Campbell Price said: 'There were several supernatural explanations ... but Egyptian stuff attracts that.'[134]

So-called cursed objects have plagued over-active imaginations since the early twentieth century. In 1909 Lord Carnarvon had just discovered a cartonnage cat coffin, painted black with yellow eyes, in the Valley of the Kings. This artefact was removed to the dig-house and placed in the bedroom of Arthur Weigall, a true believer in the curse. When he returned late at night the coffin was in the middle of the room and he fell over it, hurting his shins. At exactly the same time, the butler was stung by a scorpion and in his delirium believed he was being pursued by a grey cat.

Weigall went to bed, but took some time getting to sleep due to the butler's cries. He felt he was being stared at by a cat and just before he dropped off to sleep he swore the head of the cat coffin turned its head to look at him with a look of anger. All the while the butler was screaming about a cat.

Weigall was woken after an hour's sleep by loud bang like a gun-shot. As he woke a grey cat jumped over his bed and out of the window. The cat coffin was split in two as if the cat had jumped from 'within.' In reality, the humidity had expanded the cartonnage, causing it to burst open.

Apparently Weigall approached the window and saw his own tabby cat on the path with its back arched and glaring into the bushes, probably at the stray grey cat that had trespassed on its turf. However, Weigall and the others in the house with over-active imaginations believed the grey cat to be a malevolent spirit causing him to hurt his shins and the butler to be stung by a scorpion.[135] It is more likely, however, that the grey cat was a stray and had jumped through the window to look for food. It was startled when the coffin exploded and jumped back out of the window, further frightening the house tabby.

The curse of the mummy still appears in tabloid papers in an attempt to attract readers. In 2018, *The Sun* ran with the headline 'Ancient Evil?

Mystery 9-foot black sarcophagus in Egypt OPENED – despite warnings over ancient curse.'[136]

The story was that 'defiant' scientists opened a stone sarcophagus that had been discovered in an excavation in Alexandria. The sarcophagus was filled with water from a local sewage pipe and the remains of three bodies were discovered inside. The bodies appeared to have been those of army officers, including one with an arrow injury to the head. The sarcophagus and the bodies were then removed to Alexandria's National Restoration Museum.

Despite *The Sun's* best efforts, making reference to the so-called curse of Tutankhamun and the numerous horrible deaths associated with the tomb (see following chapter), there was not enough evidence (or any evidence) of a curse for other news outlets to pick it up. However, *The Independent* followed up with a story about how thousands of people had signed a petition to be allowed to drink the water from the sarcophagus 'so we can assume its powers and finally die.'[137] The likelihood that this water was sewage from a nearby pipe does not seem to have deterred them from making their bizarre request.

Conclusion

Mummies are an integral aspect of Western culture although their evolution has been a lot slower than that of zombies and vampires. Their popularity in the horror genre was very much tied with the archaeological work being carried out in Egypt at the same time. However, as the horror genre became stale, it developed into a comedic, farcical character before becoming a staple in children's media. The gradual changes in the approach to, and the reception of, mummies have been instigated by changing representations in the press, movies and literature. This has resulted in a change in the response to mummies by the public and changes in how mummies are treated by professionals.[138]

Mummies have been presented in three main ways: the evil baddie who kills people, the friendly clown, and the evil but ineffectual creature[139] who inspires sympathy. A perfect example of this evolution is Tutankhamun, the catalyst for the mummy in the media. He was a young man who died at only eighteen years old, and was left alone in the tomb for 3,500 years. The sympathy wanes once we realise how many treasures are associated with him,[140] and it seems more important to retrieve these treasures. He is then a creature to be feared as rumours of a curse associated with his tomb take root.

Sympathy was once again directed towards him when it was believed he was the victim of murder, but though archaeologists tried to prove this was the case, evidence suggests he was in fact the victim of a fatal accident. This was revealed in the BBC One documentary *Tutankhamun: The Truth Uncovered* (2014) in which a virtual autopsy showed that he had suffered a fractured knee just prior to death.

> Tutankhamun suffered from multiple physical disorders, and it is possible that some of them may have cumulated in an inflammatory, immunosuppressive syndrome, which would seriously undermine his health.
>
> We can imagine a young, frail king, who walked with a cane due to Köhler Disease II (osteonecrotic and sometimes painful) together with oligodactyly in the right foot and club foot in the left.
>
> A sudden leg fracture, perhaps from a fall, would be life-threatening when combined with a malaria tropica infection.[141]

Although not a murder victim, such evidence presents him as very human and therefore someone with whom to empathise. Even people who know little about archaeology or Egyptology will know of Tutankhamun and his 'cursed tomb' or 'cursed mummy'.

Mummies, like the other reanimated corpses in this book, have become part of a common parlance, with the elderly or particularly thin people being unfavourably compared to mummies. Homer Simpson in *The Simpsons* for example, tells the elderly Mr Burns: 'You are a senile buck-toothed old mummy.'[142]

Anyone unfortunate enough to be injured, will, while wrapped in bandages, also be compared to a mummy. Many parents have also been bombarded with hundreds of terrible mummy jokes from their young children (for example: 'What kind of music do mummies like? Wrap music') indicating that mummies are not a thing to be terrified of but something that can be laughed at.

Since the 1960s mummies joined the Halloween market in the USA and this has spread throughout the English-speaking world where they are sold to scare people throughout October (see figs. 2, 5 and 13). Mummies are also the simplest costume for a parent to throw together at the last minute. All that is needed is a couple of rolls of toilet paper and due to this children associate toilet paper with mummies.

In the words of Freddy from *Scooby Doo and the Mummy Too*: 'Well, gang, I guess that wraps up the mystery – and the mummy too!'

Chapter 2

Unwrapping the Mummy Myth

Introduction

The mummy myth popular in the West originates from ancient Egyptian mummies, even though mummification has been practiced for thousands of years all over the world. This is where the myth of the reanimated mummy differs remarkably from zombies and vampires, which are a melting pot of ideas, myths and legends from different parts of the world that have been incorporated into Western popular culture.

It is important to make it clear precisely what the definition of a mummy is. Mummification is essentially the preservation of a body, including the soft tissues, through drying or embalming. This can happen naturally, through drying in the sun, being buried in sand, ice, or peat bogs or through human intervention.

When considering mummies as reanimated corpses in Western popular culture the focus is on those that have been preserved through human intervention rather than naturally created mummies. Mummified remains are in some cultures an active part of religion and ancestor cults, and while these corpses are not thought to reanimate they are considered 'human' enough to be included in daily activities.

Although not directly linked with the mummy myth popular in Western culture, a short discussion on different cultural approaches to the dead may put the modern Western fascination into perspective.

Mummies as Part of Everyday Life

Jeremy Bentham

A wonderful mythical 'mummy' is that of Jeremy Bentham, which is on public display in the South Cloisters at University College, London.

The myth generally states that Bentham wished to be mummified so he could attend university meetings even after his death.

As with most myths, the facts are often altered in the retelling. The body of Jeremy Bentham is indeed on display, but is known as an auto-icon, which has his preserved skeleton dressed in period costume with a wax head created by French sculptor Jacques Talrich in place of his real head.

His head was preserved using a technique popular with the New Zealand Maori, but was not considered to be executed well enough.[1] It was originally displayed beneath his feet although this is no longer the case. He has only ever attended one meeting since his death on 6 June 1832, and that was in 2013, as a surprise for Dr Malcolm Grant for his final council meeting as UCL's Provost (see fig. 3).[2]

The myths surrounding Jeremy Bentham have mostly come through mistellings of a part of his will:

> The skeleton he will cause to be put together in such a manner as that the whole figure may be seated in a chair usually occupied by me when living, in the attitude in which I am sitting when engaged in thought in the course of time employed in writing. I direct that the body thus prepared shall be transferred to my executor. He will cause the skeleton to be clad in one of the suits of black occasionally worn by me. The body so clothed, together with the chair and the staff in my later years borne by me, he will take charge of and for containing the whole apparatus he will cause to be prepared an appropriate box or case and will cause to be engraved in conspicuous characters on a plate to be affixed thereon and also on the labels on the glass cases in which the preparations of the soft parts of my body shall be contained ... my name at length with the letters ob: followed by the day of my decease. If it should so happen that my personal friends and other disciples should be disposed to meet together on some day or days of the year for the purpose of commemorating the founder of the greatest happiness system of morals and legislation my executor will from time to time cause to be conveyed to the room in which they meet the said box or case with the contents therein to be stationed in such part of the room as to the assembled company shall seem meet.[3]

He had not stipulated therefore, that he was to attend meetings, but had hoped that, should his friends gather to remember him, then they would bring his remains to be part of the event.

Vladimir Lenin

Another famous 'mummy' is that of Vladimir Ilych Lenin, the first Soviet leader. His body was carefully embalmed and his appearance preserved when he died in January 1924. Initially he was embalmed in order that the public could come and pay their last respects during the four day state funeral. However, the people kept coming in their droves and fifty-six days later he was still on display, preserved due to the cold winter temperatures. It was only at this stage they decided to permanently preserve his body.

The mausoleum on Red Square was opened in August after a number of chemists had worked day and night to embalm the body to the highest standard. Like Egyptian mummies, all of Lenin's internal organs were removed and his skeleton and soft tissues preserved.

The lab in Moscow that carried out the embalming gained a good name for itself and was also responsible for embalming the Vietnamese president Ho Chi Minh, Bulgarian leader Georgi Dimitrov, and North Korean leaders Kim Il-sung and Kim Jong-il, as well as Soviet dictator Josef Stalin, whose embalmed body lay alongside Lenin's between 1953 and 1961.[4]

Today the body of Lenin remains in excellent condition, and every eighteen months it is taken from the mausoleum to be re-embalmed and washed by the Center for Scientific Research and Teaching Methods in Biochemical Technologies in Moscow. The process includes: 'submerging the body in separate solutions of glycerol solution baths, formaldehyde, potassium acetate, alcohol, hydrogen peroxide, acetic acid solution and acetic sodium. Each session takes about one and a half months.'[5]

It currently costs the Russian government thirteen million roubles (£165,000) per annum to preserve the body. The embalming method used was innovative and the first two scientists to work on the body were Vladimir Vorobiev and biochemist Boris Zbarsky. Alexei Yurchak, professor of social anthropology at the University of California, Berkeley, explained in an interview: 'They have to substitute occasional parts of skin and flesh with plastics and other materials, so in terms of the original biological matter the body is less and less of what it used to be. That makes it dramatically different from everything in the past, such as mummification, where the focus was on preserving the original matter while the form of the body changes.'[6] However, despite this, more than two-and-a-half million people visit the mausoleum to see the body of Lenin every year.

Indonesian Ma'nene Ritual

A particularly interesting modern ritual concerning the preserved dead is the Ma'nene ritual, also known as the Ceremony of Cleaning Corpses, in Toraja, South Sulawesi, Indonesia.

The ritual is one in which the mummified remains of ancestors are exhumed in order to wash them, dress them, do their hair,[7] or share a cigarette with them. If coffins are damaged they are repaired or replaced and the mummies are then paraded through the streets.

This has been practiced in this region of Indonesia for the past 900 years, and is celebrated every three years. Shortly after death the bodies are treated with formalin, which is a mixture of formaldehyde and water. This halts the decomposition and eventually the soft tissues begin to mummify. It is believed that death is the start of a journey and it is important that the families take care of the afterlife of their ancestors. The associated rituals are therefore rather lavish in order to assure a better afterlife for the deceased.[8]

Following death the fresh mummy is likely to be stored for two years, during which time they are referred to as a 'sick person' who is 'resting'. Once the family has saved the thousands of dollars required for the funeral, and to gather relatives from all over the country, they will hold the final funeral. At the funeral there is a ritualistic buffalo fight before the buffalos are slaughtered. The last breath of the first buffalo sacrificed represents the end of the 'resting' period for the 'sick person.' The more buffalo that are sacrificed the smoother the deceased's journey will be into the afterlife.[9] Once they are buried they can be certain they will see them again at the Ma'nene ritual.

If someone dies away from their village then as part of the ritual their descendants will walk them from their place of death back to their village where their spirits can rest in peace.

The Ma'nene ceremony enables the family to once again see and interact with dead relatives who may have died decades ago, or as little as three years before.[10]

Ancient Egyptian Mummification

As we have discussed briefly some ways in which the preserved dead are incorporated into day-to-day life we now turn our attention to the ancient Egyptians, the source of the ambulatory corpse of movies and literature. It is important to describe how the ancient Egyptians preserved the bodies of their deceased to provide context for the genre.

Although thousands of mummies, both animal and human, have survived, there is no contemporary written record describing the technique. The most complete record is from Herodotus, a fifth century BCE Greek Historian, who described the process in his *The Histories*.[11] Through comparison with surviving mummies it is clear that Herodotus' account is a reliable source.[12]

The mummification process was only reserved for the wealthy. Poorer members of ancient Egyptian society continued to use simple pit burials where the bodies of the dead were laid into a pit dug into the desert sand with no human intervention on the preservation. There were three standards of mummification: the best designed to make the deceased look like a god, and two cheaper options.

Mummification was carried out by priests and the High Priest was responsible for the wrapping itself, which was carried out while wearing a mask of the jackal-headed god of embalming, Anubis.

The most expensive mummification process was designed to create an 'Osiris' out of the deceased; in short they were going to make the deceased into a god. One of the first processes was to remove the brain through the nose of the deceased. It was believed all thought processes and emotions happened in the heart and not the brain, which was, therefore, superfluous to requirements.

To do this the ethemoid bone at the top of the nose was broken, and the brain was removed in pieces using a hooked instrument. An alternative method was to pour a juniper oil and turpentine liquid up the nose. This dissolved the brain, which was then poured out through the nostrils.

Next a cut was made in the left flank using a flint knife, enabling the embalmer to remove the contents of the abdomen. The heart was left in place as the seat of all emotion. The organs removed were preserved, wrapped and stored in canopic jars, which were placed in the tomb near the body. The body cavity was then cleansed, first with palm wine and then an infusion of pounded spices. The abdomen was then stuffed with little bundles of natron wrapped in linen and left to dry. Once it was fully dried out, the cavity was filled with a mixture of aromatic substances, linen or sawdust in order to give the empty abdomen shape before it was sewn up.

Once the organs were removed and the cavity stuffed with natron packages, the body was packed for 35–40 days in natron, a natural salt substance from the Wadi Natron. After forty days the body was removed from the natron, washed and prepared for wrapping. Wrapping took another 30–35 days, making a total of seventy days for the whole process. The seventy-day period was religiously significant as it further associated the body of the deceased with the god Osiris.

In the Middle Kingdom (2040–1782 BCE), a cheaper mummification option was introduced which did not involve the removal of the internal organs. Instead a mixture of oil of cedar and turpentine was injected into the body through the anus, which was plugged up to prevent the liquid escaping. The body was then packed in natron for forty days, after which the body was removed and the liquid was drained out bringing the liquefied organs with it (although some mummies have shown it does not dissolve evenly and the rectums are clogged by partially dissolved internal organs).

The ancient Egyptians were not afraid of death and they were not squeamish about human remains. There is even evidence that after the bodies had been wrapped they were returned to the family for burial. Sometimes family tombs were only opened every couple of years for interments and in the interim the mummies were kept in the home (not much different from the Indonesian people discussed above). There are examples of mummies with children's doodles on the feet and legs indicating they were in the living areas of the home and were, in essence, part of the household.

The Curse is Born

Although, as discussed, mummified remains are venerated all over the world, only Egyptian mummies are reanimated in Western popular culture.

Unlike other cultures, mummification in ancient Egypt died out in the Graeco-Roman period (332 BCE-30CE) more than 2,000 years ago. Additionally, mummies in Egypt were never a part of the everyday lives of the community, even when the practice was more widespread. Once the dead were buried, the idea was they would remain buried for eternity. However, tomb robbers and archaeologists had different ideas and exposed the mummies to the modern world.

So where exactly did the idea of a reanimated mummy come from? This idea is a modern construct and has absolutely nothing to do with ancient Egyptian society, culture or beliefs. The theme of a reanimated mummy is one that developed alongside the so-called curse of the mummy, or the Egyptian curse, which was also a modern construct rather than an ancient one. To identify the origins of the reanimated mummy we need to investigate the myth of the curse.

Curses Written in Tombs

All curse theories state that the 'Egyptian curse' originated with curses written inside the tombs to warn against disturbing the dead. The most famous of such 'curses' was apparently found inscribed on a clay tablet in the tomb of Tutankhamun in the Valley of the Kings, Luxor, stating, 'Death will slay with its wings whoever disturbs the peace of the pharaoh.' Some even go so far as to say this tablet was catalogued along with the other artefacts from the tomb and was translated by the famous linguist Alan Gardiner.[13]

None of this is true. There is no record of this tablet at all. There are no photographs and no written notes regarding it.[14] Many curse conspiracists believe this is an institutional cover-up, though, in fact, this specific item does not actually exist.

It is often stated that Howard Carter, the excavator who discovered the tomb, allowed the rumours of the curse to circulate without debunking them, as a deterrent to tomb robbers who may have had their eye on the treasure buried within.[15]

The origin of the so-called Tutankhamun curse, 'Death will slay with its wings whoever disturbs the peace of the pharaoh', can be traced to an American occult novelist, Marie Corelli, and not the tomb of the king. She made her name when, in 1923, she wrote to the *New York Times* following their report of Lord Carnarvon's illness: 'According to a rare book I possess, which is not in the British Museum, entitled *"The Egyptian History of the Pyramids"* (translated out of the original Arabic by Vortier, Arabic professor to Louis XVI of France) the most dire punishment follows any rash intruder into a sealed tomb … that is why I ask "Was it a mosquito bite that has so seriously infected Lord Carnarvon."' When he died a few days later, Corelli was labelled a clairvoyant for her premonition.[16]

Further doubt is thrown on the truth behind this curse, as there were discrepancies in the news reports from the 1920s. A further curse was reported as being written above the door to Tutankhamun's tomb, on magical bricks within,[17] or on the mud-brick entrance to the so-called treasury within the tomb: the reports were unable to agree. The curse however, was alleged to say: 'It is I who hinder the sand from choking the secret chamber. I am for the protection of the deceased.' One reporter embellished the curse by adding his own little addendum: 'and I will kill all those who cross this threshold into the sacred precincts of the royal king who lives forever.'[18]

Other reports state that the inscription was written on the underside of a candle near the Anubis figure within the treasury, or on the rear of the *ka* (spirit) statue guarding the door to the burial chamber. This particular curse added: 'It is I who drive back robbers of the tomb with flames of the desert. I am the protector of Tutankhamun's grave.'[19]

However, this is a mistranslation of the inscription, written on a reed lamp near the Anubis statue in the tomb, which reads: 'It is I who hinder the sand from choking the secret chamber, and who repel the one who would repel him with the desert-flame. I have set aflame the desert(?), I have caused the path to be mistaken. I am for the protection of Osiris [the deceased].'[20] This is a spell protecting the dead rather than a curse for those entering the tomb.

Surely, the inconsistencies on the location where this curse is reportedly written, as well as the specific words used, should ring alarm bells. Not to mention the fact that in all of the work that has been carried out by professional archaeologists, Egyptologists and linguists on the tomb of Tutankhamun no inscription of this kind has been found anywhere. The work of the Griffith Institute to ensure photographs of every object found in the tomb are online means that this can be checked by the public.[21] Even this does not stop people claiming that the curse has been institutionally covered up.

But why should fact get in the way of a good curse story? These curses and theories have been quoted so often they are now considered fact and accepted by many people to the extent that some visitors to Egypt refuse to go into the tomb 'just in case'.

Although reports of the curse recorded in Tutankhamun's tomb were fabricated, the tombs that *do* have curse texts are completely overlooked and are unknown to those who believe the Egyptian curse to be real.

Curses were never written in royal tombs as the entrances were generally hidden and they believed them to be safe from robbery. Non-royal tombs, on the other hand, had a funerary chapel over the burial shaft where members of the family gathered to make offerings and celebrate certain festivals with their ancestors. These were more likely to be robbed and therefore needed another layer of protection. However, the curses were not successful as a deterrent to tomb robbers as nearly all tombs, including that of Tutankhamun, have been robbed over the centuries.

The curse in one tomb states: 'As for anyone who enters this tomb unclean, I shall seize him by the neck like a bird, he will be judged for it by the great god.'[22] Another example, belonging to the fourth-dynasty (2613–2498 BCE) tomb of the Priestess of Hathor, Lady of the Sycamore, Nesysokar from Giza is more elaborate: 'O anyone who enters this tomb, who will make evil against this tomb, May the crocodile be against him on water, and the snake against him on the land, May the hippopotamus be against him on water, the scorpion against him on land.'[23]

Her husband, Pettety, also had a similar deterrent inscribed in his tomb[24] to aid in his protection: 'Listen all of you! The priest of Hathor will beat twice anyone, any one of you who enters this tomb or does harm to it. The gods will confront him ... the crocodile, the hippopotamus, and the lion will eat him.'[25]

The tomb of Ankhi, from Saqqara, provides a warning to potential tomb robbers: 'Every workman, every stonemason, or every man who shall [do] evil things to the tomb of mine of eternity by tearing out bricks or stones from it, no voice shall be given to him in the sight of any god or any man.'[26]

The sixth-dynasty (2345–2181 BCE) tomb of Harkkhuf, in Aswan, also has the formulaic curse: 'As for anyone who enters this tomb unclean, I shall seize him by the neck like a bird, he will be judged for it by the great god.'[27]

A tomb in the cemetery of the Meidum pyramid is also reported to have had a curse tablet in the antechamber which stated the spirit of the dead will 'wring the neck of a grave robber as if it were that of a goose'. There were apparently two bodies in the tomb; one the victim of the curse. As he reached towards the mummy's jewellery a stone fell from the ceiling and killed him.[28]

These curses do not make the headlines. They are specific about who will be punished and how. Often it is stated a god will do the actual punishment rather than the deceased (or indeed their mummy).

The Curse Catalyst

The so-called curse really leapt into the limelight when Lord Carnarvon died in 1923. His death is still regularly quoted as 'proof' that the curse of Tutankhamun is real (fig. 4).

George Edward Stanhope Molyneux Herbert, 5th Earl of Carnarvon, first travelled to Egypt in 1903 due to his poor health. It was a common health resort as the winter weather in Egypt was better for poor health than the damp climate of the UK. Lord Carnarvon was a wealthy aristocrat who lived at Highclere Castle in Hampshire. He was the financial backer behind Howard Carter, who initially was excavating nobles' tombs at Deir el Bahri before discovering the tomb of Tutankhamun in the Valley of the Kings. They worked together from 1907 until the tomb was discovered in 1922.

At the time of his death he was under a great deal of stress due to political strife between his protégé Carter and the authorities and he was not in the best of health when he arrived in Egypt initially.[29]

Lord Carnarvon was bitten by a mosquito, and while shaving he nicked the top off the bite. This then became infected and he contracted septicaemia, lowering his immune system further. He died on 5 April 1923 of pneumonia. *The Daily Mail* ran with the story that the mosquito had drunk Tutankhamun's embalming fluids which in turn contaminated Carnarvon, although how they would have known this is never made clear. Following the autopsy of Tutankhamun, which showed a scar on the face of the boy king, curse theorists have said the mosquito bite was in the same place as this scar, thus providing[30] extra fodder for the theory.

Carnarvon's death was not a sudden event but had rather been a slow build-up of the symptoms of septicaemia. According to the reports of his son, the 6th Earl of Carnarvon, there were twelve days of progressing symptoms: '"I feel like hell," the fifty-seven-year-old Earl said one morning at breakfast. At the time he already had a temperature of 104 and shook with chills. The next day his condition improved. Then the high fever returned. It went this way for twelve days. The doctors determined that Lord Carnarvon had cut himself shaving, opening an old wound with his razor. But that would hardly have caused the fever to linger for so long.'[31]

The symptoms of septicaemia are varied and can range from fever and chills to increased heart rate, confusion, nausea and vomiting, a rash and shock. If untreated it can lead to sepsis and can, as we have seen here, be fatal.[32]

It is often reported that at the exact time of Carnarvon's death the lights in Cairo inexplicably went out and Carnarvon started speaking in tongues.[33] The 6th Earl of Carnarvon stated: 'We asked the Cairo electric company, and they knew of no rational explanation for the lights going out and then on again.'[34]

There are a number of inconsistencies regarding these strange events. For example, there are conflicting reports about the exact time the power went off, which throws doubt on its significance. Lord Carnarvon's death certificate states that he died at 1.45am, whereas in his memoirs his son stated the lights went off shortly after at 2am, quarter of an hour after the death. Also, as Carnarvon left his bed he grabbed a torch from his bedside, indicating that perhaps out of habit a torch was kept nearby for power cuts, which even today are regular in Egypt.

The *Daily Express* reported at the time that the electricity went off just prior to his death, at 1.40am.[35] Although only a few minutes out, it is impossible to say the lights went out at the *exact* time of death which is one of the 'facts' stated as proof of the curse.

Another strange event is the death of Carnarvon's three-legged dog, Susie, in the UK. It is often reported that Susie howled and died at exactly the same time as her master. It is unlikely that there were any witnesses to the death of Susie as the main reporter of the incident was Lord Carnarvon's son, who was a true believer in the curse of Tutankhamun and who was in Egypt at the time of his father's death.[36] There are also a number of inconsistencies with this timing.

As mentioned, Carnarvon died at 1.45am in Cairo. Susie stood up, howled and keeled over dead at 3.55am in the UK. The 6th Earl states in his memoirs that the UK was two hours ahead of Cairo, meaning at was 1.55am Cairo time when Susie died, ten minutes after the death of Lord Carnarvon.

However, in 1923 GMT (Greenwich Mean Time) was in fact two hours *behind* Egyptian time, so the dog died at 5.55am Egyptian time and not 1.55am, a full four hours after the death of Lord Carnarvon.[37] Once these inconsistencies are investigated the evidence is not as compelling as perhaps it first appears.

Further 'strange events' are regularly quoted as proof of the existence of the curse. The first was that on the day the entrance to the tomb of Tutankhamun was discovered Howard Carter's pet canary was devoured by a cobra. Carter describes the incident in an article in *Pearson's Magazine* in 1923: 'But it was at this point when the nerves of all of us were at extreme tension, that the messenger brought news of the tragedy. The man, who was most breathless, told me the cobra had entered the house, passed down the passage, made its way to the room where we are now sitting, coiled up the leg of that table on which the bird cage was resting, and killed my pet!'

The canary had been seen by the Egyptian workmen as an omen of good luck and they were somewhat distressed at this turn of events, 'becoming downcast, [and] saw in the death of the bird a portent of evil omen in spite of the treasures spread out before them … had the Jinn which had protected the tomb for 3,000 years become enraged and hostile?'

In order to appease the workmen Carter contacted Lady Evelyn Herbert in the UK and got her to send a new canary. 'With the coming of the bird, cheerfulness returned to the staff.'[38]

The cobra was a symbol of ancient Egyptian royal protection, believed by some to represent the spirit of Tutankhamun,[39] giving a clear, but unheeded, warning to the archaeologist.

Weigall boldly adds that the royal cobra 'killed the symbol of the excavator's happiness displayed by the bird.'[40] Arthur Weigall is an unusual character in the cursemania story. He travelled to Egypt as a representative of the *Daily Mail* newspaper. He had worked as Chief Inspector for Antiquities in Upper Egypt in the early 1900s and it was thought he could get the inside 'scoop' on the tomb.

However, he was never actually part of the excavation team. In some records he denies the existence of a curse associated with the tomb, but was able at a later date to recall numerous details which helped to fuel the rumours with some form of authority. He is also sometimes cited as a victim of the curse, as described in the previous chapter, even though he was instrumental in its creation.[41]

Shortly after Carnarvon's death psychics and spiritualists appeared claiming to have had premonitions, or claiming they provided warnings to him. One such psychic, Cheiro (*Ki-ro*), claims to have received a premonition through automatic writing from Meketaten, a daughter of Akhenaten, Tutankhamun's father. Cheiro had allegedly been using the hand of the princess as a paperweight (see previous chapter) until just prior to the discovery of Tutankhamun's tomb.

The message Cheiro received, and which he claims to have passed onto the doomed earl, 'was to the effect that on his arrival at the tomb of Tutankhamun he was not to allow any of the relics found in it to be removed or taken away. The ending of the message was that if he disobeyed the warning he would suffer an injury while in the tomb – a sickness from which he would never recover, and that death would claim him in Egypt.'[42]

The earl, however, was not deterred from continuing work in the tomb of Tutankhamun, rather like all the archaeologists in the movies discussed in the previous chapter. Another psychic and palm reader, Velma, also claimed that Lord Carnarvon visited her on more than one occasion and was given the warning: 'I do see great peril for you ... most probably – as the indications of occult interest are so strong in your hand – it will arise from such a source.'[43]

Although this is a rather vague warning, at the second meeting, using a crystal ball, Velma described a vision which she pre-empted with the words: 'To Aton ... only god ... Universal father.' The vision in the crystal ball then apparently cleared, revealing an image of a golden mask being placed over the head of a king, which Velma believed represented the burial of Tutankhamun. The image changed to that of Howard Carter and the archaeological team carrying out their work amid a number of spirits in the tomb who, 'demanded vengeance against the disturbers of the tomb.'[44] Amidst the chaos stood Lord Carnarvon as the benefactor of the excavation. This vision was recognised by Velma as a dangerous omen,[45] and once more the popular and fashionable Amarna connection was referred to (at the time of the earl's death the Amarna period of Egyptian history was popular following the discovery of tomb KV55 (the Amarna tomb) in the Valley of the Kings in 1907, and the discovery of Tutankhamun's tomb added fuel to this obsession with the period.)

Though, historically, Tutankhamun was the product of the Amarna period, he was not a believer in the religion of his father. He had in fact restored the traditional polytheistic religion of Egypt. Surely, therefore, any curse or omen concerning the period of Tutankhamun's burial would invoke the newly reinstated god, Amun, rather than the god of his father, Akhenaten, the Aten, who had been deposed a decade earlier.

Questions also have to be raised as to why Lord Carnarvon was the first victim of the curse. Although he was the money behind the excavation, it was the archaeologist Howard Carter who carried out the work and had the most hands-on experience with the contents of the tomb, and indeed the mummy, of the Egyptian king. Surely he should have been a more fitting victim.

It is suggested in the unpublished memoirs of Sir Thomas Cecil Rapp (1893–1984), the British vice-consul to Cairo, that Carter was rattled at the death of his friend and benefactor: 'He [Carter] was suffering too from a superstitious feeling that Lord Carnarvon's death was possible nemesis for disturbing the sleep of the dead, a nemesis that might also extend to him. But he was to survive for seventeen years.'[46]

Carter, however, in his own words presents the opposite view. He is reported as stating that: 'It is not my intention to repeat the ridiculous stories which have been invented about the dangers lurking in ambush, as it were, in the Tomb, to destroy the intruder. Similar tales have been a common feature of fiction for many years, they are mostly variants on the ordinary ghost story, and may be accepted as a legitimate form of literary amusement … all sane people should dismiss such inventions with contempt.'[47]

Another source quotes Carter as saying: 'It has been stated in various quarters that there are unusual physical dangers hidden in Tutankhamun's tomb – mysterious forces, called into being by some malefic power, to take vengeance on whomsoever should dare to pass its portals. There was perhaps no place in the word freer from risks than the tomb.'[48]

It seems quite telling that Carter himself dismisses the curse theories, and it is only third-parties writing about him who claim he believed it. Carter being scared for his own life adds weight to the 'Curse of the Mummy' narrative.

Regardless of the minor detail that the most likely victim of a curse of Tutankhamun survived for seventeen years after the event, practically every aspect of the death of Carnarvon has been used as 'proof' of the curse. His last words, which were no doubt prompted by fever and delirium, have also been used to prove the case. Carnarvon said on his deathbed: 'A bird is scratching my face. A bird is scratching my face.'[49] This has been linked to a First Intermediate Period tomb inscription which claims Nekhbet, the vulture goddess, will scratch the face of anyone who does anything to a tomb.[50]

Could it be simply have been that, with a high fever, septicaemia and pneumonia, the fifth Earl of Carnarvon had itchy skin which, in his delirium, was likened to a bird? Of course, this scenario would not fit in with the curse theory narrative, much of which is taken directly from the nineteenth-century novels discussed in the previous chapter with warnings from psychics and mediums, dead animals and, of course, ominous last words.

Early Curse Research

In the same way that the genuine curses on tombs are often ignored, unusual deaths of Egyptologists prior to the discovery of the tomb is also largely unstudied.

Vandenberg, however, redresses this in his *The Curse of the Pharaohs*. He demonstrated that for many years before Tutankhamun scholars were struck down by an 'Egyptian curse', which, he stated, 'always struck men who had spent long years in Egypt and were somehow involved in excavation.'[51]

His research included case studies of eminent Egyptologists like Heinrich Brugsch (1827–1894) who became more delusional the longer he stayed in Egypt. According to records, Brugsch left Egypt abruptly in order to take up Lepsius' position in Berlin at the university. Lepsius was still in the post at the time with no intention of leaving. Brugsch then stated that if he was not given the Berlin post he would take a similar one in Paris, even though he had not been offered one.[52]

Vandenberg then discusses an unidentified paralytic disorder which was responsible for the death of Champollion in 1932 soon after his return from Egypt,[53] as well as Emery in 1971, who suffered paralysis on the right side and lost the ability to speak. The next day he died and it was recorded in the newspaper *Al Ahram:* 'This strange occurrence leads us to believe that the legendary curse of the pharaohs had been reactivated.'[54] It sounds more likely, though, that Emery, aged sixty-eight, suffered a stroke.

Vandenberg also claims that many Egyptologists die of fever and delusions, sudden terminal cancers and circulatory collapse, quoting as proof the deaths of Belzoni in Sierra Leone in 1823, George Möller at age forty-four in 1921, and James Henry Breasted in 1935.[55] This so-called 'proof' of the curse is tenuous as there are few similarities in their deaths and they are not likely, therefore, to share a common cause.

Following the discovery of the Tutankhamun's tomb in 1922 the misplaced publicity surrounding the curse intrigued and terrified generations of people. The theory was believed to such an extent that anyone who was working in the tomb, or with the artefacts within, and who died afterwards had their death reported as resulting from the curse. Some of the claims of deaths associated with the so-called curse were, however, ludicrous.

Charles Kuentz, Pierre Lacau, Bernard Bruyere and Alan Gardiner died more than forty years after the tomb was discovered and have been reported as being victims. Additionally, a number of the people who were said to have died as a consequence of the curse were advanced in years (more than eighty years old) or had travelled to Egypt as a remedy for ill health, which was not uncommon in the 1920s.

The most famous victim of the curse, as discussed earlier, was George Herbert, 5th Earl of Carnarvon, who died in April 1923 at the age of fifty-seven. He provided the funding behind Howard Carter's excavation of the tomb and was therefore one of first people to enter, and to benefit from its discovery. He had initially travelled to Egypt for his health, following a serious car accident that left him underweight and susceptible to chest infections. He died of pneumonia and septicaemia in Cairo. Howard Carter, the chief archaeologist, died in 1939, some seventeen years later, aged sixty-five. One would have thought he would have been struck down sooner, considering the extensive work he carried out in the tomb and then post-excavation on the artefacts.

Others who also worked closely with the artefacts died even later than Carter: Harry Burton, the official photographer of the artefacts, died in 1940, aged sixty; Alfred Lucas, the Director of the Chemical Laboratory of the Egyptian Government Antiquities Service, who conserved the objects, died in 1950 aged seventy-nine; Reginald Engelbach the Chief Inspector of Antiquities, died in 1946 aged fifty-eight. Douglas Derry from Cairo University, who examined the mummy of Tutankhamun, passed away in 1969 at the ripe old age of eighty-seven, and Jean Capart – who died in 1947 aged seventy – showed the treasure of Tutankhamun to Queen Elizabeth of Belgium (who was never thought to have been affected by the curse). Gustave Lefèbvre from the Institute of France and the Chief Curator of Cairo Museum, who was responsible for the organisation of the exhibition, died in 1957 aged seventy-eight; Pierre Lacau, was ninety-two when he died in 1965, and Bernard Bruyere was over eighty when he died sometime after 1965. The final victim of the curse, Alan Gardiner, who was responsible for translating all the written inscriptions, died in 1963 aged eighty-four.

This list of mainly elderly men dying between fifteen and forty years after the tomb was discovered does not present a very convincing case for this curse being a real and effective phenomena. In the 1920s the average age of death for men was fifty-seven,[56] and the majority of the so-called victims surpassed this by many years. Those who claim that the curse was a genuine thing to be feared often leave out the ages of many of these so-called victims. Egyptologist Nicholas Reeves comments: 'It cannot be denied, however that death was peculiarly selective in his choice of victims, and surprisingly long in coming for those who were perhaps closest to the work.'[57]

The curse did not just affect archaeologists but anyone who came into contact with the tomb or its artefacts. Even if they suffered an illness or a misfortune, conspiracy theorists and journalists would pounce on it as a result of the curse. So, for example, the Head of the Department of Egyptian Antiquities at the Louvre, George Bénédite, suffered a fall and a stroke following a visit to the tomb. Result of the curse. The Assistant Keeper of the Department of Egyptian Antiquities at the Metropolitan Museum in New York, Arthur Mace, died shortly after visiting the tomb, aged fifty-three of pleurisy, a condition he had long before the tomb was discovered.[58] A result of the curse. Some tried to add further intrigue to Mace's death by stating that he died in the same hotel as Lord Carnarvon[59] although he died at home in England.[60] The son of an American financier, George Gould, was said to have collapsed with fever after visiting the tomb in 1923. He died of pneumonia.[61]

The Carnarvon family were once again targets of the so-called curse when Lord Carnarvon's younger brother, Aubrey, died in 1923[62] at forty-three years old, of blood poisoning following the removal of his teeth in a misguided attempt to cure blindness.[63] Carnarvon's wife, Lady Almina, died six years later, in 1929. She, like her husband, died following an insect bite. Howard Carter's secretary, Richard Bethell, also died in 1929[64] of natural causes at the Bath Club aged forty-six years old.[65] His father, Richard Bethell, Lord Westbury, distraught with grief, killed himself by jumping from a window, aged seventy-eight. Then tragically on the way to the funeral an eight-year-old child was run over by the hearse.[66] Neither Lord Westbury nor the child had entered the tomb.

The list of curse victims goes on, but there are no similarities or patterns in the deaths, misfortunes, ages or time-lines that would genuinely support the theory of a curse being cast on anyone who entered the tomb. Moreover, following its discovery hundreds of visitors from nobility and royalty all around the world came to see it. Not all of them were struck down by the curse and many survived well into old age.

Scientific Studies

The curse of the mummy, or the curse of the Egyptian tomb, has plagued Egyptologists relentlessly since 1922. In 1934 Egyptologist Herbert Winlock tried to disprove it once and for all. He drew up statistics demonstrating that the curse of Tutankhamun was fabrication. His findings showed that twenty-six people were at the opening of the tomb and yet only six had died within a decade. There were twenty-two at the opening of the sarcophagus and only two died, and of the ten at the unwrapping of the mummy not one succumbed to death.[67]

He also added a list of some of the so-called victims of the curse, adding details which debunked these claims. For example, he reported that George Gould was ill before he even travelled to Egypt, Arthur Weigall was only allowed in the tomb as a member of the general public and had nothing to do with the tomb itself, Ali Fahmy Bey, who was shot by his wife in the London Savoy hotel shortly after visiting the tomb,[68] had only visited the tomb as a tourist and was not involved in the excavation, and workmen in the British Museum handling objects from the tomb were said to have died as a result of the curse although there had never been any Tutankhamun artefacts in the museum. He also made a general comment that many people visiting Egypt at the time were elderly and suffering with their health.[69] He felt this was compelling enough to show that the curse was fabricated.

That was not the end of the matter, however, and in 2002 a further scientific study was carried by an Australian scientist, Mark Nelson. His study investigated the length of time between exposure to the tomb and death. There were twenty-five people listed in the research who were potentially susceptible to the curse and included those who were present at the opening of the third door on 17 February 17 1923, those at the opening of the coffins on 3 February 1926, and those present at the unwrapping of the mummy on 11 November 1926. The study showed that of these twenty-five exposed individuals the mean age of death was seventy years old, and the average length of time between exposure to the tomb and death was thirteen to fifteen years, indicating that, scientifically, there was no proof of a curse causing the death of those present in the tomb.[70]

Biological Warfare

All angles of the curse have been studied over the years, though whether this was to prove or disprove is not always exactly clear. One of the most recent lines of enquiry is into germs, diseases or bacteria present in the tombs which could have contributed to the 'suspicious' deaths often associated with the curse.

There are four main theories which developed from these studies. One is that Tutankhamun himself died of an infectious disease and the bacteria that had caused it was still alive and infected those who discovered the tomb. Alternatively, it is thought that bat guano in the tomb was the cause of breathing problems; this aggravated previous ailments and ended in death. However, prior to the opening in 1923 the tomb had been air tight and there were no bats in the tomb. Following the opening bats were reported as flying around after dark, and Carter was said to have removed them each morning.[71] In the 1960s the theory of radiation was introduced, and it was thought to have been used as a natural protection against tomb robbers.[72]

The line of enquiry into bacteria was one that even caught the interest of Howard Carter, but he dismissed the theory: 'out of five swabs from which cultures were taken, four were sterile and the fifth contained a few organisms that were undoubtedly air-infections unavoidably introduced during the opening of the doorway and the subsequent inspection of the chamber, and not belonging to the tomb, and it may be accepted that no bacterial life whatsoever was present. The danger, therefore to those working in the tomb from disease germs, against which they have been so frequently warned is non-existent.'[73]

Conan Doyle, author of Sherlock Holmes and a staunch believer in the curse – as well as fairies and ghosts – was questioned about the death of Carnarvon and believed it was down to 'elementals': 'An evil elemental may have caused Lord Carnarvon's fatal illness. One does not know what elementals existed in those days, nor what their form might be. The Egyptians knew a great deal more about these things than we do.'[74]

As recently as the 1990s[75] further research was carried out on ancient Egyptian mummies, and in particular the *aspergillus* bacteria. Three forms of the bacteria have been discovered in mummies: the *aspergillus nigers, aspergillus ochraceus* and *aspergillus flavas*. The theory was originally suggested by Dr Ezzedin Taha in 1962. He demonstrated that *aspergillus nigers* may have affected the health of those working with Egyptian papyri. The symptoms were skin rashes and laboured breathing and he suggested this could be the cause of many health problems with archaeologists in general.[76] Taha suggested the bacteria may have been disturbed when the tombs were opened, becoming airborne. The bacteria was then inhaled by archaeologists, which may have been the cause of illness, organ failure, and even death if the individual was already weakened.

Various researchers have supported the findings. Merk studied rocks and dust from the tombs and found spores of two forms of *aspergillus* and *cephalosporium*. Both of these are dangerous to humans.[77] Hradecky studied food from earthen pots at various Egyptian grave sites and discovered that the bacteria was still potent and had remained so for thousands of years.[78]

These findings are interesting, and the idea of natural bacteria is a plausible theory as to the cause of death. However, without exhuming those who are thought to have died due to the curse it is impossible to prove.

Other scholars believe the ancient Egyptians actually placed poisonous substances within the tombs in order to cause harm to anyone entering into them. Lord Carnarvon's teeth are often stated as proof of this as they had chipped every few days, which some have interpreted as a sign of deep infection[79] or slow gradual poisoning.[80]

Zahi Hawass commented on entering the twenty-sixth dynasty tomb of the vizier Zedkhonsuefankh under king Apries (589–570 BCE) and his wife Naesa: 'At that moment of discovery, I felt as though arrows of fire were attacking me. My eyes were closed and I could not breathe because of the bad smell. I looked in to the room and discovered a very thick yellow powder around the anthropoid sarcophagus. I could not walk and did not read the name of the owner. I ran back out because of this smell. We brought masks for the workers who began to remove the material. I found out it was hematite, quarried nearby in Baharia.'[81]

Although there was a noxious substance within the tomb it is impossible to tell if it was placed there intentionally. It is suggested that as the archaeologists removed more than sixty bags of the powder it may have been left by the workmen and was excess material left over from painting the tomb.[82]

However, this is not the only tomb that has left the archaeologists feeling unwell. Sami Gabra, excavating in the ibis necropolis of Tuna el Gebel in the 1940s, reported that his team all had violent headaches and shortness of breath after working in the necropolis. The workers blamed this on a curse of the ibis-headed god of wisdom, whereas Gabra believed it to be noxious gases. To counter this he evacuated the tomb and left it open for a few days before returning to work.[83]

Some researchers have run with the idea that poisons were placed in the tomb as a deterrent to tomb robbers. Vandenberg believed it was a form of nerve gas that could kill instantly and he used this theory to explain why Horemheb did not desecrate Tutankhamun's tomb. [84] This theory is intriguing, but is not borne out by the evidence. As nearly every tomb was robbed, including Tutankhamun's, there should be a trail of dead robbers as proof of this toxic nerve gas. Additionally, the reuse of items from earlier burials raises the question as to how they overcame this deterrent to remove objects.

In the 1940s the theory of the power of radiation was popular. Radium is obtainable from uranium core available in roughly the same areas as gold mines, as well as in some forms of granite, which was regularly used by the Egyptians. In 1949 Professor Bulgarini believed the burial chambers were lined with stone heavy in uranium, creating a radioactive field, so when the archaeologists entered they died from radiation poisoning.[85] As this is not yet supported by the archaeology it is not a widely accepted theory.

Conclusion

Despite all the research that has gone into the theory of the curse of the pharaohs, or curse of the mummy, and the fact that it has uncovered little evidence, there are still those who believe it to be real. Careless words from archaeologists themselves can add fuel to the flames of this theory. For example, in his book *The Curse of the Pharaohs*, Zahi Hawass sends very mixed messages. He states categorically: 'I have never had an experience that I would attribute to an ancient curse.'[86] But in the chapter entitled *My Real-Life Brushes with the Curse* he lists a number of 'strange coincidences', which, to the impressionable minds of the children the book is aimed at, can perpetuate the idea that it is in fact a real thing.

He also refers to the discovery of four statues in the tomb of Inty-Shedu from Giza (2613–2498 BCE). On the day the discovery was to be announced to the world, 12 October 1992, there was a massive earthquake in Cairo and the announcement was postponed. On the new announcement date Hawass had a heart attack and the announcement never happened. Hawass glibly states: 'Maybe Inty-Shedu was shy and didn't want everyone paying so much attention to him.'[87]

He states that when he first started excavating it was his job every year to take the newly found artefacts to the Cairo museum. On that day in year one he was told his cousin had died. On the same day in year two he found out his uncle had died. And in the third year he heard his cousin had died.[88] He does not explain whether they actually died on that day, or if he had been told of the deaths by his relatives as he entered the city after working in the desert for months. He then uses a series of bad dreams following his decision to display the mummies of two children from the Valley of the Golden Mummies, which he interpreted as them asking him to display their father with him.[89] A cursed mummy or a guilty conscience?

So how do we get from the curse of the Egyptian tomb to the reanimated mummy popular in the Western media? The curses that do exist in Egyptian tombs do not state the mummy itself will wreak vengeance, but they seem the obvious choice of a protagonist for authors and movie makers.

When looking at the 'evidence' of the curse and its victims it is left ambiguous and can be questioned. In fiction, however, by presenting a mummy as fulfilling the curse there is little ambiguity. Add to that the horror of a 5,000-year-old corpse coming to life and the movie makers and authors were clearly onto a winner.

Unlike the origins or vampires and zombies, the reanimated mummy has very little by means of 'truth' behind it. Yes, mummies are real things and can be seen in museums the world over, but nowhere other than Western popular culture do they emerge from their sarcophagus and start killing people. Of all the reanimated corpses discussed in this book, the mummy as a theme is the newest and the furthest removed from its origins.

Chapter 3

Zombies in Modern Western Culture

In the last decade or so zombies have increased in popularity in Western media in the form of movies, television shows, cartoons and books. That said, however, zombies have been a part of Western culture for more than a century. Before going into the history of the modern cult of the zombie it is essential to identify exactly what a zombie is.

Dictionary.com has a number of definitions, the first being associated with Haitian Voodoo. It is described as 'the body of a dead person given the semblance of life, but mute and will-less, by a supernatural force, usually for some evil person,' or indeed 'the supernatural force itself.'

In the *Encyclopaedia of Science Fiction* the editor, Peter Nicholls, explains the social status of fantasy figures, including the zombie, in the modern world: 'Vampires are aristocratic, drinking only the most refined substances, usually blood. In the iconography of horror, the vampire stands for sex. The werewolf, who stands for instability, shapeshifting, lack of self-control, is middle class and lives in a dog-eat-dog world. The zombie or ghoul, who shambles and rots, is working class, inarticulate, dangerous, deprived, wishing only to feed on those who are better off; in the iconography of horror the zombie stands for the exploited workers.'[1]

The term zombie has also been identified as, 'a person whose behaviour or responses are wooden, listless, or seemingly rote; or automaton,' which is directly connected to the idea of a Voodoo zombie but in common vernacular. In Canadian slang the term zombie was also used to describe an army conscript assigned to home defence during the Second World War.[2]

Although zombies appeared in literature long before the first zombie movie in 1932 (*White Zombie*) the connection between the media genre is cyclical. Early literature inspired the movies, which inspired graphic novels, which in turn have inspired television series, the popularity of which inspires books based on the television shows or movies.

Literature

Zombies were introduced to the West in 1929 with W.B. Seabrook's book *The Magic Island*, which described Haitian zombies that were slow, practically brain dead and used to work on the fields as slaves. He claimed this to be 'true, without fiction or embroidery'.[3] 'It seemed that while the zombie came from the grave, it was neither a ghost nor yet a person who had been raised like Lazarus from the dead. The zombie, they say, is a soulless human corpse, still dead, but taken from the grave and endowed by sorcery with a mechanical semblance of life – it is a dead body which is made to walk and act and move as if it was still alive.'[4]

These zombies were either employed for some criminal act or sent to work on heavy tasks and beaten like animals if they did not perform the tasks adequately: 'As the zombies toiled day after day dumbly in the sun, Joseph sometimes beat them to make them move faster.'[5] The zombies retained no memories prior to being dead, and when confronted by family members they failed to recognise them, and only showed any recognition when faced with their own graves.

This captured the imagination of the Western public who had feasted on stories of vampires, ghosts and monsters for decades. In the 1930s zombies appeared in pulp fiction, though they did not crave the taste of human flesh until Romero's 1968 movie *Night of the Living Dead* (discussed below).[6]

Another early short story, which later became the inspiration for the 1943 movie *Revenge of the Zombies*, produced by Monogram, was Thorp McClusky's 1939 tale *While Zombies Walked*. It was first published in the September 1939 issue of *Weird Tales* magazine, a fantasy and horror periodical founded by J. C. Henneberger and J. M. Lansinger in 1922 and published until its last issue in 2014.

While Zombies Walked tells the tale of Anthony Kent, who travels to the south of the US to find out why Eileen, his fiancée, has broken off their relationship. She had gone to the south to take care of an uncle who had suffered a stroke, and had written to tell Kent that she did not wish to see or hear from him again.

When Kent arrived in the town, 'He saw men working, men who were clad in grimy, dirt-greyed garments that were an almost perfect camouflage.'[7] When he asked one of the workers for directions the man did not acknowledge his presence. Upon closer inspection Anthony noticed, 'Above the man's left temple, amid the grey-flecked hair, jagged splinters of bone gleamed through torn and discoloured flesh! And a greyish ribbon of brain-stuff hung down beside the man's left ear! The man was working in the cotton – with a fractured skull!'[8]

The zombie workforce in *While Zombies Walked* was led by an evil pastor, Reverend Barnes, who tortured his slaves through the use of a Voodoo doll. This almost anti-Christian theme is one that is revived in the movies of the genre following Romero's 1968 classic movie.

There were a number of early zombies in short stories, including *The Facts of the Case of M. Valdemar* by Edgar Allen Poe (1845). In this tale the narrator wants to create a zombie with the power of mesmerism (hypnosis). His friend, M.Valdemar, who is dying from an illness, agrees to allow the narrator to mesmerise him. At the moment just before death Valdemar is hypnotised and remains in the state until he dies. His corpse is able to answer questions posed to him and remains in this period of undeadness for seven months. At this point, it is decided to wake him up, at which point the decomposition of his body seems to catch up and the body dissolves on the bed.

H.P. Lovecraft also wrote zombie short stories including *Herbert West–Reanimator*, published in 1922. It was originally published as a series of six stories and has since been made into the movie *Re-animator*, in 1985, directed by Stuart Gordon, with a sequel, *Bride of the Re-animator* (1990). Lovecraft explores the notion of scientifically reanimating corpses using a specialist serum and is greatly influenced by Shelley's *Frankenstein*. Initially they are forced to rob graves, with varying levels of success, until they start murdering people in order to experiment on their corpses. All of the reanimated corpses are violent and go on a killing spree, and all bear cannibalistic tendencies. This horror is realised at the end of the fourth instalment, *Six Shots by Midnight*, in which a boxer killed in a fight is reanimated and attacks a local child: 'Looming hideously against the spectral moon was a gigantic misshapen thing not to be imagined, save in nightmares – a glassy-eyed, ink-black apparition nearly on all fours, covered with bits of mould, leaves, and vines, foul with caked blood, and having between its glistening teeth a snow-white, terrible, cylindrical object terminating in a tiny hand.' Unlike the post-Romero zombies, this reanimated corpse was killed with six shots from a gun.

In Robert E. Howard's *Pigeons From Hell* (1951) the *zuvembie*, a specific form of female zombie, was killed by the lead from a bullet. 'A *zuvembie* is no longer human. It knows neither relatives nor friends. It is on with the people of the Black World. It commands the natural demons – owls, bats, snakes and werewolves. And can fetch darkness to blot out a little light. It can be slain by lead or steel, but unless it is slain thus, it lives for ever, and it eats no such food as humans eat.'[9]

A *zuvembie* was created through voodoo rituals and a specially produced elixir, and also had the ability to control a freshly dead human for as long as they remain warm.

In recent years the Jane Austen romantic classic *Pride and Prejudice* (1813) was rewritten as *Pride and Prejudice and Zombies* (2009) by Seth Grahame-Smith, which sees Elizabeth Bennet and Mr Darcy killing zombies in between at-home visits and ball attendances. This was subsequently made into a movie in 2016 with Matt Smith and Lily James and directed by Burr Steers. There were mixed reviews at the cinema and the film made a loss. It cost \$28m to make and only grossed \$16m at the box office.[10]

The story follows the original plot of Mrs Bennet trying to marry off her five daughters at the start of the eighteenth century, but with the added twist of being set in the zombie apocalypse. All of the Bennett sisters have learned martial arts in China, which comes in useful when having to fight the undead. But Charlotte Lucas (played by Aisling Loftus) sums up the juxtaposition of this early eighteenth-century world and the post zombie apocalyptic world when she declares at the ball: 'Zombies or no zombies all women must think of marriage, Lizzie.' The zombies are slow and lumbering, but they are also able to communicate. Zombie Mrs Featherstone is about to impart a secret to Elizabeth Bennet when she is taken down by Fitzwilliam Darcy (played by Sam Riley).

Such a parody of a classic is not new and the plot of the 1943 movie *I Walked with a Zombie,* for example, was taken from Charlotte Brontë's 1847 novel, *Jane Eyre*. However, the zombies in this film were slow and listless, and closer in character to the traditional Haitian zombie than those of brain-eating monsters.

One of the most inspiring books to emerge from the zombie genre is Daniel Drezner's *Theories of International Politics and Zombies* (2011), in which he presents political theory in the context of a zombie outbreak. He outlines a number of political theories and how they would fare within such an apocalyptic situation. Although a tongue-in-cheek, pseudo-academic book, it explains political theory in an easily accessible manner.

Drezner presents different political standpoints in regard to their opinions of the undead. For example, the realist is someone who sees very little difference between humans and zombies. Humans have a natural lust for power and zombies have an instinctual lust for brains. Both power and brains are a 'scarce resource' and therefore both are susceptible to opportunistic behaviour.[11] The liberal approach to the zombie apocalypse, however, would be to try to force cooperation through sanctions; though there are few sanctions that would successfully persuade a zombie to cooperate.[12] The constructivist theory emphasises that most people, or indeed governments, abide by social norms to prevent being ostracised by other people/nations. Therefore, according to this view, zombies are made more terrifying because their ever-expanding community goes against all social norms in their pursuit of human brains.[13]

Whereas the majority of movies show a world without government intervention, *World War Z* presents what is likely to happen in the event of a zombie apocalypse. In order to distract the world from close scrutiny, China, where the virus originates, begins an international conflict with Taiwan, a technique witnessed throughout every election campaign. The United States government abandons North America and holes up in Honolulu, whereas in South Africa they leave survivors stranded in order to use them as bait to attract zombies away from the government safe zones. The Chinese Politburo, while in a safe place, sends waves of conscripts into the undead areas to keep them satiated. However, in all these movies what is always glossed over is that when the government sends in hundreds of soldiers they are in effect increasing the zombie horde rather than diminishing it.[14]

Moving away from political strategy, Scott Kenemore (2015) published *The Zen of Zombie: (Even) Better Living Through the Undead*, a self-help guide to happiness through channelling your inner zombie and learning to move at your own pace, playing to your strengths and being adaptable.

There is even a zombie cookbook, *The Art of Eating Through the Zombie Apocalypse* by Lauren Wilson, with more than eighty recipes with titles like 'Overnight of the Living Dead French Toast', 'No Knead to Panic bread', and 'Honey and Blackberry Mead'.

Classic zombie genre novels have also saturated the market over the past thirty years and many of them follow common plot lines. For example, Brian Keene's *The Rising* (2004) follows a group of individuals in the zombie apocalypse who join forces to go on a quest. Jim starts a journey across the USA to save his son, who lives in New Jersey with his ex-wife. Along the way he meets a priest, Thomas Martin, an ex-prostitute and heroin addict, Frankie, and a scientist responsible for the outbreak, Professor Baker. However, a key difference with *The Rising* from others in the genre is that the zombie affliction affects all creatures, not just humans. Therefore the countryside and the woods offer danger in the form of deer, squirrels and even birds. Another main difference is that once a human or animal dies, their bodies are taken over by sentient beings from the 'void'. The precise nature of these beings is never fully explained, but they are intelligent life forms and able to communicate with each other. They track the living, they can drive, and they can set traps and sieges to catch their quarry. *The Rising* presents an ambience of complete hopelessness with the characters realising the inevitability of turning into a zombie.

In recent years there has been a plethora of post-zombie apocalyptic novels following a band of survivors as they go on a mission to find a loved one or head somewhere safe, but there have been a few which are narrated from the viewpoint of the zombie itself. One such viewpoint can be found in Stephen Kozeniewski's *Braineater Jones* (2019). Jones is a detective in 1934 USA who is determined to discover who murdered him and dumped him in a swimming pool: 'I woke up dead this morning. Yesterday Morning. All Hallows' Eve. Whatever you want to consider it. Not dead tired. Not dead drunk. Dead. Dead. As in no pulse, no breathing, dead as a doornail dead. I mean, I've woken up a lot – I assume – and who really thinks about whether they're breathing or not?'

In this post-zombie apocalypse there is an undead quarter, which is where Jones heads to. This is essentially a detective novel, with a severed head for an assistant, and to keep his zombie brain-eating tendencies at bay, Jones has to drink liquor on a daily basis.

Zombie, Ohio: A Take of the Undead, by Scott Kenemore (2011) is also written from the viewpoint of the zombie. When college professor Peter Mellor dies in a car accident but walks away he does not remember what happened and has to deal with the zombie apocalypse from the point of view of a self-conscious zombie. He is shunned by his friends, he is concerned that he can see his brain due to his head injury, and he is not happy at being addicted to brains. He also slowly realises that the fatal car accident was not an accident and starts to investigate the truth behind it. The sequel, *Zombie, Illinois*, follows a pastor, a reporter and a female musician who are fighting to survive the zombie apocalypse: a common plot line. They also turn investigator when they realise there is a conspiracy to take over Chicago and they need to join forces, despite their differences, to prevent it from happening. In 2014 *Zombie, Indiana* was published as the third in the series.

Graphic Novels

Graphic novels have been a great source of zombie stories, some of which have later been adapted into TV series. Robert Kirkman's and Tony Moore's *The Walking Dead* graphic novel series was commissioned in 2010 by AMC into a television show, which at the time of writing was entering its eleventh season.

The first of the comic books, *Days Gone Bye* (2010), follows police officer Rick Grimes, who wakes from a coma to discover the hospital abandoned and the world overrun with the walking dead. After realising his family has fled, he decides to travel to Atlanta, which, he has been informed, is protected by the government. Upon arriving, however, he discovers the city is also overrun and he narrowly misses being overwhelmed by zombies. He is rescued by Glen, an ex-pizza delivery guy, in the nick of time. He takes Rick to a camp where other survivors are waiting for the government to rescue them. When they arrive at the camp Rick discovers his wife, Lori, and son, Carl, are safely there. The camp is inevitably attacked by zombies, forcing them to leave in order to find somewhere safer to stay.

Their ensuing adventures are the focus of the remaining graphic novels and, subsequently, the TV series. The first season covers their journey to the Centre of Disease Control, which is putting out a broadcast attracting survivors to Atlanta. However, when they arrive at the CDC they realise it's not the answer to their problems as it's overrun with walkers and unable to help.

The zombies in *The Walking Dead* are presented as soulless, focusing purely on the kill. The drawings show a distinct difference between the living and the dead, with the zombies' eyes being a key feature. These zombies are what Ben Muir refers to as Supernatural Zombies,[15] essentially caused by 'death'. In the *Walking Dead* there is no reason provided for the start of the apocalypse, and everyone has the potential to become a zombie when they die.

In February 2019 Fox promoted the upcoming ninth TV series with the first *The Walking Dead Immersive Art Gallery*, which was open for two days in the Truman Brewery, Brick Lane, London. The exhibition had a series of interactive set and prop replicas, immersive artwork and fan art. There was a recreation of the room where The Governor (David Morrissey) lived in seasons three to five of the TV show. Here visitors could join the wall of decapitated walker heads as well as examine a replica of the motorbike ridden by Daryl (Norman Reedus). There were also a few live walkers re-enacting the escape from Terminus scene from season four and other classic zombie kills. Visitors were also able to have a 'make-under' with the SFX make-up artists and be turned into a zombie.

The Walking Dead franchise has grown to colossal proportions since the first graphic novel, with a spin-off series, *Fear the Walking Dead* (2015 to present), which acts as a prequel to *The Walking Dead* (at the time of writing this was just at the end of season five). A second spin-off series, The World Beyond aired in 2020, and a trilogy of movies starring Andrew Lincoln as Rick Grimes, following his departure from *The Walking Dead* in 2018 is planned.

The smaller universe of Chris Roberson's and Michael Allred's *izombie*, on the other hand, presents a completely different approach to the zombie apocalypse. Rather than a post-apocalyptic scenario with the living fighting the dead, the dead are functioning and live and work amongst the living undetected. This universe also started life as a graphic novel focusing on the world of the main character, Gwen Dylan, a zombie who works as a grave-digger and who, after dark, digs up the corpses in order to snack on their brains. The side effect of this diet is that the final memories of the deceased filter into Gwen's subconscious. Those who were murdered or wronged in some way seek revenge or retribution via Gwen. She is accompanied in her detective activities with her friends, a ghost, Ellie, who lives at the cemetery where Gwen works, and a were-terrier called Scott, affectionately known as Spot. To complicate matters further there is a group of hot vampire girls terrorising the town, and a couple of vampire hunters who have tracked them through time.

This idea of functioning zombies is a relatively new approach to the zombie genre, with the first *izombie* graphic novel being published in 2011. In 2015 the idea was turned into a Netflix series of the same name. In the television series there were, however, some substantial changes to the plot. The main character, Olivia (Liv) Moore (Rose McIver), was a zombie who absorbed the memories of the brains she consumed and solved their murders, but the similarities end there. Instead of sneaking around a graveyard for food, Liv Moore works for the county morgue and therefore has a ready supply of brains. There were no other supernaturals living in the world, just zombies who were identified by their pale skin, and white hair, but otherwise were functioning and could hide in plain sight. 'Tan and Dye' became the zombie motto in this universe.

The only 'traditional' zombie behaviour was evident when zombies had not had their monthly brain ration or if they were threatened or angry. The longer they go without food, the more personality and social functionality is lost until they are reduced to a shambling zombie in the mindless pursuance of brains.

This development of the zombie genre, in which the undead are unidentifiable from the general community, plays on fears of the enemy within following the 9/11 attacks and the subsequent war on terror. In the same way that it is impossible to identify the fundamentalist terrorist within the community, it is impossible to identify the zombie who is one meal away from meltdown.

This is not a modern innovation to the zombie genre, but rather a reverse of an old one. In Romero's *Land of the Living Dead* (2005) the zombies start displaying signs of remembering their past lives. One zombie, Bub, salutes a member of the military, in reference to his own military past. He seems visibly hurt when the officer refuses to return the salute as Bub was undead. Other aspects in the movie which indicate zombies remember their pasts can be seen with zombies playing instruments in the street, and a zombie in the service station responding to the customer bell.[16]

Another alternative approach to the zombie graphic novel genre was *Resurrection Man* (2012) by Dan Abnett, Andy Lanning and Fernando Dagnino. This is about Mitch Shelley, who has the ability to self-resurrect and, therefore, comes back to life every time he dies. The twist in this graphic novel is that every time he resurrects he has a new super power, as well as compulsions to be in particular places and to help particular individuals. He has vague memories of his own past, but due to his multiple deaths his soul is considered overdue, and throughout the series he is being chased by the 'guys upstairs' and 'those downstairs', who will stop at nothing to capture him.[17]

Television Series

Traditional zombies based on Haitian zombies are rare on both the small and the big screen, but they do sometimes make an appearance. *American Horror Story: Coven* (series 3, 2013) introduces the traditional zombies who are brain-dead slaves rather than brain-obsessed monsters. The Voodoo queen, Marie Laveau, played by Angela Bassett, was able to raise the dead remotely and send them wherever she needed them to be. They were mindless beings until she gave the word and they would then do her bidding, which was to terrorise and kill the witches in the coven.

The sheer horror of the power of zombification was seen in episode eight, *The Sacred Taking*. Delphine Lalaurie (played by Kathy Bates) had drunk an immortality elixir prepared by Marie Laveau, who then slaughtered her family and buried her alive. One hundred and eighty years later her grave is opened and she emerges, alive and really annoyed. In this episode Delphine is decapitated by Marie and her still living head is delivered to the doorstep of the coven, thus demonstrating the power of the elixir.

American Horror Story: Coven also showed the witches practicing the art of resurgence: essentially the art of bringing living beings back to life as part of their training. Throughout this series a number of characters are brought back to life and are able to function as humans with little to distinguish them from the living other than the scars associated with their deaths. Only one character, Kyle Spencer (Evan Peters), returns from the dead with mental impairment due to the inadequacy of the witches carrying out the rituals to bring him back.

The British contribution to the zombie TV series was *Dead Set*, written by Charlie Brooker and directed by Yann Demange. The five-part series aired in 2008 and ran for five consecutive nights. It took place on the set of the *Big Brother* house and was produced by Zeppotron, one of the companies involved in the real *Big Brother* show.

The contestants in the reality TV show carry on as normal, not realising that the world outside has fallen victim to the zombie apocalypse.

73

When a member of the production staff enters the house it is the last safe place in the television studios. Once the zombie apocalypse enters the Big Brother compound the traditional tropes come into play: planning a supplies run and dealing with a zombie infiltration of the safe environment. The most effective aspect of the Brooker contribution to zombie lore was the volatile characters and the almost consistent bickering and arguing throughout the series as they try to figure out what to do. Although exaggerated, it is the most 'realistic' approach to how ordinary British people would react in this situation.

Dead Set was well received by the public and was even nominated for a BAFTA for best drama serial. In 2019 Charlie Brooker announced that Netflix would premiere a Brazilian series, *Reality Z*, which was based on *Dead Set* and was due to be produced by Brazilian production company Conspiração's Production. By the end of 2019 this still had not been released and no final date had been announced.

Netflix has, however, produced three series of a zombie comedy-horror show with a difference called the *Santa Clarita Diet*. The zombies in this series are also fully functioning and completely unidentifiable from the living. They do, though, need a diet of human flesh, and as they are essentially reanimated corpses their bodies are putrefying and so extremities and other body parts can fall off, mostly to comic effect.

The series was created by Victor Fresco and stars Drew Barrymore and Timothy Olyphant as the lead couple, Sheila and Joel. The writers deviated from the traditional theme of a virus resulting in the dead rising; instead Sheila goes through a 'transformation' with an excessive amount of vomit before a creature with legs – like a meatball spider – is evacuated. Subsequently she dies and comes back to life within minutes, and thereafter craves human flesh. Her husband, Joel, is on board to support her in her new life and they continue with their jobs as estate agents and their role as parents to a teenage daughter. To feed her, Joel and Sheila accidently become serial killers, as fresh flesh is the only thing that satisfies her.

The show's creator, Victor Fresco, and producer, Tracy Katsky, said: 'Like our audience, we were all-in on Sheila and Joel. Their relationship, in the face of incredible adversity, was inspiring to write and to watch. Mostly, they were funny, which in a comedy is important.'[18]

Similar to the AMC's *The Walking Dead* (discussed above), the SyFy channel commissioned five series of *Z-Nation* in 2014. This was set three years into the zombie apocalypse. As is quite common in the zombie genre, what instigated the outbreak is not discussed until the very end of series one.

The show was created by Karl Schaefer and Craig Engler and has more comedy than *The Walking Dead* with scenes showing zombie strippers, zombies on speed and viagra and someone exploding a zombie with a fire extinguisher. Each episode is a self-contained story within a greater plot in which the group of survivors find themselves in different situations such as in a nuclear power plant which is about to melt down, in a women-only compound where all men are 'removed', and a zombie tornado.

The premise of the show is to transport Alvin Bernard Murphy (played by Keith Allan), a prisoner who had been forcibly experimented on in order to identify a cure for the outbreak. He was injected with a vaccination and bitten. Murphy survived the zombie bites and is the last human to do so. He is being escorted from New York to the Centre of Disease Control in California by a group of survivors. This was also the plot of series one of *The Walking Dead* television series. Throughout the *Z-Nation* series Murphy morphs into a zombie/hybrid, with his skin changing colour, zombie instincts and ability to mind control other zombies. *Z-Nation* also introduces the concept of zombie animals with a zombie bear being used to execute rogue men in the all-female camp in episode eleven of season one, and a zombie sheep on the attack in episode five of season two. The animals in subsequent episodes included camels, racoons and cows.

Their journey is overseen and guided to a certain extent by PFC Simon Cruller, aka Citizen Z, played by D.J. Qualls, who is situated at the NSA outpost at Northern Lights in the Arctic Circle. He is the sole survivor at this outpost and throughout the series he slowly goes insane through loneliness, with nothing but a husky, Pup, for company.

Z-Nation was written for the small screen but following its popularity, a series of prequel graphic novels were written in 2017 by Craig Engler and Fred Van Lente. They were set one year after the apocalypse, and two years before the first series of the television show.

At the time of writing (2019) Karl Schaefer had just released a spin-off show, *Black Summer*, on Netflix, which he describes as 'a straight up scary zombie show that was as realistic as possible, but still different than what you've seen before.'[19] *Black Summer* moves away from the humour and comedy of *Z-Nation* to something more 'traditional'. It is a prequel to *Z Nation* and explains what happened in the first summer of apocalypse.

In the last few years there have also been a number of similar television shows and movies following the plot line of the dead returning from their graves some years after burial. They are exactly as they were prior to death regardless of how long it has been, but with no explanation as to why they have returned. There were two films called *The Returned:* one is French (2004) and the other is Spanish-Canadian (2013). There were also two television series, one French – *Les Revenants* (2012) – and the other from the US called *The Returned* (2015), which is a remake of the French one. There was also a series of four books by Jason Mott based on the same theme.

A similar idea is presented in *Glitch* (2015–2017), an Australian television show set in the fictional town of Yoorana, Victoria. Seven people all return from the dead, crawling out of their graves and then wandering, dazed, through town. They are initially gathered by the local policeman, James Hayes (Patrick Brammall), who starts to unravel who they are and why they are back. He tries to keep their resurrection a secret from his work colleagues, and confides in the local doctor, Elishia McKellar (Genevieve O'Reilly). The whole situation is further complicated by James' first wife being one of the resurrected, and the fact that one of the resurrected, a nineteenth-century landowner and mayor of the town, Patrick Fitzgerald, 'escaped' and is causing havoc with the help of an aborigine teenager who turns out to be a descendant.

Japanese anime has unsurprisingly embraced the zombie genre. *High School of the Dead* follows the lives of five high school students as they try to survive once their school has been overrun by zombies. The apocalypse was caused by a pandemic which turns humans into zombies. As with most zombie survival tales, they leave the high school with the aim of going to a so-called safe-place, stopping at a shopping mall and police station along the way. *High School of the Dead* started life as a manga series by Daisuke Satō before being serialised into a twelve-episode anime series by Madhouse in 2010.

Another school-based zombie show that started as a manga series is *School-live*, in which a number of school girls are the sole survivors of a zombie apocalypse and live at Megurigaoka Private High School. Once the zombies overrun the school the main character,

Yuki Takeya, is in denial about the situation and tries to maintain the pleasant school life-style, aided by her classmates. The serialisation of the manga was in 2012 and it was adapted for the screen in 2015. A live-action film was also released at the beginning of 2019.

South Korean anime movie, *Seoul Station* (2016), follows the life of a woman trying to survive once Seoul has been overrun by the undead. It was written and directed by Yeon Sang-Ho and acts as a prequel to Sang-Ho's previous film, *Train to Busan*. The story centres on a young woman who has run away and is trying to survive at Seoul Station. A father is there looking for his daughter and discovers she is working as a prostitute. Just as he plans to reunite with her the zombie apocalypse starts and they are then faced with a different kind of survival.

Gungrave (2003) is a Japanese TV series based on a computer game and tells the story of Brandon Heat, who was murdered by his best friend and Mafioso, Harry MacDowell, and was reanimated as an almost invisible zombie-creature. This is set thirteen years after his death and is a story of revenge against the friend who murdered him. The series was directed by Toshiyuki Tsuru and written by Yōsuke Kuroda and is very similar to the plotline of *Braineater Jones* discussed above.

Movies

The popularity of the zombie TV series is a fairly recent phenomena compared with zombie movies, which have been popular since the 1930s. During this ninety-year history there have been spikes of popularity: between 1969 and 1977, for example, more than thirty zombie movies were released throughout the world (Spain, Italy, Mexico, England, and USA).[20] In the last twenty years zombies have become the most common form of apocalyptic cinema plots[21] and a *USA Today* article stated, 'In the world of traditional horror, nothing is more popular right now than zombies. The living dead are here to stay.'[22] It is thought that more than one third of all zombie movies were made in the first decade of the twenty-first century.[23] It may be a case of quantity over quality, however, as Russell states: 'Zombies feel no pain, which must be a blessing considering how many crappy movies they're roped into.'[24]

Although zombies have been popular in cinema in the latter half of the twentieth and beginning of the twenty-first centuries, in the 1930s, when they first hit our cinema screens, zombies were not as popular as vampires, who were seen as superior.[25] The earliest zombie movie, in 1932, was Victor Halperin's *White Zombie*, which shows plantation slaves as zombies, thereby acknowledging their African roots.[26] There is also a short story of the same name by Vivian Meik, first published in 1933, which featured scores of zombies being used to cultivate the land. It also featured the concept of the zombies being released, and allowed to die once their zombie master had been killed. They were each in turn touched by a crucifix before they died, sending the message that Christianity was the answer to the abomination of the undead.

There are, however, only a couple of zombie movies that acknowledge the Haitian origins of the zombie as slaves. This theme is emphasised in *Sugar Hill* (1974) and in *Demoni 3* (1991), which present zombies as slaves, complete with manacles.[27]

This origin of zombies as mindless slaves has, to a certain extent, dictated zombie characteristics. In the majority of movies zombies are unable to think or communicate. They move slowly and, by rights, should not be a dangerous enemy unless the living are trapped and outnumbered. Paul Waldmann observed, 'in truth zombies should be boring … what's remarkable is that a villain with such little complexity has thrived for so long.'[28]

Perhaps their similarity to humans is the catalyst for their popularity. The thought that it *could* happen is what makes the genre interesting. Others think such movies are emphasising the need for community; ie, people banding together against the common enemy, be it the walking dead, ghouls, zombies, or the undead. The alternative to this outlook is an 'I'm alright Jack' world where everyone looks out for themselves, resulting in more fighting amongst the living. Muir makes this point when he says, 'Survival … is about surviving and you're only going to do that if you completely and unequivocally look after number one.'[29] In *28 Days Later*, the female lead, Selena, played by Naomi Harris, starts the movie with this attitude and makes it clear she will kill anyone 'in a heartbeat' who holds her back. By the end of the movie she realises that family and community are in fact essential for survival.

A classic zom-rom-com movie, *Shaun of the Dead* (2004), has this idea of community at its heart. Throughout the film there is conflict within the group of survivors who all have a shared history: Shaun's mother and stepfather, his best friend and ex-girlfriend, and his ex-girlfriend's flatmate

78

and her boyfriend. However, by the end they all realise that in order to survive they need to cooperate and Shaun (Simon Pegg) comments: 'As Bertrand Russell once said, "the only thing that will redeem mankind is cooperation". I think we can all appreciate the relevance of that now.' Of course, being a comedy this idea of cooperation is taken one step too far when four people are all helping to fire one shotgun.

At the end of Ruben Fleischer's comedy, *Zombieland* (2009), Columbus says, 'without other people you may as well be a zombie,' as he realises the people he is thrown together with are like family. The sequel, *Zombieland 2: Double Tap*, was released in 2019 and is set ten years after the first film. The four survivors – Tallahassee, Columbus, Wichita, and Little Rock – have set up home in the White House, which has been abandoned since the apocalypse started. The movie is about the continuing frictions between the makeshift family, evolving zombies and other survivors.

Whilst such a revelation as community matters is presented as something surprising in zombie movies, generally the majority of people behave in an altruistic way and help each other following disasters such as earthquakes or bombings. It is, in fact, more unusual for people to behave as selfishly as they are depicted in most movies,[30] such as Serena at the beginning of *28 Days Later,* and the Saviours, led by Negan, in *The Walking Dead* (season eight), who terrorise and torture other survivors in a display of supremacy.

Conflicting groups, though, make for more interesting movie plots and in *Night of the Living Dead* (1968) seven people trapped in a farmhouse with the undead outside find it difficult to cooperate. This results in two different groups, with one 'gang' on the ground floor and one in the basement, ruled by different people. In *Dawn of the Dead* (1978) and *The Walking Dead* some within the survivors' groups were considered undesirable and therefore not worthy to be accepted into the safety of the main group. This results in either the 'undesirable' group being left to the zombies and their subsequent deaths and then reanimation, or, as in season eight of *The Walking Dead*, a full-on war between the Saviours (the bad guys) and the groups from Alexandria, Hill Top and the Kingdom (the good guys).

But though community is often at the heart of most zombie movies, other themes have been explored. Between the 1930s and 1960s the zombie genre grew and evolved with the zombie masters being either mad scientists, Nazis or even aliens from outer space. In the 1950s representations of zombies resulting from alien invasion or nuclear experimentation were seen as metaphors for the Cold War.[31]

This was to change with George A. Romero's classic, *Night of the Living Dead* (1968) in which the dead are risen but have no master as they are simply following their own base desires. Romero's two films – *Night of the Living Dead* and *Dawn of the Living Dead* – were iconic and laid out the rules for zombies, which have been followed in cinema and television since their release. These are:

- The dead rise from the grave although the reason behind this is not always given. This has been attributed to space,[32] nuclear radiation, toxic waste, a computerised pulse,[33] a virus,[34] acne,[35] or divine retribution;
- Their sole purpose is survival through eating of the living;
- A person bitten by a zombie will die and become a zombie;
- They are slow and dim-witted;
- They cannot be injured but can be destroyed by a blow to the head;
- It is possible to kill some but not all of them as the zombie population continues to grow with each death.[36]

This list of rules is now so ingrained that the majority of movies and television series follow them. However, as the zombie genre continues to grow in Western cinema, variations are being explored to keep the genre fresh. There are, though, always constants in order to fit the genre: that they start some time after the outbreak once civilisation has been threatened;[37] and they almost never show the catalyst.

Many critics believe Romero's movies included themes of post-colonialism, psychoanalysis and Marxism, and some people believe there was an anti-Christian theme throughout the movies. There was an element of hope to the 1960's zombie: they were easily outwitted, slow on their feet and could be destroyed by a blow to the head. Romero did not refer to them as zombies, instead using the term ghoul or walking dead.

Romero's zombies were very human in their nature, which made them more disconcerting. Unlike vampires, they could go out during the day and were not immobilised by garlic, holy water or mirrors. Turning the monster into humans meant that there was no concept of 'them and us', or good versus evil: the potential to be a zombie was in all humans. Some have stated that this was a somewhat defeatist approach, as everyone was destined to die and eventually become a zombie, regardless of what actions were taken. Such hopelessness was seen by some as a rejection of Christianity. In such a post-zombie-apocalyptic world God will not, and cannot, help the living and this is emphasised in Romero's *Dawn of the Dead* (1978) with the explanation: 'When there's no more room in hell, the dead will walk the earth.'

The anti-Christian rhetoric is further highlighted when zombies attack people praying, as well as priests and those seeking sanctuary in a church, all of which are traditionally instrumental in defeating supernatural creatures. *Dawn of the Dead* even includes a zombie nun and zombie Hari Krishna, showing that devotion to religion is no barrier to the zombie.

A cult zombie film from 1973, *Psychomania*, focuses on this idea of a hopeless world. The film follows a biker gang known as the Living Dead. The leader of the gang, Tom Latham (played by Nicky Henson), has learned the secret of eternal life from his mother, and convinces the gang to commit suicide via a number of bike stunts. They all return to life and 'terrorise Shepperton', which was the location of the film studio where the film was made. Latham's mother turns herself into a frog in order to stop the biker gang who then turn into stone.[38] It is also said that there are a number of sub-texts within the movie which have contributed to its cult status. For example, the relationship between Tom and his mother is considered Oedipal, and the fact that suicide is considered the answer to initiate a rebirth is a reflection of the boredom of 1970s' youth.[39] Furthermore, this rebirth then demonstrates the gang's descent into selfishness and 'infantile hedonism' as they smash up supermarkets and drive recklessly.

In Danny Boyle's *28 Days Later* (2002) such anti-religious rhetoric is continued as, in one of the earliest scenes, the Irish Catholic protagonist, Jim, played by Cillian Murphy, enters a church for refuge. He is attacked by a Catholic priest, and despite initial misgivings is forced to kill him. This is considered to be a representation of a world without God and therefore without hope.[40]

The zombies in *28 Days Later* were also different to traditional zombies in that they were not slow and ambling. It has been questioned whether they were zombies at all as they are not really dead but rather infected with the Rage Virus. However, this has become a classic zombie movie regardless of this debate.

In *Hollywood Wants to Kill You* the virus that created the zombies in *28 Days Later* is described: 'The result is an epidemic (a local outbreak, in this case confined to the UK) of zombie humans displaying symptoms that suggest a combination of rabies and Ebola. It's not pretty.'[41]

The zombies in *28 Days Later* could sprint, they had quick instincts, and they were strong, thus showing an even more terrifying aspect to the genre. In many zombie movies they move slowly and can be easily outrun. This is in line with what 'reality' would be should the zombie apocalypse happen. Zombies are essentially decomposing corpses; the degradation of their bones and muscles would render them slow moving and they would get slower as decomposition continued. It would also be the case that the condition of the body at death would affect the initial speed of the reanimated corpse. For example, an elderly person will move slower upon reanimation than a young, fit individual.[42] But when did reality matter when making a movie?

28 Days Later also breaks with tradition by showing the catalyst of the zombie apocalypse, and placing the blame solely at the door of mankind. A chimpanzee is freed from a laboratory by animal rights activists after being infected with the Rage Virus, which makes it angry and bloodthirsty. It then infects other victims, who in turn cannot talk, bear no resemblance to their former selves and have an instinct to kill and eat other humans.

Although the victims become infected while still alive, in all respects they are zombies in that they have lost all that makes them human, and humane. Ben Muir claims they are humans 'who have been infected with some form of virus that has made them crave human flesh and become a bit grumpy.'[43] It is believed by some that following a spate of anthrax attacks in 2001 there was an increased fear of biological attacks and biological warfare and this leaked into zombie movie genre,[44] including *28 Days Later*.

Juan Carlos Fresnadillo's *28 Weeks Later* (2017), the sequel to *28 Days Later*, is thought by some to be a social commentary on the Iraq War,[45] showing the USA's heavy-handed approach. In the movie the US army is situated in London and is trying to contain the zombie outbreak. When the outbreak spirals out of control the Americans are given the order to shoot everyone, whether they are infected or not. Scarlet, an army doctor played by Rose Byrne, explains: 'It all makes sense.

They're executing Code Red. Step I: kill the infected. Step 2: containment. If containment fails, then step 3: extermination.' But even firebombing London does not stop the infection reaching Europe.

It is thought that through the representation of the zombies as 'evil' and a threat to our way of life they are deserving target for extermination. Dehumanising the 'enemy' makes killing them a lot easier and 'permits otherwise principled individuals to engage in acts of brutal violence against the perceived "other".'[46] It then becomes a moral obligation to destroy the enemy first and ask questions afterwards. It is only in the movie *Shaun of the Dead*, and in the television show *Z-Nation* that characters show any distress at having to kill undead humans. Bishop states that zombies are presented as the 'ultimate foreign other' who lack any human identity, even though they were human at one point.[47] In the event of a zombie apocalypse this would be a constant conflict within the community.

This is made clearer in *The Rezort* (2015), in which the reanimated dead are exploited. They are confined to an island known as the Rezort where holidaymakers can partake in zombie hunting as an alternative safari adventure. However, due to action by an Undead Rights Activist, the security system fails and suddenly they are actually fighting for their life. The real twist in the plot, however, is the discovery that the company in charge of The Rezort are ensuring they have enough zombies for their enterprise by making new zombies out of displaced people.

Moving away from the horror genre, the relatively modern zom-rom-com (zombie romantic comedy) is gaining traction. This tongue-in-cheek approach to zombies was introduced in the 1980s starting with Michael Jackson's *Thriller* video (1983). What followed was a number of spoof movies such as *I was a Teenage Zombie* (1986), and *Chopper Chicks in Zombietown* (1989). These spoof movies take zombies from horror into comedy. One of the main differences is that zombies do not only eat other humans, but other animals as well. In *Redneck Zombies* (1989) a zombiefied dwarf eats a cow and another zombie starts munching on his own body parts.[48]

A classic film from the UK is the chaotic *Cockneys vs Zombies* (2012) directed by Matthias Hoene and starring Alan Ford, Harry Treadaway and Michelle Ryan. In this comedy a group of East End bankrobbers not only have to escape the police but find themselves in the middle of the zombie apocalypse. The criminal gang only decided to rob the bank to get enough money to save their grandfather's care home. Once the zombie apocalypse starts the gang decide to save their grandfather and the other elderly residents from the zombies, although in reality the octogenarians are much more capable than the young gang. 'Built on the smart idea that one of the few sections of society unable to outrun zombies are OAPs, a gang of retirement home residents call up the bulldog British spirit to repel an undead invasion, while a gang of likable young 'uns find their failed bank heist becomes a secondary issue to marauding flesh-eaters.'[49]

Another British zom-com is the Christmas musical movie *Anna and the Apocalypse* (2017) in which the zombie apocalypse hits the small town of New Haven. Anna needs to get across town to get to the high school to be somewhere safe. She has to fight through zombies, zombified Santas, elves and snowmen. The film was billed as 'Shaun of the Dead meets La La Land.'[50]

A similar British zombie musical was the short film *Zombie Musical*, which was released in 2001 and directed by Ryan McHenry. A group of high school students struggle to survive the zombie apocalypse, as well as the inevitable humans gone bad, through singing and dancing.[51] In 1965 the musical *Nudist Colony of the Dead* was released in which a group of nudists commit suicide when their colony is closed down to house a religious retreat. They then return en masse to terrorise the new inhabitants through singing.[52]

Further elements were added in Jonathan King's *Black Sheep* (2006), with its advertising slogan 'There are 40 million sheep in New Zealand and they are pissed off'. The movie essentially was the tale of genetic engineering gone wrong, resulting in a flock of zombie sheep. One bite from these over-aggressive farm animals saw the victim start developing into a sheep, starting with the injured limb, thus adding an element of the werewolf myth into the zombie myth. Billed as a comedy horror, *Black Sheep* reflects the fears in society of genetic engineering and the potential of creating 'monsters', in addition to the fear of being outnumbered and unable to tell the 'bad' sheep from 'good sheep'.

Another spoof animal zombie movie was *Zombeavers* (2014) which sees a group of college kids who go to a lakeside cabin for the weekend unaware of the zombie beavers in the vicinity. The beavers had been infected by accidental spillage of toxic material into the lake. One bite from these undead creatures not only renders the victim as undead but also turns them into a beaver, complete with huge flat tail and protruding teeth.

These were not the first films to feature members of the animal kingdom as zombies. In the six *Resident Evil* movies (2002–2016) not only are humans able to turn into zombies but also dogs and birds, adding a different dimension to the fear.[53] A classic animal zombie movie, and a novel by the same name, is Stephen King's *Pet Sematary*. The story is about a rather sweet pet cemetery which local children from the town of Ludlow, in Maine, have used to bury their pets for decades. However, there is a darker side to the cemetery: anything buried in the older part will come back. Initially, Louis Creed buries their family cat, Church, in this part of the cemetery to avoid having to tell his daughter that it got killed on the road. When his younger son, Gage, is also killed in an accident, Louis exhumes him and reburies him in the old burial ground. However, both Church and Gage are different when they return.

This theme of 'them and us' is a common one in zombie media, with 'them' being either the zombies or an undesirable group of survivors. However, deeper political messages are also identified in these popular cult movies. Romero's sequel to *Night of the Living Dead, Dawn of the Dead* (1978), takes place in a shopping mall with the zombies mindlessly wandering the corridors. The zombies are believed to represent a Marxist working-class society.[54] This Marxist approach to the zombie genre was a reaction to a capitalist society in which the population has become dehumanised and mindless, governed by corporate overlords and ever-growing commercialism.[55] Francis Gooding comments: 'Completely over determined in its meanings, it also contains an allegory of the emptiness of consumer culture: a picture of the doomed fantasy that the privileged can maintain their control of the world's wealth; a commentary on class and race distinctions; a morality tale about cruelty; manifestations of a lingering death of communism.'[56]

It is thought that this was meant to be a commentary on the West's obsession with a consumerism that was growing in the late 1970s. It is also suggested that the film *28 Weeks Later* was a commentary on the apparently 'unstoppable, global spread of Starbucks.'[57] This global spread is represented by the global threat posed by a zombie infection as zombies can spread throughout the world in a matter of hours due to the extensive flight network. One zombie outbreak can be a global phenomenon within a day.[58]

It is even possible that many zombie movies play on our feeling of being overwhelmed by the sheer number of people we are surrounded with on a daily basis; for example, on public transport or in busy tourist areas.[59] The most terrifying aspect of the zombie genre is that they can emerge from within the human population and everyone has the possibility to become a zombie. Film critic Barry Keith Grant, on discussing the *Invasion of the Body Snatchers*, a movie about alien invasion, commented that the B-horror movie conveys 'its paranoid scenario of the horror within the normal.'[60] This could easily be applied to the phenomena of the zombie.

Although there are numerous 'rules' to zombie movies, many writers try to shake this up by changing some of the chief characteristics. For example, in 2009's *Doghouse* the zombie virus only affects women, whereas in Jay Lee's *Zombie Strippers* (2008) the virus turns men into zombies but women into philosophical pole dancers.[61]

Sometimes small differences are introduced which completely alter the traditional movie tropes. In the majority of movies zombies move at a very slow speed – Brooks states it is 'barely one step per 1.5 seconds'[62] – whereas in the movies *World War Z* and *28 Days Later* zombies move with almost superhuman speed so that the living and the dead are more evenly matched.

In the 1950s the fear of zombies was in the 'depersonalisation' of the human once it became a zombie.[63] Losing one's individuality was a great fear for the audiences and that is what made them terrifying. In the TV show, *izombie*, however, the undead maintain their personalities, and if they 'tan and dye' they can go undetected in the real world for as long as they can consume at least one brain a month. This takes the genre to an even more disturbing level as it is impossible to identify the living from the dead.

In *Night of the Living Dead* another level of fear was added to the zombie as they were able to use tools. In *World War Z* they even started working as a team and were able to create an undead ladder in order to penetrate the walls of Jerusalem. This is more frightening than the idea of an empty shell of a human with no characteristics or intelligence. Using tools closes the gap between humans and zombies and makes them a more dangerous adversary.

Finding a cure is a common plot line within the genre. But a cure for zombieism is in fact a cure for death itself. Often, people will hide

Mummies

(*Right*) **Fig 1**: Coffin for modern mummification. Copyright Summum. Used by Permission. (All Rights Reserved)

(*Below*) **Fig 2**: Mummy Plant Pot. Canada, Halloween 2019. (Photograph Courtesy of David Valentine)

(*Above*) **Fig 3**: The Jeremy
Bentham Auto-Icon
on a meeting at UCL.
(Photograph Courtesy of
UCL Museums)

(*Left*) **Fig 4**: Lord
Carnarvon's grave on
Beacon Hill at Highclere.
(Photograph by the author)

Zombies

(*Above*) **Fig 5**: Halloween Zombies, Canada 2019. (Photograph courtesy of David Valentine)

(*Right*) **Fig 6**: Mariachi Band at the Toronto Zombie Walk, 2011. (Photograph by Stacie DaPonte. Wikimedia Commons)

(*Above*) **Fig 7**: Decontamination Suits at the Toronto Zombie Walk, 2011. (Photograph by Stacie DaPonte. (Wikimedia Commons))

(*Left*) **Fig 8**: Zombie Island Massacre (1985) Film Poster. There is only one zombie in this film, which is part of a voodoo ritual. (Courtesy of Free Classic Images https://freeclassicimages. com/Film_Posters.html)

Vampires

(*Above*) **Fig 9**: Whitby Abbey, Yorkshire. (Photograph by the author)

(*Below*) **Fig 10**: The Circle of Lebanon, Highgate Cemetery, where the Charles Fisher Wace Mausoleum is located. (Picture by Michael Reeve, Wikimedia Commons)

(*Above*) **Fig 11**: Bran Castle Romania. (Photograph by the author)

(*Left*) **Fig 12**: Dracula's House, Sighisoara, Romania. (Photograph courtesy of BKB Photography)

Fig 13: The Dracula Experience at Dracula's House, Sighisoara, Romania. (Photograph courtesy of BKB Photography)

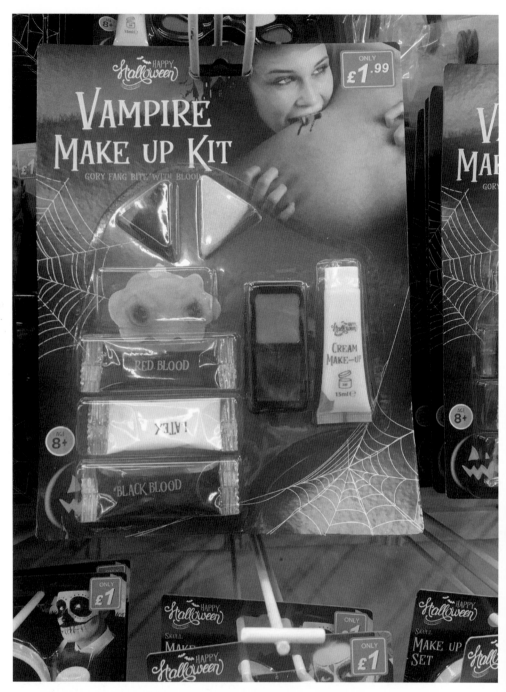

Fig 14: Vampire Make-Up Kits, Halloween 2019. UK. (Photograph by author)

infected friends and family in the hope that they can be returned to the land of the living.[64] In *World War Z* they are successful in their quest for a cure. Although there is a 100 per cent infection rate when a zombie bites a human, only healthy humans are targeted by the undead. The way of avoiding the undead is to be vaccinated with a fatal illness and thus rendered invisible to the zombies. So rather than death by zombie, death by disease is preferred.

In *iZombie* Liv Moore's colleague, Dr Ravi Chakrabati, is looking for the cure to her condition, and manages to find a temporary reprieve. In season one Ravi discovers a cure, but only has two doses, neither of which ends up curing Liv Moore as intended. Once a zombie is injected with the cure it becomes human again, albeit for a limited time. In season four another 'cure' is discovered when it is noticed that those who suffer with the fictional Freylich syndrome are immune to the zombie virus, and eating their brains can cure the condition.

The 2017 movie, *The Cured*, is the only one that deals with the time after a cure has been found for the zombie condition, and the social issues that arise from that. The cured zombies are discriminated against by society due to the number of people who were killed by zombies. *The Cured* was written and directed by David Freyne and grossed $323,776 worldwide. This is an interesting take on the genre as it hints at the zombie apocalypse being a humanitarian disaster rather than a security threat to the state. The rehabilitation of the cured zombies addresses the issue that zombies are in fact people with an 'illness' and is perhaps a more realistic representation of what would happen in a zombie apocalypse. This theme emerges sometimes in TV zombie shows and films. For example, in *The Walking Dead* (season two) Hershel keeps the zombies of his friends and family in the barn in the hope that there will one day be a cure ('we don't shoot sick people') raising the ethical question of the humanity of zombies. This humanity is perhaps what makes zombies an ideal horror character as they are essentially human and a mirror of ourselves and what we can/will become.[65]

International Zombies

Zombies have not just lumbered onto the screens of English-speaking nations. They are also starting to infiltrate international cinema.

In 2013 *The Rise of the Zombie* introduced Indian cinema to the zombie genre. This was directed by Luke Kenny and Devaki Singh, but it was not received well by the critics and had very limited release. In the film wildlife photographer Neil Parker is an exceptional talent but is a lot less successful with his personal life. His girlfriend leaves him and he goes on another isolated assignment where he is camping in the woods. However, a bite from a mosquito changes him into a zombie-type creature.

This is the only zombie-based Bollywood movie and also one of the first to suggest the zombie virus can be transferred by the bite of a mosquito. A terrifying thought. Muir however points out that should the zombie apocalypse happen, 'some insects aid in decomposition. Something that is generally overlooked by popular media in the depiction of the undead is that they will most likely be surrounded by flies and will have other insects living in or on them. Zombies are rotting flesh and this will attract some insects to them … the flies who eat the zombie flesh may then be able to transmit the virus.'[66]

The first Swedish zombie film was *The Zombiejäger* (2005) directed by Jonas Wolcher. There is a zombie outbreak in Gothenberg and three mercenaries are hired to contain it. The three 'heroes' start a hunt for the necromancer who is actually raising the dead. This film was not received well by critics: 'Silly, grim and totally witless, it looks like it was conceived down the pub and shot during the next day's hangover.'[67]

French film *Night Eats the World* (2018), directed by Dominique Rocher and written by Jérémie Guez, Guillaume Lemans and Rocher, is an interesting twist on the zombie genre and an adaptation of Pit Agarman's novel. Sam visits his ex-girlfriend's flat in Paris to pick up some possessions, but she is in the middle of a house party. He gets a nosebleed and shuts himself away in a back room where he falls asleep. When he wakes the next morning the house is empty. He finds his zombified ex-girlfriend in the hall as he ventures from the apartment. The film then follows his life as he lives in the flat, protecting himself and the flat from the zombies. There is very little dialogue and very few characters, but the film offers an almost realistic approach to the aftermath of a zombie apocalypse.

Netflix has produced the French-language Canadian movie, *Ravenous* (2017), directed by Robin Aubert and starring Marc-André Grondin, Monia Chokri, and Brigitte Poupart. The film is set in a small town in Quebec and looks at how they deal with a zombie attack. There are a few survivors in the town and they have a small patrol who attempt to keep the town safe. What follows is a standard survival movie with the survivors in the town fleeing and meeting other survivors along the way. Some of the tropes used have been compared to the 1968 *Night of the Living Dead*. The only twist is that, at the end of the movie, newly formed zombies are seen standing around a stack of chairs with a parrot on top. Though the significance is not explained, gives the impression the zombies have a form of religion and are therefore sentient.

In his review Robert Everett-Green believed this film to be an allegory for Quebec politics. The zombies with their own possessions and the possibility of a religion were a threat to the native culture. He stated: 'Imagine the Quebec homeland being overrun by a hegemonic tribe with its own culture, and its own irresistible method of converting the inhabitants into beings such as themselves. That is the worst Québécois nightmare, from the Conquest of 1759 to the arrival of niqabs on the streets of Montreal.'[68]

Erotic Zombies

Vampires are often associated with sex and so it seems almost natural that there is a market for vampire pornography (see chapter five). But though zombies are not naturally considered to be sexy and erotic there are a surprising number of movies of zombie erotica.

Porn of the Dead (2006), for example, is a hard-core pornography zombie flick directed by Rob Rotten. There is little plot or dialogue, 'just a lot of sex between blokes in decontamination suits and various zombie women covered in boot polish and blood.'[69]

A more plot-led film is the Italian *Porno Holocaust* (1981) in which scientists visit an island 'inhabited by a radioactive, mutant zombie with a huge penis.'[70] What ensues is a lot of sex and killing as the zombie goes on the rampage. The following year another Italian movie was released called *Erotic Orgasm* in which a witch creates zombie sex-slaves.

A soft-core offering is *Orgy of the Dead* (1965) which features a number of topless zombies dancing on gravestones. A couple who were killed in a car crash are forced to watch this undead dance-off.[71] The 1977 French movie *Naked Lovers* sees a man haunted by the zombie of his dead wife whenever he tries to sleep with his new wife: 'The rest of the movie concentrates on a series of sexual couplings intercut with hard-core close-ups of throbbing genitalia.'[72]

The Necro Files (1997) was a low-budget erotica film which starts with a rape scene. When the offender, Logan, is shot and killed by the cops he returns as a zombie and continues his spree of sexual assaults 'with a decaying face and an oversized penis.'[73]

Games

Moving to a more sedate pastime, Zombies are also popular in the board game market, with one of the most complex being Plaid Hat Games' *Dead of Winter: A Crossroads Game,* a multi-player game of strategy and survival. The manufacture description states that it 'tests a group of survivors' ability to work together and stay alive while facing crises and challenges from both outside and inside.' The players work together towards the main survival goal, but each player also has a personal secret which could be a 'psychological tick that's fairly harmless to most others in the colony, a dangerous obsession that could put the main objective at risk, a desire for sabotage of the main mission, or worst of all: vengeance against the colony.' [74]

Zombie Dice is a less complex game with the goal of eating brains and not being shot. In this game the player is the zombie and is playing against other zombies. There are thirteen custom dice which represent the victims and you keep rolling the dice until the shotgun symbol ends your turn. In each turn you take three dice from the box and roll them. A brain symbol is worth one point, and footsteps allow you to reroll this particular dice. If a player gets three shotgun blasts during their turn, it is over and they get no points. Whichever player collects thirteen brains first wins.

There are even solo zombie games such as *Dawn of the Zeds*, from Victory Point Games. The virus, or poison, known as 'Zombie Epidemic Disease' (ZEDs) starts the zombie apocalypse although in true zombie trope fashion it is not clear how the disease spreads. The objective of the game has players running the town of Farmingdale, while at the same time trying to survive in the zombie apocalypse. The player must defend the town against the zombie invaders and lead local people in the war against the Zeds dealing with zombie incursions, supply and ammo shortages, and hopefully finding the cure for the infestation.

Zombies are also popular with the video game market with numerous cross-overs from the small and big screen. These include *World War Z*, *Resident Evil* and *The Walking Dead*. Numerous new games were introduced in 2019 including *7 Days to Die*, which 'finds you seeking food, shelter, and water in Navezgane, Arizona, as you work to survive as long as you possibly can against the harsh new environment and the austere hordes of zombies that want nothing more than to have you for lunch.'[75]

Lollipop Chainsaw follows in the wake of zom-coms with the players taking on the role of zombie-hunting cheerleaders. 'It's a high-energy romp through a world of peace, love, rainbows, and gore, and certainly the cure for the common zombie game, especially if you love bubbly characters and personalities like Juliet's.'[76]

A less tongue-in-cheek game is *Days Gone*, where the player is a biker-turned-outlaw who is searching for his wife. In order to reach her he has to encounter 'freakers', or the undead. The game was developed by SIE Bend Studio and released in April 2019. Although there were mixed reviews in the UK it was the best-selling physical game in the release week.[77]

Romero is acknowledged in *Dead Rising*, in which the players are trapped in a shopping mall that's crawling with the shambling undead. This was initially released in 2006, and has since had four games plus two remakes: *Chop Till you Drop* (2009) and *Off the Record* (2011). The game was so popular that in 2010 a Japanese movie, *Zombrex: Dead Rising Sun*, was released, based in the *Dead Rising* world.

An alternative to becoming a zombie-slayer is *Stubbs the Zombie in Rebel Without a Pulse*, created by Wideload Games in 2005. It allows the player to become a zombie with the objective of not only killing humans and eating their brains, but also looking for love.

There are also video games for children, with the latest (at time of writing) being *Plants vs Zombies*. This was produced by PopCap Games, originally for Windows and OSX, although as the franchise developed it has expanded to a number of consoles and handheld devices. In the game the player is a homeowner who is protecting their homes during the zombie apocalypse. They are aided in their battle by plants bearing special skills, such as being able to launch projectiles. This franchise was originally launched in 2008 and in September 2019 the latest instalment, *Battle for Neighborville*,[78] was released.

Live Action

For those who want some realistic live action zombie apocalypse activities there are plenty of options, ranging from passive experiences to those of a more immersive nature. Since 2001 in Toronto there has been a zombie walk through the streets with hordes of people dressing as the undead (see fig. 6). Some are ambling along, others are lying on the floor waiting to reanimate. The Zombie Walk started initially as a promotion for the Trash Film Orgy, a midnight film festival held in Sacramento, California and has caught on. Participants in the Zombie Walk obviously take part for fun but for some it helps them 'express cultural anxieties over death and warfare.'[79] (See fig. 7.)

For runners there is the 5km zombie inflatable survival run – organised by UK Running Events – where the runner not only has to scale over inflatable obstacles but also 'survive eight zombie-filled "infected" zones … our Zombies will aim to remove your three "lives" from your tag belt, as you run past them.'[80]

Alternatively, runners can download the *Zombies, Run!* exer-game created by Adrian Hon of London games studio Six to Start and the author Naomi Alderman in 2012. Alderman explained how she took a beginners course in running and when they were asked why they wanted to run one woman answered 'to escape the zombie horde'. This gave the inspiration to start the app.[81] The advertising strapline states: 'You tie your shoes, put on your headphones, take your first steps outside. You've barely covered 100 yards when you hear them. They must be close. You can hear every guttural breath, every rattling groan – they're everywhere. Zombies. There's only one thing you can do: Run!'[82]

The player will hear one of 200 missions they are expected to carry out while out on a run, either outside or in the gym. The player takes on the role through the missions as Runner 5, receives instructions from Able Township and collects supplies to build up a survival base. Whenever the runner hears zombies behind them they must speed up. The missions are written by Naomi Alderman and her team, and includes guest writers such as Margaret Atwood and Andrea Phillips. There are a total of seven seasons with approximately forty missions per season.

The *Zombies, Run!* app was well received by the general public and was the highest-grossing health and fitness app sold by Apple within the first two weeks.[83] Alderman believes the success is because *Zombies, Run!* is: 'the first fitness game with a real story, not a marketer's idea of a "story" which means picking one of three "cool characters" to be your "coach". Games are great at motivating action. But stories add meaning to your action. That's the sweet spot I think we've hit.'

In 2012 a spin-off app called *Zombies, Run! 5K Training* was launched and offers a 'Couch to 5K' programme for new runners which has twenty-five missions that will take eight weeks to complete.[84]

For a more immersive experience there are *Zombie Experiences*. These are three-hour events where the visitor is trained to hunt and kill zombies before being immersed in the 'experience', which takes place in nine different scenarios including an asylum, bunker, factory, forest, and a shopping mall. The experience is completely plot driven, with make-up and professional special effects. All participants are furnished with laser weapons that record the hits (and misses) and the experiences can also involve survival techniques.[85]

Another option is to be a zombie for a day at *The London Tombs*, which is promoted as London's scariest attraction. This six-hour experience enables the visitor to witness the specialist FX make-up artists do their work as they transform them into zombies and then take part in a live show 'scaring loved ones and strangers alike.'[86]

The Zombie Uprising company offers something similar but with different scenarios including a circus, a clinic, a sanctuary, or a barracks. 'You and your teammates will be armed with a single weapon and given a mission. From there you will have to battle and reclaim the outbreak zones that have become infested with the walking dead … if fear doesn't get you something else will.'[87]

Zombie Combat Paintball is another means of acting out zombie apocalyptic fantasies in a night-time experience. The activity is described on the website as: 'Using our Zombie Graveyard Paintball arena we are able to offer a Zombie Themed Paintball Experience using our two storey Church as well as Crypts, Coffins and a Graveyard! You will split into two teams of survivors to battle it out for life supplies whilst trying to avoid our resident Riot Zombie who can be fired on but that will just make him angry and faster. If he gets you .... you're out. In this Creepy Graveyard within the middle of the Forest this is a truly Awesome Paintball Game.'[88]

Better Safe than Sorry

For some, the zombie apocalypse is more of a reality than these experiences would suggest. In 2013 hackers from Montana, USA, were able to hack into Montana Television Network and convinced a number of viewers that the zombie apocalypse was actually happening.[89] They interrupted a talk show with the message that 'dead bodies are rising from their graves and are attacking the living ... do not attempt to approach or apprehend these dead bodies as they are considered extremely dangerous.'[90] Even though most of us are aware there are no cases of actual corpses rising from the dead as zombies this does not prevent insurance companies cashing in and ensuring against the zombie apocalypse. My Zombie Insurance charges between $0.99 and $2.99 for different insurance plans. These include insurance against zombie bite, the transmission period and defensive combat against zombie attack liability.[91]

So what is the reality behind zombies? Could the insurance companies be onto something? Zombies and the possibility of a zombie apocalypse have become the subject of a number of university studies to demonstrate political theory, as well as the impact it would have on states and their populations. For example, in Canada the universities of Carleton and Ottawa state: 'An outbreak of zombies infecting humans is likely to be disastrous, unless extremely aggressive tactics are employed against the undead ... [A] zombie outbreak is likely to lead to the collapse of civilisation, unless it is dealt with quickly.'[92]

At Utah State University Dr James Powell has created a human vs zombie game to look at survival and contagion rates. Another social studies course at Michigan State University used the zombie apocalypse to investigate the effect of catastrophes on societies and social behaviour.[93]

Even the United States Center for Disease Control, a US government body, has launched *Preparedness 101: Zombie Apocalypse*, which helps people prepare for disaster.[94] They have used zombies in their campaigns for some time with the strapline, 'if you're ready for the zombie apocalypse, then you're ready for any emergency,' which was aimed at expanding their reach for their emergency preparation advice.[95]

Different approaches to such an apocalypse vary. The neo-conservative approach would be to throw as much military power as possible at the problem until it is 'solved', whereas it is suggested that the realist view to the zombie apocalypse would less cataclysmic: 'To them, a plague of the undead would merely echo older plagues, from the Black Death of the 14th century to the 1918 influenza pandemic.'[96]

One thing the movies do not prepare us for is that should a zombie apocalypse happen the political response would not be quick as policies would need to be addressed and passed. Movies tend to go straight into the post-government apocalypse where there is no law and order, or even insurance companies with which to file your claim.

Chapter 4

Identifying Zombie X

As we saw in the previous chapter zombies are a huge part of modern Western culture and feature in literature, movies and common parlance. It is often thought that Lafcadio Hearn introduced the term zombie to the West in an article in *Harpers* magazine (1889). He had recently arrived in Martinique, where the term zombie applied to goblins, ghosts and monsters, so it seems unlikely he brought this term with its current meaning.

One of the earliest records of the word *zonbi* (an alternative of zombie) actually appears in 1797, when travel writer Moreau de Saint-Méry refers to it as a 'returned soul'.[1] The word had also appeared in *History of Brazil* (1819) by Robert Southey when he was discussing an ex-slave republic in Penambuco. Zombi was the name of the chief, which in Angolan meant 'deity'. However, the Catholic Portuguese, who had colonised Brazil and Angola in 1500, interpreted the word zombi as another word for devil,[2] which fits with their idea of pagan religions. 'From deity to walking corpse is a very large leap'[3] and indicates that the origin of the word and the origin of the zombie as we know it are very different.

In modern Western culture the 'zombie' morphed from mindless slave to brain-eating monster, from the result of a man-made virus to functioning corpses, and from zombie sheep to virus-carrying mosquitos. However, the origin of the zombie myth is far removed from these evolving characteristics of the Western zombie and this chapter will investigate the form that 'Zombie X' took.

To identify this we need to travel to sixteenth-century Haiti in the Caribbean. It was known then as San Domingue and in 1697 had been given to France in the Treaty of Ryswick. Under the control of the French the island became economically viable through the use of African slaves to working on plantations. Some African nationalities were favoured over others for their perceived 'qualities'. The Senegalese, for example, were thought to have superior morality and taciturn character. The population from Sierra Leone and the Ivory and Gold Cost were thought to be stubborn and most likely to revolt and run away, whereas those from Nigeria were considered more likely to commit suicide.[4]

By the eighteenth century there were thought to be 500,000 African slaves in Haiti but only 50,000 French masters. Haiti was an important island economically for France. The export of indigo, cotton, coffee, cacao, tobacco and sugar generated two-thirds of the country's international trade income.

However, with such a disparity in numbers, in 1791 there was the first inkling of a slave revolution. It took thirteen years to come to fruition, when the island gained independence. The French withdrew in 1803 and Haiti was declared independent in January 1804. This was the only successful slave revolution in history. It was violent and characterised by torture and bloodshed, but in the end the French were simply outnumbered by the slaves by ten to one and were overcome.

Following the revolution many ex-slaves returned to the land to produce food for national markets, refusing to work for international traders. By 1825 only £2,000 of exports were generated, a small fraction of the £163 million during the height of the French colony. Haiti was once again occupied in July 1915 when the US Marines landed under the orders of President Woodrow Wilson. However, due to civil unrest the US withdrew and Haiti has been self-governed since 1934.[5]

Religion

Under the seventeenth-century French colonists, the African slaves had Catholicism forced upon them: 'the West Indians generally associated the terrors of African witchcraft and the horrors of their American slavery with the demons of Christianity.'[6]

Traditionally, in such colonial situations belief systems are often the last aspect of culture to disappear, and in this instance resulted in a juxtaposition of West African traditional belief systems and Catholicism. This new Haitian religion is commonly known as Voodoo (or vodou).[7] The word comes from the Fon language of Dahomey, an African kingdom that was absorbed into the French Empire in 1894, and means 'god' or 'spirit.'[8]

Voodoo is more than a religion. It is a way of life with no separation of the sacred and the secular. Every worshipper can be 'possessed' by a *loa* (god, demon or spirit) and therefore can essentially become a god and be touched by the spirits on a very personal level.

In Haiti, Catholicism and Voodoo are very closely intertwined, and some Haitians believe that to 'serve the *loa* you have to be Catholic.'[9] *Loa* characteristics are closer to the idea of Catholic saints than deities and include ancestors as well as divine spirits.[10] St Patrick, for example, who chased the snakes from Ireland, is considered by Voodoo practitioners to be an incarnation of the snake-god Damballah-Wèdo. The Lady of Sorrows is worshipped as Ezili-Freda-Dahomey because the jewellery and sword adorning the saint in one specific painting are similar to that of the Voodoo *loa*. Papa Legba, the most powerful *loa*, who represents the sun and guards the gateway between the material and the spiritual world, is connected with both Christ and St Peter.[11] Baptism is also an essential part of the Voodoo religion, not only for worshippers but for the *loa* and the cultic objects (drums, necklaces, clothing etc.).[12] In fact, Monseigneur X commented that Voodoo practitioners: 'worship the pictures of saints and one might say no saint in the calendar is excepted from the attention unless it be those whose likenesses have not been imported into the country.'[13]

Even Catholic and Voodoo calendars coincide and Voodoo practitioners close their sanctuaries during the forty days of Catholic Lent. Additionally, during Lent there is a very special Voodoo festival known as Rara, specifically for the Haitian peasant class, with processions and rituals carried out for the Voodoo *loa*. It is, though, very much connected with the Christian calendar, with the culmination of the festival being Holy Week. During the slave era Holy Week was a time of holiday for the slave populations and this festival remains to this day a reminder of that time in their history. Spiritually the angels, saints, and Jesus enter into the underworld on Good Friday.[14] During Holy Week Voodoo icons and statues are covered with a sheet in the same manner as icons in Catholic churches.

Following the 1791 revolution the ex-slave population bonded over their shared African heritage and their shared Catholic and Kongolese religion, known as Voodoo. The slave revolution unnerved the slave owners of America and this fear was transferred to the reception of this semi-pagan religion. *The Encyclopaedia of Religion and Ethics* (1908–1922) describes it: 'Voodoo is devil-worship and fetishism brought from the Gold Coast of Africa by negro captives to the United States and West Indies. Its chief sacrifice is a girl child, referred to by the initiates as the "goat without horns" [...] there is a regular priesthood to intimidate and rob the devotees.'[15]

Emergence of Zombies

It is from this religion and the slave community that the zombie originated. The fate of the zombie and that of a slave were considered similar: torn from their families, removed from society and forced to work for another after spending time confined in a coffin (slave ship).[16] Following independence from America in 1934 the cult of the zombie really took root amongst the black Haitians, formulated from the fear of further enslavement,[17] to which death was the only release.

The Haitian zombie is very different to the zombies of Western culture. A traditional Haitian zombie is a recently deceased individual who is abducted by a *bokor* (priest). Through a series of 'magic' rituals the *bokor* can enslave the deceased by removing their soul and free will in order to do his bidding or be sold as slave labour. A Haitian zombie does not feast on brains or kill humans. Instead a Haitian zombie simply works tirelessly.[18] When the *bokor* has achieved his aims with the zombie he can sell it to another owner, or even to a butcher for meat.[19] This is even more worrying for the general population as there is the fear that eating the flesh of a zombie could result in illness or death. Some have viewed this aspect of zombification as a reference to Christian communion whereby the body and blood of Christ are consumed: essentially a man who died and returned to life and therefore something not to be trusted.[20]

Not all zombies are left to this fate. Some are released by the *bokor* and are able to return home. Release can be the result of various actions. A zombie could, for example, be released should they consume salt, which immediately enables the zombie to realise their current situation, and to attack and ultimately kill their slave master. The zombie then returns to their grave where they once more turn into a rotting cadaver.[21]

Other ways in which the zombie could be released include the death of the *bokor*, the zombie astral (an element of the soul) being freed from its container, the zombie being removed by his/her family, or through divine intervention.[22] However, even when a zombie has returned home they do not regain their original faculties and instead remain in the catatonic state both mentally and physicaly, which can result in their capture once more. Most *bokors* claim that returning a zombie back to their pre-zombie state is not in fact possible.[23] This concept of a living death is considered horrific to most Haitians; as indeed it would do in most cultures.

Various anecdotal records exist of people being made into zombies who have later escaped and returned home, but no stories or evidence exists of zombies actually held in captivity.

According to popular Haitian belief, many zombies were said to be forced to work in the fields, whipped mercilessly and fed the bare minimum, which was a clear reflection of life in the Santa Domingue slave colony.[24] However, if controlled by a *hungan* (a priest who practices black magic) the zombies could be used to commit crimes on his behalf. For example, some zombies, known as *zombi-graines*, were said to have stolen flowers from the neighbour's coffee plants and grafted them to the *hungan's* plants, therefore increasing his productivity and wealth.[25]

The fear of being made into a zombie slave for eternity is such a central part of Haitian culture that zombification (the act of making a zombie) is a crime under the 1883 Haitian Penal Code (Article 246). While the victim is technically alive the crime is treated as murder,[26] stating: 'Also to be termed intention to kill, by poisoning, is that use of substances whereby a person is not killed but reduced to a state of lethargy, more or less prolonged, and this without regard to the manner in which the substances were used or what were their later results […] If following the state of lethargy the person is buried, then the attempt will be termed murder.'[27]

A number of secret societies, including the *zobop, bizango, cochon gris* and *secte rouge* have all been implicated in the crime of zombification. These societies are themselves illegal under sections 224 and 227 of the penal code.[28]

Whilst the Haitian community fear being zombified, they do not fear the zombies themselves. Instead they have compassion and pity for them. The fear of losing liberty and being controlled by another is a greater fear than that of the zombie.[29] In fact, in reported cases of returning zombies (see below) families took them into their homes to care for them.[30]

Such an altruistic act can be difficult for the families. 'Socially' the returning zombie is no longer classified as a human. At some point in the past they died and were buried, and so have lost their place in society. The returning zombie has no place to return to and is therefore ostracised by society and termed 'zombie' for the rest of their returning existence: ie, they are stuck between death and life.

This fear of being controlled after death by a *hungan* or *bokor* manifests itself in another aspect of the Voodoo belief system: that of the *Expéditions* or Sending of the Dead. This is when the spirit of a deceased individual is sent after another individual in order to possess them.

There were different means of sending the dead after a victim. One way of ensuring the deceased remained near the proposed victim was by hammering two nails into a beam in their house.[31] At other times the Catholic Saint Expedit, the patron saint of speedy cases, would be called upon to send the deceased to the victim as the saint was viewed in the Voodoo religion to be a great sorcerer.[32] He would work in collaboration with the Voodoo Bawon Sam'di, master of the gods. Such *Expéditions* result in the victim being possessed by the 'dead'. Most cases are fatal and see the victim grow thin, spit blood and then die shortly afterwards.

Some of these possessions of the dead can be cured by a *hungan* with a series of medicinal herbs and a talisman to ward off the 'dead',[33] or by locating the nails in the beams of the house which can simply be removed. Other possessions, however, are not so easily remedied. In some cases a powerful *mambo* (priestess) will perform an exorcism comprising numerous superstitious rituals including feeding the victim garlic, encouraging a hen and a cockerel to peck grain from their body, and showering themselves with leaves and vegetation. A particularly telling aspect of the exorcism is when the *mambo* appeals to higher deities: 'I ask you for the life of that man there, I buy him cash, I pay you. I owe you nothing.'[34] This indicates that it was generally believed that the purchasing of the soul or sanity of the man was possible with money, even from a god. This shows that the fear of losing liberty (mental or physical) in life or death has firm roots in the religious beliefs of the Haitians.

South African Zombies

Although there is little doubt that the Western zombie originates in Haiti there are similarities in South Africa and a strong association with the fear of slavery. Witches are the equivalent of the *bokor* and they are said to produce *ditlotlwane* (zombies) by capturing the victim's shadow or aura, allowing them to slowly take control of different parts of the body until they have complete control. The witches then cut out their tongues so they are unable to communicate.[35] To fool the victims' families they leave an icon with them so they believe they are dead and bury them. [36]

Accusations of witchcraft and of keeping zombies are often made against neighbours and relatives, particularly the *nouveau riches* as well as 'prosperous outsiders', who are thought to gain their wealth by putting the zombies to work in the fields. It is thought that this may have originated from the memories of slavery and absentee landlords who become wealthy off the backs of slave workers.[37]

Niehaus carried out anthropological fieldwork in the 1990s in Impalahoek, in the Bushbuckridge municipality of Limpopo. He recorded twenty-seven accusations of witchcraft before 1960 against neighbouring groups. There were five accusations of zombie-keeping, but these were made against very poor individuals who were thought to resort to using zombies to increase their yield and thereby even out the inequalities within the community. Since 1960 accusations have increased, with 197 people accused of witchcraft and thirty-nine accused of keeping zombies.[38] It was widely reported that sixty-nine per cent of the victims of the witches were children,[39] and most of the accused witches were between fifty to seventy years old. The accusations arose from suspicion at how they managed to make ends meet without family to help them or how they managed to achieve difficult tasks by themselves.[40]

This practice continues into the modern era. Since 1986 activist members of the African National Congress (ANC) carried out witchcraft-eradication campaigns around the countryside to eliminate immorality.[41] It is thought that witches were metaphorical representations of white slave masters in the minds of the villagers, while zombies represented the slaves. Between 1978 and 1985, when migrant workers commuted by newly constructed railways, it was believed that witches were transporting the zombie workers by train in the dead of night. These trains were also said to abduct people who wandered around at night, and when asked if they wanted a 'single or 'return', if they answer 'single' they were killed and joined the zombie hordes on the trains. To further add to the belief, these zombie workers only required maize porridge for sustenance, the same food that the slave workers survived on.[42]

Case Studies

Only four cases of zombification have been examined and reported by doctors, all with intriguing results. A true case of zombification can only be identified when there is no evidence of mental illness in the individual. It is therefore not surprising that at the time the 1883 Haitian Penal Code (Article 246) was introduced there appeared to be more cases of zombieism as mental illnesses often went undiagnosed.

Three cases of so-called zombies in Haiti were re-examined in 1996–7 in their homes with their families offering information on the process: they were Francina Illeus, a thirty-year-old woman, Wilfred Doricent, a twenty-six-year-old man, and MM, a thirty-one-year-old woman.

Francina Illeus died following an illness which resulted in her suffering digestive problems. She died at home and was buried the following day in the above-ground family tomb. Her body was identified as dead by a local magistrate. She was recognised in the village three years later, mute and unable to feed herself. She walked slowly with her head down, appeared to be oblivious to the world around her, and did not answer any questions when addressed.

Her identity was corroborated by her family and family friends, who recognised her by a scar on her temple. Upon examination, her tomb was discovered to be full of rocks and the family immediately accused Francina's husband of zombifying her in retribution for an affair she had. Francina was submitted to a psychiatric unit in Port au Prince, where doctors claimed she was 'unremarkable' and offered the final diagnosis of catatonic schizophrenia, which was 'a not uncommon psychiatric illness'[43] in the region.

The next zombie to be examined was Wilfred Doricent who, at eighteen, became ill and died. Shortly after death his body bloated quickly. He was buried in the family tomb near the house. Although according to custom the tomb would normally be watched on the first night, in Wilfred's case this tradition was not carried out. Nineteenth months later Wilfred was seen by his father in the local market place. Wilfred accused his uncle of zombifying him, though he was unable to describe the process of zombification or recall the nineteen months that had elapsed since his funeral. He had injuries to his wrists consistent with being chained, and he also had a small hole, 5mm in diameter, in the centre of his chest. He walked slowly and his family claimed he needed assistance in bathing. They also felt the need to shackle his feet to prevent him from hurting himself in his zombified state.[44]

Other relatives and villagers confirmed the identity of Wilfred and the uncle was arrested and given a life sentence for zombification. His justification was jealousy of his brother who was literate and had registered all the family land in his name. In 1991 Wilfred's uncle escaped prison during political unrest, but was later traced and interviewed. He claimed his confession was given under torture and that he was innocent of the charges. A female cousin who owned the land upon which the tomb was situated refused to allow it to be opened and examined upon Wilfred's return. Medical examination of Wilfred produced the diagnosis of organic brain syndrome and epilepsy. Administration of medication (phenytoin 100mg) reduced his epileptic fits to once a month.

The third case of zombification is MM, who was eighteen when she became ill with fever and diarrhoea following a prayer meeting for a neighbour who had been zombified. Her body swelled up before she died, in a similar manner to Wilfred, and she was buried in the traditional manner. Thirteen years later she appeared in the market place stating she had been held as a zombie 100 miles north of her village. In the intervening years she claimed to have had a child with another zombie. She was released by the *bokor's* son upon the *bokor's* death. After her return, her brother, a Protestant priest, recognised she was a zombie and held healing services in her honour. Before her death she was described as a shy but friendly girl, whereas on her return she laughed and giggled inappropriately and asked random questions. She had no obvious injuries except for a small, round scar on her chest, approximately 10mm in diameter and also comparable to Wilfred.

The medical diagnosis was given as a learning disability, perhaps caused by foetal alcohol syndrome. However, the plot thickened when the researchers returned with the girl to the market place, where she was recognised as a simple local woman who, nine months previously, had been enticed away by musicians during the Lenten festival. There were essentially two families claiming that MM was their relative and accusing the other family of zombification. Then MM's brother and daughter were contacted. They bore a family resemblance to her. MM recognised her daughter but still insisted her father was a zombie. It was clear to the researchers that MM had simply wandered away from home, or been abducted, and then a second family mistook her for their deceased relative.[45] DNA testing proved she was likely to be the mother of the child claiming to be her daughter, but was not related to the two men claiming to be her brothers.[46]

A fourth case – that of Clairvius Narcisse[47] – was examined by Colombian-Canadian anthropologist Wade Davis. He was pronounced dead in a US-run hospital by two doctors, one American. He was suffering from digestive disorders, uremia, pulmonary edema, hypothermia, respiratory difficulties, rapid weight loss and hypotension.[48] He also showed symptoms of blue skin (cyanosis) and tingling sensations (paresthesia).[49] He was buried in 1962, but in 1981 a man approached his sister, Angelina, in the market place, claiming to be Clairvius Narcisse and introducing himself by a childhood nickname. He recalled being a zombie and accused his own brother of the act. Narcisse claimed he had worked on a sugar plantation for two years until the death of the master set him free, and recalls his sister crying as he was pronounced dead.[50] He did not recall how long he was in the tomb, but estimated three days before he heard his name called, the sound of drums and the *bokor* singing. As he emerged from the tomb he was grabbed, beaten, blindfolded and led away.[51] He was identified by more than 200 village residents who all believed he had returned from the dead.[52]

It is intriguing that two of the victims of zombification – Wilfred and MM – both presented a small round wound on their chests that could not be explained by their relatives or by the medical examiners. They spent time speaking with *bokors* who claimed to carry out zombification and they also could not explain the wounds.[53]

The most obvious question is how a *bokor* can make 'zombies' from the corpses of deceased villagers. The answer lies both in religious belief and scientific study.

Making a Zombie

In Haiti there are two theories regarding how to make a zombie: one is that through magic the *bokor* can raise the dead and turn them into zombies; the other theory is that the *bokor* poisons an individual, who becomes ill and then appears to die. There is a funeral and the deceased is placed in a traditional tomb, comprising an above-ground concrete structure next to the house. These were susceptible to being broken into and it was in this way that the bodies were removed by the *bokor*.[54] Generally *bokors* work in secret because of the dark nature of their work, in particular keeping their recipes and potions secret. It is thought many *bokors* are however, charlatans or conmen.[55] Sometimes the families thrust a knife into the heart of the body of deceased family members to ensure they are truly dead, or even decapitate the deceased in order to prevent their bodies being zombified.[56]

In the Voodoo religion the human body is comprised of five elements: the *corps cadavre* (body), the *n'ame* (spirit of the flesh which enables the body to function) the *z'etoile* (star of destiny which resides in the sky), the *gros-bon-anj* (an animating principle) and the *ti-bon-anj* (free will, moral awareness and energy).[57] The *gros-bon-anj* enters the body at conception and after death it spends seven days near the body. The *ti-bon-anj* is believed after death to go under the water to enter the spirit world, whereas the *gros-bon-anj* remains near the body for a period of seven days.[58] The *gros-bon-anj* provides the individual with their life force and following death it returns to the sky to join the *loa,* becoming one themselves.[59]

In order to make a zombie the *bokor* needs to capture the *gros-bon-anj* and keep it locked in a container known as the *zombie astral*. This is essentially a soul without a body, meaning a zombie is a body without a soul.[60] This would then be stored in a vessel, which may also include skull shavings, herbs, perfumes, alcohol, cemetery earth and other ritual powders.[61] The skulls used were charged with a 'specific strength, job or problem to treat.' These bottled zombies were then presented as good luck charms.[62]

Elizabeth McAlister did fieldwork in Haiti and was presented with such a bottle: 'The mirrors around the centre of the bottle are its "eyes for seeing" and will identify any force coming at me with malevolent intent. The scissors lashed open under the bottleneck are like arms crossed in self-defence. The dollar bill in the bottle instructs the zonbi spirits to attract wealth. The herbs are for the zonbis to heal me of sickness and disease, while the perfumes are to make me attractive and desirable.'[63] McAlister was informed by the *bokor* St Jean that she could now ask the zombies for anything that she wanted as they were trapped in the bottle and were under his control, which he 'subcontracted' out to her. These were spiritual rather than physical zombies.

The *bokor* can capture the *gros-bon-anj* while the victim is alive, rendering the individual as apparently dead, or it can be captured shortly after death while it remains close to the deceased. To capture the *gros-bon-anj* poison can be laid in the shape of the cross near the door of the deceased. To create a zombie the *bokor* can simply waft the jar containing the *gros-bon-anj* beneath the nose of the corpse.[64] Alternatively, the *bokor* can release the *gros-bon-anj* into insects, animals or other humans.[65] In order to prevent the *gros-bon-anj* from re-entering the deceased's body when it is removed from the tomb a severe beating is administered (as Clairvius Narcisse recounted as part of his own zombification). The *gros-bon-anj* must also be prevented from returning to its source (i.e., god) hence it is captured within the seven-day period following death. The *n'ame* prevents the cadaver from decaying.[66]

The more practical method of zombifying a corpse is for the *bokor* to apply zombie powder to the skin of the deceased, which results in the loss of free will of the individual. Some Haitians believe this change from human to zombie is caused by poisoning, which is identified in the Penal Code as part of zombification and, therefore, murder.[67] Victims are not generally chosen at random by the *bokor* but have normally committed some social *faux pas*, such as theft or adultery,[68] and are accused or tried by the community. In this way, zombification could be used to maintain social order.

In the 1980s Wade Davis (see above) was sent to Haiti by Nathan Kline and David Merrick to obtain zombie powders, the antidote and the method of preparation. He was able to acquire five examples of zombie powder. He believed the *bokors* did not produce zombies from the recently deceased but rather poisoned individuals and then merely revived them.

The idea of poison being able to simulate the appearance of death is not a new one, and appears in Shakespeare's *Romeo and Juliet* (Act IV, Scene 1):

> And this distilling liquor drink thou off;
> When presently through all thy veins shall run
> A cold and drowsy humor, for no pulse
> Shall keep his native progress, but surcease:
> No warmth, no breath, shall testify thou livest;
> The roses in thy lips and cheeks shall fade
> To wanny ashes, thy eyes' windows fall,
> Like death, when he shuts up the day of life.

Davis based his theory of poisoning on a comparison between the descriptions of zombie behaviour and the symptoms of those with fugu (puffer fish) poisoning.[69] In this way he had a clear idea of what he was hoping to find.

Initially he was expecting to discover the zombie powder to be made from a plant known as Datura or 'the Holy Flower of the North Star', which he knew grew in Haiti. One of the species was known as the *concombre zombi* (zombie cucumber).[70]

In the native tribes of America the Datura plant was closely associated with death, and in Peru it was thought that those under the influence of the plant could locate the tombs of their ancestors.[71] Furthermore, the *Datura stramonium* plant was used by tribes in Africa, including the Hausas of Nigeria, who used it in ritual beverages, the Fulani, who used it in rites of passage into manhood, and in West Africa it was used in criminal poisonings.[72] As the majority of the population of Haiti comprised black Africans, Davis expected that some of the cultural practices may have transferred.

Within twenty-five minutes after taking the poison, the body becomes paralysed, although the brain is fully conscious for a further few hours. The victim eventually dies of a heart attack or from suffocation. However, if the victim survives for twenty-four hours they are likely to fully recover.

In Japan, the fugu is a delicacy and can only be prepared by specialised chefs as it contains lethal levels of tetrodotoxin. Despite this precaution some 200 cases of fugu poisoning a year are reported, and fifty per cent of them are fatal,[73] some within sixteen minutes of consuming the poison.[74] Tetrodotoxin is a volatile poison and is not a drug that can be taken for recreational purposes:[75] gram for gram it is more lethal than cyanide.

The feeling after consuming fugu can be warmth, flushing skin, paraesthesia of the tongue and lips, and a sense of euphoria, none of which are unpleasant. Such poisoning is recognised by the lips and tongue starting to go numb within twenty minutes of eating the fish. Before full paralysis sets in the victim may experience headaches, difficulty in walking, and paraesthesia in the face, hands and feet. The increasing paralysis is followed by respiratory problems, convulsions and mental impairment. It can take between twenty minutes and eight hours to die.[76] In some cases it has been known for a victim of fugu poisoning to be declared dead only to 'come back to life' before the funeral. It is, therefore, possible to administer a non-lethal dose of tetrodotoxin and the victim can recover with little mental impairment.[77]

Although the methods utilised by the *bokor* are said to be secret, Davis was able to obtain the examples by claiming he wanted to 'use it on an enemy',[78] while on another occasion he admitted that he was conducting scientific research. Over the course of a few weeks in 1982 he was able to purchase the zombie powder but was not able to witness how it was prepared. There are a number of ethical concerns regarding Davis' fieldwork practices. He seemed to forget he was dealing with the abuse of human beings when he commented that: 'All that remained to accomplish as far as he [Kline] was concerned was the documentation and medical study of a victim as it [sic] came out of the ground.'[79]

It seems he was unable to witness this element of the research and one wonders how he tried to persuade the *bokors* to do this to a local victim. He describes in the *Serpent and the Rainbow*[80] how a young girl was exhumed in front of him while he was communicating with the *bokor*. During the ceremony to produce the zombie powder, her skull was crushed and added to the mix and her bones placed upon a grill.[81] Considering such a process was illegal, and unquestionably immoral, it is surprising that, as a scientist, Davis went ahead with the process.

This young girl's body was violated once more for the preparation of the antidote for the zombie powder. This contained six plants (*aloe vera, guaiacum officinalem cedrela odorata, Capparis cynophyllophora, Amyris maritima* and *caparis sp.*) as well as sea water, cane alcohol, perfume and a material from the apothecary called Black Magic.[82] This antidote was only administered to a victim who thought that he/she had been poisoned and indicates that it was more of a placebo than a genuine medical cure.

The samples collected by Davis were examined and shown to contain evidence of three types of dried puffer fish – *Diodon holcanthus L, Diodan hystrix L. and Spheroides testudineus L.* – as well as numerous variations of plant materials, amphibians (including the toad *bufo marinus*), reptiles (including lizards), an arachnid, a centipede, an annelid (polychaete worm,) and dried human bone and flesh.[83] Human remains are such a common feature in Voodoo magic that most tombs have been broken into to obtain ingredients for magic. Two common ingredients, *Datura metel L.* and *Datura stramonium L,* are hallucinogens that can cause amnesia, and a third ingredient, *Mucuna pruriens*, can also have hallucinogenic effects.[84] Other ingredients, including a tree frog (*Osteopilus septentrionallis Dumeril* and *Bibron*), can cause temporary blindness or paralysation (*Hermodice carunculata*),[85] and *bufo marinus* can produce nausea, breathing problems, prickling skin and turn the lips a shade of blue.[86] All of the ingredients are broiled until they take on a soft, oily consistency before they are ground down to a powder.[87]

Tetrodotoxin from the puffer fish was thought by some to be the active ingredient, which can account for some aspects of traditional zombie behaviour.[88] Such zombie behaviour included a vacant stare, clumsy actions of a repetitive nature, nasal intonation and extremely limited and repeated speech patterns.[89] Whilst a zombie can generally speak, eat and hear when people speak, there is complete memory loss and no awareness of their situation.[90]

However, the levels of tetrodotoxin within the samples were so low that when tried on mice they showed no evidence of intoxication.[91] Critics of the theory emphasise that the samples studied had high alkaline levels (pH10), which made the tetrodotoxin unstable and ineffective as a poison.[92] In alkaline environments tetrodotoxin decomposes irreversibly and therefore is not effective.[93] Davis responds to this criticism by highlighting that the poisons are in the form of powders, which do not have a pH. Additionally, they are administered to the individual through abrasions in the skin and the blood prevents the denaturation of the tetrodotoxin. However, the counter-argument is that the powder is not wholly free from water and therefore can be unstable in a humid environment, which could cause denaturation.[94] Unfortunately, the only references for Davis' findings are his own works[95] and cannot be verified.

Poisoning from tetrodotoxin causes the peripheral nerves to become paralysed, resulting in suffocation as the respiratory system stops working.[96] A sub-lethal dose, however, will instead cause the appearance of death as the respiratory system slows. Davis believed that this apparent death was used by the *bokor* to create their zombies. A poisoned individual presenting the appearance of death was buried, later retrieved by the *bokor* who then revived the individual. Often deaths in Haiti are pronounced without the input of a medical professional, and normally buried within a day, so it is possible that not everyone who is buried is in fact dead, and could therefore be revived by a *bokor* upon retrieval.[97]

There are numerous anecdotal cases of zombification from Haiti, some more credible than others, although they are mostly concluded to be mistaken identities. Some estimate there are as many as a thousand new reported cases each year.[98] Davis identified one case that appears to support the theory of tetrodotoxin poisoning. That is the case of Clairvius Narcisse who died in 1962, and then approached his sister, Angelina, in a market place in 1982, as discussed above.

Davis views the case of Clairvius Narcisse as a classic case of tetrodotoxin poisoning, which often starts with tingling of the skin and respiratory paralysis, and believes that Japanese records of Fugu poisoning read like cases of zombification:[99] 'A gambler [...] died by eating fugu, and the body was placed in storage for the officials to examine. About seven days later the man became conscious and finally recovered. The victim claimed to have recalled the entire incident and stated that he was afraid he would be buried alive.'[100]

Studies were done on rats that had been injected with the zombie powder to see the results of poisoning. One of the zombie powders did appear to sedate one of the rats, but the doctor emphasised that the powder used was crude in nature and no firm conclusions could be drawn from these results.[101] Davis claims that, from studies on the rats, it could be ascertained that 3.5g could render a 73-kg human comatose.[102]

Davis's record of the tests was more successful, though his writing style is more anecdotal biography than academic reporting. He reports that when the powder was applied to the skin of the rat, it stopped all activity within fifteen minutes, and after forty minutes only moved when 'stimulated', before remaining immobile for as long as six hours. After six hours there was no movement, but there was still a trace of a heartbeat. They apparently remained in this state for twenty-four hours.[103] Similarly, when a monkey was treated with the powder, it became sedated within twenty minutes and lost all of the aggression Davis had previously witnessed.[104]

Evidence also shows, however, that tetrodotoxin does not withstand high temperatures for long periods. Short periods of 100–116°C are acceptable, but anything longer will incinerate the poison, indicating that it would not survive the preparation process.[105] Additionally, the scientists who studied two of these powder samples make it clear that 'neither of them contained anything more than insignificant traces of tetrodotoxin,'[106] which would not produce 'any significant biological effects.'[107]

Many of the other ingredients of the zombie powder were skin irritants. Davis was unable to ascertain the exact method of introducing the powder to the individual, but speculated that the powder could be sprinkled where the intended victim was likely to walk, or it could be rubbed onto the skin.[108] Davis spoke to a *bokor* in Haiti and different methods of application were suggested: e.g., scattering in a cross shape in the threshold of the door of the intended victim, placed inside their shoe or down their back.[109] The poison was never sprinkled in food as ingestion of tetrodotoxin results in complete respiratory failure within minutes and therefore would defeat the object of the process.[110]

As many of the ingredients were skin irritants this could be an effective way of getting the poison into the bloodstream. The victim scratches the skin, leaving open wounds which could leave the victim more susceptible to further administration of the poison. However, poisoning via a topical application is much less effective than when it is consumed internally.[111]

Frère Dodo, a Voodoo sorcerer turned evangelical preacher, asserts the main ingredient of zombification powder is, in fact, tetrodotoxin, regardless of Davis's findings. He explains that it is administered to the victim and then they are revived once they are retrieved from the tomb. Other *hunguns* have claimed that, rather than putting poison in the food of the victim, it is repeatedly applied to the skin, preferably with open wounds, or is blown over the victim.[112] Brain damage, such as that witnessed on Wilfred Doricent, could be due to oxygen deprivation caused by being shut in a coffin for a prolonged period of time before the tetrodotoxin poison wore off. It seemed that Clairvius Narcisse suffered from twenty-one of the known symptoms of tetrodotoxin poisoning.[113]

This suggests that *bokors* do not actually raise the dead, but instead poison an individual until their state resembles death, before reviving them.[114] However, survivors of tetrodotoxin poisoning do not resemble zombies in their behaviour. Rather they recover completely and remember their experiences. It is suggested that one of the ingredients in the antidote could be responsible for the prolonged lethargic state.

When the antidote to the poison is administered, the poison has already damaged 'part of the brain which governs speech and will power. The victim can move and act but cannot formulate thought.'[115] The antidote, however, is not consistent. The ingredients and preparation techniques vary from region to region. The antidote fed to most zombies upon revival is a paste of sweet potato, cane syrup and *Datura stramonium* or *Datura metel*, which contain atropine and scopolamine and which could be the active ingredients to counter the poison.[116] These latter two active ingredients are, however, psychoactive drugs and therefore the dosage makes the victim pliable, meaning he or she can be easily led away.

The question seems to remain unanswered as to whether zombies actually exist in Haiti, and whether any zombie powders have the potential to be effective. Some people automatically dismiss it as folklore and mythology, but it has to be considered and accepted that many Haitians believe the zombie phenomenon to be a very real one, and there is a lot to be said for the power of belief.

It has been suggested that the idea that the *bokor* poisons their victims until appear dead allows Haitians, 'to hold on to a magical belief yet give it the appearance of scientific respectability.'[117] Further suggestions are that the belief in zombies and the power of the *bokor* itself is responsible for the symptoms; essentially through the power of suggestion. It is a known phenomenon that beliefs can be 'viral' as the more someone is exposed to a particular belief the more likely they are to accept it, even if there is no logic to it.[118]

This process is called 'Voodoo death', whereby the victim believes they have been cursed, given the evil eye or marked as a potential zombie by the *bokor* due to their unacceptable behaviour. This belief can then leave them open to pathological infections or make them more susceptible to poisoning. In the cases of Clairvius Narcisse and Francina Illeus, they were already isolated from the community due to their actions and anti-social behaviour. They were not liked by the villagers and there was strife within their families (due to the former's rift with his brother regarding land, and the latter's extra-marital affairs).

It is said that Narcisse was sold to the *bokor* by his brother for zombification. If this was the case, it is unlikely he would have been supported by the villagers if this act was not sanctioned by others. When Narcisse first fell ill this social situation may have made him believe he was being poisoned by a *bokor* and was on the route to zombification.[119] Davis also suggests that this was an effective method of social control and was nothing short of 'legitimate capital punishment'. Narcisse mentions in his recollections that before he became ill and died he had gone through a tribunal with the 'masters of the land' who were the initiated members of the secret societies, in particular the Bizango society. Zombification may be illegal in Haiti, but it is still a form of societal punishment.[120]

Davis's study, however, is considered at best controversial, and at other times contradictory to other reports. For example, the Rara musicians of Haiti view the utilisation of zombies (zonbi) in a totally different way to Davis. Rara is an annual religious festival specifically for the poorer classes. The procession goes through villages with Rara bands playing music and singing songs. Rituals are carried out to Voodoo deities at significant places such as crossroads, bridges and cemeteries.[121] One of the secret societies associated with the Rara is the Chanpwel, and one of their beliefs is that spirits of the recently deceased (zonbi/zombie), are obliged if they were Voodoo to work for the living Voodoo practitioners.[122] The protestant dead however have no such obligation and if a protestant zombie is captured they become agitated and refuse to work, and even refuse the final meal that will release them. As one record states, 'Simeon was left with a stubborn zonbi on a hunger strike.'[123] According to this Rara leader, Simeon, only lazy people would object to being called upon as a zonbi as 'they feel happy because they didn't like to sit around doing nothing.'[124]

Capturing zombies for the Rara requires the help of the *loa*, and before entering the cemetery it is necessary to ask the *loa* Bawon for permission to remove the spirits of the recently deceased from the cemetery. Bawon will give permission, as well as deciding the number of zombies who are allowed to be removed.[125] To identify the presence of a zombie, the Rara pick up handfuls of earth from the cemetery. When it is too hot to touch, the zombie is close and can be captured and placed inside a bottle.[126] The Rara carefully choose the zombies according to their talents and skills. Simeon states: 'I sell zonbi. If somebody wants a zonbi to drive a car, I have to give them a chauffeur's zonbi. If somebody needs a zonbi to do business, I have to give them a market-woman's zonbi. Somebody who was a market-woman who had a bar and restaurant. You can't take the zonbi of somebody who was a tailor and give it to somebody who wants to be a chauffeur. That won't help him. What's he going to do with that?'[127]

It is clear that these zombies are not the reanimated corpse, but rather the spiritual possession by a zombie spirit. The Rara musicians were at times possessed by a zombie spirit, enabling them to play for hours during the Easter weekend.[128] The only time they seemed to use the body was in order to make use of the deceased's particular talents. But they would wait for a year before opening the tomb in case they were afflicted by the 'bad air'.

Others who may also be considered ideal zombie possibilities were those who died before their time; the young, for example. Often these unexpected early deaths were blamed on sorcery and so were considered unnatural. But simply dying an unnatural death was not enough to make a zombie. The power and the will of the *bokor* was also essential, and without it the victim remained dead. It was believed that only god determines the death of an individual. Therefore, if someone died at the hands of another they were said to have died 'by the hands of man' and can be used as a zombie until they die twice 'by the hands of god.'[129] Killing a person and then capturing them for use as a zombie was seen as sorcery whereas using their zombie for healing and something positive was seen as religious magic.

While the roots of the zombie are firmly in the Voodoo religion that originated in the eighteenth century, it was not until the 1960s and the anti-authoritarian movement that zombies became a cult creature entering Western culture in the form it can be found today. It reflected the need to face mortality and the fear of not finding an 'authentic' reason for being.[130]

But how did this transformation happen: from mindless cadaver being enslaved to work for the *bokor* to a dangerous, flesh-eating killer following the basest desires, with no hope of freedom, unlike the Haitian zombies?[131] Whether this was intentional is questionable. It is more likely that small tweaks in novels, short stories and movies to make the zombie more terrifying has seen a gradual change. No longer is the person in control to be feared but the monster within us all. Remember that in the modern zombie incarnation all humans will become reanimated on death and therefore the monster is in us all.

Chapter 5

Vampires in Western Media

Definition

Vampires have been popular in literature, television and movies since Bram Stoker wrote *Dracula* in 1897. They are more popular than ever today and are an evolving feature of Western culture. The term vampire has also been adopted to mean 'a person who lives by preying on and exploiting others'.[1] In Alice and Claude Askew's *Aylmer Vance and the Vampire* (1914) they state: 'There are certain people – I could think of several myself – who seem to depress one and undermine one's energies, quite unconsciously, of course, but one feels somehow that vitality has passed from oneself to them.'[2]

In the *Encyclopaedia of Science Fiction* the editor, Peter Nicholls, discusses the status that vampires hold in the modern world: 'Vampires are aristocratic, drinking only the most refined substances, usually blood. In the iconography of horror, the vampire stands for sex.'[3]

This has not always been the case. In the sixteenth century there was little difference between a vampire and a ghost and Shakespeare's *Hamlet* asks if his father's 'dead corse' (*sic.*) is roaming the castle. There is speculation as to whether this refers to a spirit or something more tangible. Shakespeare's vampires and ghosts were based on case study reports such as those of Henry More (1614–1687) who wrote of the case of Johannes Cuntius, an alderman in Pentsch, Poland, who after death caused a great deal of trouble around town. He shook houses, turned milk into blood, and desecrated the altar with blood. In some reports, though, he was less tangible and was described as a spirit that disappeared when a candle was lit.[4]

The modern vampire is generally considered to be a corpse who has risen from the dead, drinks blood to survive, is immortal and displays supernatural abilities. This is the culmination of 120 years of vampire lore.

With such a long history it has been suggested that vampires have now become generational, with each new generation preferring a different version of the vampire form.[5]

Literature

The catalyst in the West was Bram Stoker's *Dracula*, published in 1897, which started the Western fascination with the undead. It was not the first vampire story to be written, but it was the one that introduced many of the characteristics which have remained staples throughout vampire evolution. Arthur Conan Doyle, the creator of Sherlock Holmes, described Stoker's story as the 'very best story of diablerie that I have read in many years'.[6]

In the story an English attorney, Jonathan Harker, travels to Transylvania in order to help Count Dracula purchase property in London where he plans to relocate. The count is not as one would expect. He carries out many of the chores around his castle himself, such as cooking, making the beds, and setting the dining table, while chatting with Harker on a number of subjects. Harker mentions that he has no servants on more than one occasion.

However, in the dead of night the count is seen crawling down the side of the building, alerting Harker to his non-human status. Upon venturing to the crypt Harker finds a number of vampires asleep in their coffins. The truly vampiric action, however, occurs when Dracula travels to Whitby in Yorkshire upon purchasing the old abbey next door to the lunatic asylum (fig. 9).

Here we are introduced to some of Dracula's skills as he demonstrates his ability to take the form of mist, or a bat, and creates a storm to disguise his arrival into the country. At this point of the story Dracula has clearly shed his domestic persona. There are, however, limitations to Dracula's ability, as Abraham Van Helsing, the vampire hunter, explains: 'The Count, even if he takes the form of a bat, cannot cross the running water of his own volition.' There ensues a battle between Dracula and Harker, and a number of others, including Van Helsing, who all wish to protect Mina, Harker's new wife, and her friend, Lucy Westenra.

Dracula was seen as a sexual predator – something feared greatly in Victorian England[7] – as he preyed on both Mina and her friend, Lucy.

Sadly, Lucy is turned into a vampire and her fiancé, Arthur Holmwood, stakes her on what would have been their wedding night. Dracula, likewise, is killed and the world is saved.

While Stoker's *Dracula* has become the 'original' text of the modern vampire it was not the first literary vampire. Stoker himself would no doubt have been familiar with John Keat's *Lamia* (1884) and Samuel Taylor Coleridge's *Christabel* (1797–1800), two poems which feature vampires. The legend of the vampire of Croglin Grange in Cumberland, which first appeared in *Story of My Life* by Augustus Hare in the 1890s, was also well-known when Stoker was writing, as was Edgar Allan Poe's *Ligeia*, which tells the story of a vampire wife who would not stay in her tomb.

Stoker also worked with Dublin author Sheriden le Fanu, who, in 1872, wrote the vampire story *Carmilla*. This has been described as one of the most influential vampire stories ever written.[8] The narrator, Laura, recalls that as a child she had a dream of a woman coming to her bedroom and biting her on her chest. Years later an injured Carmilla is left at the castle by some travellers. Carmilla and Laura become good friends. Carmilla, however, sleeps all day and is out all night. She continues feeding from the slowly deteriorating Laura, as well as other young girls in the surrounding area. Once Carmilla is identified as a vampire her resting place is traced to a crypt in a ruined chapel in the village of Karnstein. The coffin is opened and she is inside looking to be in the best of health. When Carmilla's heart is pierced with a stake the corpse lets out a blood-curdling scream. The body is then decapitated, releasing a spurt of blood, before being cremated. The ashes are then scattered in the river.

The vampire castle in *Carmilla* is based in the Duchy of Styria, Austria, and Stoker originally planned to set *Dracula* here before choosing Transylvania. This area of Romania has since been considered to be the 'true' home of the vampire.

George Gordon Byron, more commonly known as Lord Byron, was involved in the vampire craze and penned the 1813 poem, *The Giaour,* which Stoker may also have been familiar with. He also drafted the original outline for *The Vampyre*, which was completed and published by Dr Polidori. The two had originally been friends but had fallen out. Polidori based the main character, Lord Ruthven, on Byron himself.[9] A young man, Aubrey, comes under the influence of the ruthless

Lord Ruthven, but when he realises the Lord was a vampire he tries to break free of his influence. Later, he falls in love with a girl, Ianthe, but their love is not to be. Lord Ruthven catches up with the couple and kills her. Aubrey does not realise that the Lord is responsible for her death and allows him to nurse him through his grief. In a series of events Ruthven is mortally wounded, and following burial, his corpse disappears. He returns and starts making advances on Aubrey's sister. Aubrey is unable to prevent a marriage taking place and his sister subsequently becomes a vampire, like her husband.

The inspiration for this story was thought to be an affair between Byron and Lady Caroline Lamb, and the relationship between Polidori and Byron himself, which swung between hate and hero worship.[10] The sinister figure of Ruthven, who was able to bring people under his thrall and influence, was to be the blueprint for all vampire tales to come, and so it can be said that 'Count Dracula was a metaphorical grandson of Lord Byron.'[11]

The story was published in *New Monthly Magazine* on 1 April 1819 under Byron's name, much to Polidori's annoyance. When it was published as a book it became a bestseller and it was not long before it was put onto the stage. Queen Victoria, upon seeing a version of *The Vampire*, based on Polidori's work, claimed in her diary it was 'very trashy.'[12]

It is from this first stage production of Polidori's work that the so-called 'Vampire Trap' was invented for the theatre. This was a trap door in the floor of the stage which had two spring leaves that opened under pressure and then immediately reclosed giving the impression that the actor was passing through solid matter.

Between Polidori's novel and Bram Stoker's *Dracula* there were a number of other literary vampire offerings including Count Alexis Tolstoy's (cousin of Leo) *The Family of the Vourdalak* (published in 1884), Russian writer Gogol's *Viy* (1835) and Edgar Allan Poe's *Berenice* (1833). A colossal work, which ran to 850 pages and appeared weekly for 220 weeks in a Penny Dreadful, was *Varney the Vampyre*, written by James Malcom Rymer in 1847. It remained a best seller for more than a decade.[13]

Despite the popularity of vampires in literature at the end of the nineteenth century, Bram Stoker's *Dracula* was not a bestseller at the time. That said, it was not unsuccessful and had sold 3,000 copies in the first print run. The book has not been out of print since then,[14] but it was not until movies were made of the book thirty years later that it became a genre classic.[15]

Since Stoker's *Dracula*, vampire literature has also remained popular, although a prequel to Stoker's novel was not written until 2018 by J.D. Barker entitled *Dracul*. It was shortlisted for the 2018 Bram Stoker Awards for Best Horror Novel. It tells the story of a young Bram Stoker in 1868, who spends time locked in an abbey's tower fighting against a horrific beast armed only with mirrors, crucifixes, holy water and a gun. This is designed to provide the background to how Stoker came to write his infamous vampire novel.

The nature of the vampire has varied over the decades with the vampires represented in varying degrees of evilness. In *The Dracula Tape* (1975), by Fred Saberhagen, the vampire is 'more sinned against than sinning'[16] with the destruction being caused by the vampire slayer, Abraham Van Helsing, in his single-minded pursuit of his quarry.

I am Legend by Richard Matheson (1954) tells of the last surviving human of a plague that turned the rest of the world into cannibalistic vampires. The protagonist, Neville, is immune to the virus following a bite from a vampire and has to protect his home with garlic, mirrors and crosses. During the day he turns predator and goes into the vampires' houses, staking them as they sleep. At night the vampires come to his house and try to entice him to come out. There seem to be two kinds of vampires: those who want to kill him and those who are more intelligent and who view Neville as an indiscriminate murderer who kills vampires without finding out if they are intelligent or not.[17] This was considered such a classic book that it has been made into three different movies: *The Last Man on Earth* (1964) with Vincent Price, *The Omega Man* (1971) with Charlton Heston, and *I am Legend* (2007) with Will Smith. It was also the inspiration behind Romero's *Night of the Living Dead* (1968).

Vampires were soon to be presented as 'collected', or composed, and 'sexy' and this developed into a whole genre of romantic books. The classic 'heart-throb' vampire was introduced in the movie adaptation of Anne Rice's *Vampire Chronicles,* a series of ten books written between 1976 and 2003. They are considered vampire cult classics and include *Interview with the Vampire* (1976), *The Vampire Lestat* (1985) and *The Queen of the Damned* (1988).

These books (and subsequently movies) represent an alternate underworld society with a distinct hierarchy, complex politics, jealousy, desires and affection. Her vampires were: 'romantic, aristocratic, elegant, and erudite aesthetes. Predators who are always erotic and occasionally ethical.'[18] The older these vampires got the better their taste developed. They thought the preservation of art was increasingly more important and considered themselves to be the custodians of culture.[19] The vampire Lestat is aware of how they had evolved and indeed in *The Vampire Lestat* he refers to Dracula as, 'the big ape of vampires, the hirsute Slav Count Dracula.'

The origin of the *Chronicles* was 4,000 BCE in ancient Egypt, when an evil spirit combined with the flesh of Queen Akasha and created the world's first vampire. She turned her husband into the second vampire and so the saga began. It is stated that there are 'a remarkable number of [fictional vampire universes] which coalesce in ancient Egypt, traditionally viewed as the cradle of all black arts.'[20] This was also discussed in Chapter 1 in regard to the reanimation of the mummy.

It is believed that *The Vampire Chronicles* were written as a critique of capitalism. Both the Bank of London and Rothschild Bank, where Lestat invested his money over the centuries, and Lestat himself, are described as 'immortal', lending an unnatural element to both. In Stoker's *Dracula* the count gets his money through digging in the forest, where fairy lights mark the spot, whereas the vampires in *The Vampire Chronicles* obtain their money through investments or the plunder of humans over the centuries.[21] One interesting aspect of the critique is that the horrific nature of vampires/capitalism must remain a secret in plain view for it to be successful. In *The Vampire Lestat* he reveals the nature of vampires, but is not impressed that the human audience do not care: '[They] might know the truth and prefer to remain enslaved, or at least complicit in its suppression.'[22]

Even Karl Marx in *Capital* compares the capitalist to a vampire: 'Capital is dead-labour which, vampire-like, lives only by sucking living labour, and lives the more, the more labour it sucks.'[23]

This suppression of the knowledge is made clearer in the *Queen of the Damned* when Queen Akasha teaches Lestat about poverty. He claims in *The Vampire Lestat* that: 'the poverty and filth that had been common in the big cities of the earth since time immemorial were also completely washed away.'

In the *Queen of the Damned* Akasha proves him wrong: 'She spoke slowly, close to my ear. "Shall I recite the poetry of names?" she asked, "Calcutta, if you wish, or Ethiopia; or the streets of Bombay; these poor souls could be the peasants of Sri Lanka; of Pakistan; of Nicaragua, of El Salvador. It does not matter what it is; it matters how much there is of it; that all around the oases of your shining Western cities it exists; it is three-fourths of the world! Open you ears, my darling."'[24]

In 1994 the movie adaptation *Interview with a Vampire* was released with Tom Cruise playing the moody vampire Lestat and Brad Pitt playing Louis de Pointe du Lac. This is one of the only movies that makes the homoerotic feelings obvious between the two leads. It is stated that the gay subtext is 'as bare as the time would allow'.[25] Louis allows Lestat to turn him into a vampire following the death of his wife and child so he is not really a victim of Lestat. However, throughout his undead life Louis struggles with his nature and this is most evident when they turn the little girl, Claudia, into a vampire. She suffers a great deal of angst as she will remain a child for eternity.

The relationship between Lestat and Louis is unusual. Lestat is clearly the superior but they go from mentor/mentee, parent/child, saviour/ tormentor and soulmate/enemy as Lestat teaches Louis about being a vampire. It is also suggested that the recording of Lestat's activities via cassette tape is meant to be a reflection of the Watergate scandal of 1972–1974. The original *Interview with a Vampire* book from which the movie was based was written in 1976, so was a political commentary of the time.

There is an additional element of 'death of Christianity in a secular society'[26] throughout the plot. The common trope of vampires being repelled by the crucifix is obliterated and the religious symbol does nothing against these walking undead. The use of the crucifix in repelling the vampire reinforces the assumption that the vampire is of a 'heathen' faith; essentially not Christianity. Obviously this falls apart if the vampires are of the Christian faith.[27]

Armand the vampire also emphasises this point with the line that God does not exist, and that the sun is the oldest god of all. In folklore and in the media the crucifix is something that is ineffective against an old vampire: in other words one who was turned before Christianity.[28] The cross 'emphasises the relationship between Christianity and morality on the one hand, and its inverted image in vampirism and sensuality on the other. The modern vampire myth survives by sucking the blood out of Christian taboos.'[29]

In the American television series, *Buffy the Vampire Slayer*, the taboo is further emphasised as Angel is the only vampire who is not repelled by the crucifix she wore, enabling him and Buffy to form a relationship. Also, in most vampire literature and movies – from Bram Stoker to the twenty-first century – vampires are drawn to ruined chapels, churches and abbeys as 'places where the existence of God is denied or forgotten.'[30]

While destroying one trope Rice introduces another. Vampires in her world must only drink fresh blood and Claudia is able to harm Lestat by tricking him into drinking blood from corpses that have been dead for some time. He does not, however, die as planned, and is reduced to surviving by drinking the blood of animals in the swamp where his body is dumped. Rice also introduces the notion of the rules and hierarchy of the vampire world. Claudia must answer for her crime of 'killing' another vampire and is executed by being exposed to sunlight.

Another romantic film adaptation was made of Stephenie Meyer's *Twilight* series, which sees five films and four books. These follow the blossoming relationship between vampire Edward Cullen (Robert Pattison) and his love interest, Bella Swan (Kristen Stewart). The film/novels are set in the township of Forks, Washington, because the cloud cover suits the Cullens who cannot go out in bright sunlight. Bella is a misfit, unpopular at school and a virgin, who feels there is something missing in her life. This gap is filled by the other-worldly Edward Cullen, who is from a wealthy family, but has an air of aloofness and mystery about him which she finds attractive. He is super-strong and is able to transform into a bat; rather like an 'emo super-man'.[31]

Bramesco describes it as 'an epic about one girl who wants to get laid so badly that she's willing to die to do it,'[32] as Cullen refuses to have sex with her unless she marries him as a human and then allows him to turn her to the other side. Which she does: 'She abandons all her friends and her family to sign the rest of forever away to a man she met earlier that year.'[33]

Others have suggested that the *Twilight* series advocates abuse. Bella will do anything for Edward's affection, which he withholds from her to the point where she attempts to wreck a motorcycle and jump off a cliff to bring him to her aid.[34] In the books he also acts at times like a domineering father rather than her boyfriend as he tells her off, grounds her as a punishment and even sends off her college applications.[35]

Edward Cullen also explains in the film that he is 'vegetarian', a family joke in the sense that he only drinks animal blood (rather than human), which he claims does not silence the hunger but is enough to survive on. Viewed through a vegetarian lens, this has been seen as being anti-vegetarian because it is 'a diet that leaves the vegetarian with an insatiable craving from what has been omitted; bloody meat'.[36] In the films Bella is also represented as a vegetarian.

Along similar lines are *The Vampire Diaries*, written by L.J. Smith and adapted for television by Kevin Williamson and Julie Plec. The TV series stretched to an epic 171 episodes, spanning eight seasons between 2009 and 2017. The plot follows the life of teenager Elena Gilbert (Nina Dobrev) who falls in love with Stefan Salvatore (Paul Wesley), a 162-year-old vampire. This love story is complicated by the appearance of Damon Salvatore (Ian Somerhalder), Stefan's older brother. Elena Gilbert is the spitting image of Stefan's first love, Katherine Pierce, and Damon is plotting to bring her back (although when she does return Damon has to protect Elena from her). In 2013 a graphic novel to tie-in with the television series was also introduced by DC comics. Drezner glibly observes: 'Recent literary tropes suggest that vampires can peacefully coexist with ordinary teens in many of the world's high schools, provided they are sufficiently hunky.'[37]

This in itself describes most of the vampire/human relationship genre. *Buffy The Vampire Slayer* was one of the earliest vampire shows to advocate the human girl/vampire boy relationship, and this increased in popularity with *True Blood, Twilight* and *The Vampire Diaries*, amongst others. The vampire boyfriend is normally presented as young (although chronologically old), and imbued with traditional, gentlemanly characteristics that seem appealing.[38] They are also other-worldly and therefore have the hint of exotic and dangerous about them. This has become a staple in the vampire romance genre of literature and movies.

Between 1998 and 2014 Chelsea Quinn Yarbro wrote twenty novels about the Count Saint-Germain, a vampire who was 4,000 years old and from Transylvania in Romania. The novels follow his existence through some of the most famous periods in history, including Rome during the reign of Nero, Russia in the reign of Ivan the Terrible, England between the two World Wars, Peru during the invasion by the Spanish and then present-day USA. During a stint in Egypt he practices the art of necromancy, bringing the dead back to life and creating fully salient zombies.

He requires a little blood to live and does not kill to acquire it. Many women offer it freely, or he takes it at night without waking them.

There have been many further screen adaptations of novels, including Stephen King's *Salem's Lot* (1975), which covers the story of novelist Ben Mears who returns to his home town, Jerusalem's Lot, Maine, only to discover that the residents are all turning into vampires. In 1979 the book was turned in a two-part mini-series with David Soul as Ben Mears. This was followed in 1987 with a sequel, *A Return to Salem's Lot*. In 2004 another two-part mini-series was made staring Rob Lowe.

Other book adaptations include such 'crimes against decency'[39] as Seth Grahame-Smith's *Abraham Lincoln: Vampire Hunter* (2010). In this novel the would-be president Lincoln loses his mother aged nine and later discovers this was due to vampires. He then makes it his life's work to become the ultimate vampire slayer. The author bases the story on a previously undiscovered *Secret Journal of Abraham Lincoln*. This book was made into a movie, directed by Timur Bekmambetov in 2012, with Benjamin Walker playing the lead. There were mixed reviews but the general consensus was that the film was a little lacklustre. One review in the Associated Press stated: 'What ideally might have been playful and knowing is instead uptight and dreary, with a visual scheme that's so fake and cartoony, it depletes the film of any sense of danger.'[40]

A parody along the lines of *Pride and Prejudice and Zombies* (see Chapter 3) was *Little Vampire Women* (2010) by Louisa May Alcott and Lynn Messina. This is based on the story of *Little Women*, but with the entire March family as humanitarian vampires who survive by eating small animals. Beth has a liking for kittens: 'Beth bit into a beloved kitten, her feeble fangs draining it as the creature softly mewed, but she was far too tired to have more than half and insisted Jo finish it [...] As the cost of kittens was dear, the consuming of them remained Beth's special province and she dined on them almost exclusively now.'[41] Messina changed the infamous opening line of this book to: 'Christmas won't be Christmas without any corpses [...] I don't think it's fair for some vampires to have plenty of pretty squirming things, and other vampires to have nothing at all.'

The earliest vampire literature presenting the vampire as an alien appears in the French science-fiction work by Gustave Le Rouge, *Le Prisonier de la Planète Mars* (1908). The thought power of Hindu Brahmans transports an engineer to the fourth planet from the sun

126

where he discovers bat-winged, blood-sucking creatures. The sequel, *La Guerre des Vampires*, which followed in 1909, describes the chaos that ensues when these creatures come to earth.[42] Colin Wilson's *The Space Vampires* (1976) describes the alien vampires as energy vampires who suck the life from their human victims, either leaving them dead or as slaves. Three of the vampires are brought back to earth and it is up to Commander Olaf Carlsen to save the day. This book is reminiscent of Bram Stoker's *Dracula* in that the aliens' viewpoint is not discussed. The narrative is from the human viewpoint – i.e., that the vampires are evil criminals – and there is only one line from the aliens themselves: 'all living creatures eat other living creatures.'[43] The traditional association between the vampires and sexuality also features.

Television programmes

We have discussed so far a number of screen adaptations of books about the vampire world, but there are also numerous television adaptations of graphic novels as well as literary texts. For example, a recent TV series, *True Blood* (2007–2014) was based on the Charlaine Harris *Sookie Stackhouse/Southern Vampire* literary series set in Bon Temps, Louisiana.

The TV series was produced by Alan Ball and starred Anna Paquin in the lead role of Sookie, a telepathic waitress. The plot is set shortly after the vampires have just 'come out of the coffin' and announced their existence to the world. This sees the introduction of synthetic blood, or Tru Blood, which enables vampires to assimilate within the community. The synthetic blood does not really satiate their thirst for blood, and Sookie explains that this has led to some 'unfortunate incidents'. Wright suggests this, in fact, played to a culture that 'pays more attention to appearances than to substance,' as they drink Tru Blood in public and human blood in private. The introduction of the synthetic blood allows vampires to mingle amidst the humans they crave.[44]

Sookie herself is part fairy, whose blood is very attractive to vampires. One constant trope within the vampire world of Bon Temps is that a vampire can only enter the home if invited, and the script makes a big deal about this, with Sookie inviting and revoking invitations depending on her mood, or whether she was in imminent danger.

Life for Sookie is relatively straightforward until she falls in love and starts dating 173-year-old vampire Bill Compton (Stephen Moyer), a true Southern gentleman. This relationship introduces her to the dangerous world of the vampires and their politics, as well as a number of other supernatural creatures who are also residing in her home town.

An interesting turn of events in the Sookie Stackhouse series is that vampires are as much at danger from humans as humans are from vampires. Vampire blood when drunk by humans acts as a hallucinogen and therefore there is a market in vampire blood, or 'V'. Vampires are kidnapped and drained of their blood in the same way humans are drained of theirs.

Not all vampire television series started life as a book. The BBC's *Being Human* (2008–2013) was a supernatural comedy-drama written by Toby Whithouse. There were five series comprising thirty-seven episodes in total. The premise was that three supernatural beings shared a flat: Annie Sawyer, a ghost (played by Andrea Riseborough), George Sands, a werewolf (played by Russell Tovey), and John Mitchell, the vampire (played by Guy Flanagan). They are all simply trying to maintain a normal life in a world of humans while coming to terms with their supernatural natures. There was also Canadian spin-off of the same name which ran from 2011 to 2014. It followed the same premise of a werewolf, vampire and ghost sharing an apartment. The season ran to four series with thirteen episodes in each season.

One of the most popular television shows was *Buffy the Vampire Slayer* (1997–2003) and the spin-off show, *Angel* (1999–2004). The franchise started as a movie in 1992, which, despite being slammed by critics, was developed into a long-running TV series.

Buffy Summers (Sarah Michelle Gellar) is sixteen years old and bears the destiny of being a slayer, responsible for killing all demonic creatures, not just vampires who live in her town of Sunnydale. This is a role which falls to one woman per generation and she tries to juggle this responsibility with also living a normal teenage life. 'Buffy is simultaneously a fierce, fearless (feminist?) vampire slayer and in insecurity-ridden (conventionally feminine) young woman.'[45]

The true conflict arrives in the form of Angel (David Boreanaz), with whom Buffy has a sexual relationship. Angel is a vampire with a soul, due to a gypsy curse. He is in constant conflict with his nature, hating that he needs to kill humans to survive.

The idea of bringing vampires into a totally ordinary setting, with Buffy suffering from the traditional teenage angst, was, at the time, innovative. There are no gothic castles and instead, 'alongside this ordinary world exists something extraordinary.'[46]

In 2019 *What We Do in the Shadows* was based on a film, set in New Zealand, of the same name. The TV show is filmed as a mockumentary following the lives of four vampire roommates and how they cope with modern life in New York; and more importantly how they interact with humans. They have shared a house for hundreds of years and naturally have the same arguments that any humans in similar close quarters would have.

The director of *What We Do in the Shadows*, Jemaine Clement, stated: 'We stay [close to] pretty basic 70s/80s vampire rules, with a little bit of 30s. They can turn into bats. They can't go in the sunlight; they don't sparkle in the sun, they die. They have to be invited in; in a lot of literature vampires have to be invited into private buildings, but this is a documentary so it's the real rules which means they have to be invited into any building.'[47]

Vampires are still popular and the production of vampire-themed television series shows no sign of slowing down, the latest being *Nos4A2* (pronounced Nosferatu) and based on Joe Hill's novel of the same name, and *V-Wars*, which is based on the graphic novels by Jonathan Maberry and Alan Robinson. Both were created in 2019.

Movies

Vampires have been an important part of international cinema since 1922 when the first vampire movie, *Nosferatu*, was released by the Prana Film studios. The film was based upon Bram Stoker's novel, although the main character was renamed Count Orlok. The novel had been adapted by German director Albin Grau, who had met a Serbian in World War One who claimed to be the son of a vampire.[48] Weinstock asserts that this movie was full of anti-Semitic propaganda, starting with the 'exaggerated stereotypical Jewish features, such as his disproportionately-large hooked nose and heavy eyebrows,' who 'arrives in the German city of Bremen along with the Plague,'[49] spreading death in his wake while acquiring property.

Stoker had died in 1912, and his widow, Florence, had forbidden any stage and film adaptation of the novel since his death.[50] She heard about the film *Nosferatu* after she was anonymously sent a programme claiming the movie was 'freely adapted from Bram Stoker's *Dracula*.'[51] She sued the studios for copyright infringement.[52] The case dragged on for three years, after which Prana Film Studios were ordered to destroy all copies of the film, leading to their bankruptcy. Only a few copies of this first vampire movie have survived,[53] though it is now freely available to watch on YouTube.

The film, which premiered at the Marble Hall of the Berlin Zoological Gardens at huge cost (almost bankrupting the film studio),[54] was directed by Friedrich Wilhelm Murnau, and Count Orlok was played by Max Schreck, whose name means 'Max Terror'. Like the book, the movie was the template for all vampire movies to come, although there were some departures from the original story. The ending, for example, shows Nosferatu being destroyed by sunlight after failing to return to his coffin in time, whereas in the novel he is staked.

The film was full of atmosphere and Count Orlok exudes tension and awkwardness with an exaggerated countenance (a feature of the silent movie era). Roger Ebert, a film critic emeritus, wrote of *Nosferatu* in 2007: 'Here is the story of Dracula before it was buried alive in clichés, jokes, television skits, cartoons and more than 30 other films.'[55]

The name *Nosferatu* refers to the 'Bird of Death' though the character of Count Orlok was distinctly rat-like in his appearance and a far cry from the suave vampires of the later representations. These non-human characteristics make the count more disturbing as he is functioning on a basic, animalistic level. Today Schrek still 'exudes a weird magnetism almost erotic in its intensity.'[56]

Stoker's *Dracula* introduced the word *nosferatu* as an alternative to vampire. It was mentioned twice in the novel: 'when you had died, have become nosferatu,' and 'the nosferatu do not die like the bee when he stings once.' It was claimed that the word had its origins in the Romanian language although linguists have been unable to trace it.[57] It is possible that it may have come from the Greek work *nosophorus* or plague carrier.[58]

Despite the film's notoriety, this awkward, rat-like version of the vampire was immediately replaced with one who was much more refined. In 1979, however, Werner Herzog released *Nosferatu the Vampyre* as a tribute to Murnau's 1922 film. It was essentially a remake of the film with a few updates to bring it into the modern world.[59] The main difference between the 1979 remake and the original is that Count Orlok was given depressing soliloquies about the state of being immortal, which would have been impossible in the silent movie era. The lead character was played by Klaus Kinski who 'with his pronounced lips, deep-set eyes, and overall cretinous energy [...] was perfect for the job of resurrecting the mouldering corpse of the original vampire.'[60]

The Murnau classic was once more resurrected with *Shadow of the Vampire* (2000) directed by E. Elois Mehige, written by Steven Katz and starring John Malkovitch as Murnau and William Dafoe as Schreck. The film tells the behind-the-scenes story of the making of *Nosferatu* in 1921.[61] In the film Schrek is hiding true vampiric tendencies and the film crew are living a real-life horror film.

Following the Stoker estate law case against Prana Film Studios, Hamilton Deane received permission from Florence Stoker to turn *Dracula* into a stage play. He wrote the play himself in three acts and removed all the scenes from Transylvania, instead moving all the action to London.[62] The play was not received well by the critics when it was released in 1927, but it remained at the Lyceum until 1939. It was this stage play that made Count Dracula 'suitable' for the Victorian drawing room by introducing the now synonymous opera cloak with the high collar. As Dracula could only come out at night this was seen as suitable attire for a man about town. The outfit also set the vampire apart from the rest of society as he was always attired thus. Indeed, Bela Lugosi's Dracula went as far as wearing this outfit and his medals in the coffin.[63]

The introduction of the cloak meant that Dracula could 'disappear' on stage (with the use of a trapdoor).[64] Another use of the cloak was the same way a Victorian lady used her fan, to hide behind and mask kisses and other illicit behaviour. It is used this way in many of the early films.[65] The cloak also gave the character the added drama of resembling a bat when he raised his arms. This connection with bats is a common theme throughout vampire movies and books. In Justin Richard's book, *The Parliament of Blood* (2008), however, the wolf bat was actually the saviour of the human race, as they fed on vampires' blood, draining them of life force and leaving them as a pile of dust.[66]

The first movie to be made with permission from the Bram Stoker estate was Tod Browning's 1931 *Dracula*. This film started many of the stereotypes associated with the Dracula franchise, including a lack of reflection, his ability to hypnotise mortals,[67] and to disintegrate in the morning light.[68] These were all tropes that were to remain with the vampire genre until the modern day.

Part of the fear of vampires was their ability to control the mind and the body of humans,[69] making them forget, providing false memories, or making them compliant. This skill is used in rather sinister fashion in the book *Carrion Comfort* (1989) by Dan Simmons, in which the vampires use their 'ability' to plant racial hatred in the minds of people across the world: 'The German Willi inspires Nazism and thrives on concentration camps; Nine and Melanie, purring southern belles, manipulate racial hatred in the United States. Along the way, for exercise, they foment such apparently isolated catastrophes as the murders of John Kennedy and John Lennon.'[70]

Returning to Ted Browning's 1931 *Dracula*, the lead was played by Bela Lugosi, dressed in a tuxedo, white bow tie and medals, with immaculately slicked-back hair that is not disturbed even when feeding. Lugosi had been playing Dracula in the Broadway production, which had been running since 1927 and coincided with Deane's play at the Lyceum.

Stoker's original book had once more been rewritten for the American movie market,[71] though Lugosi did not speak English and throughout his career never felt the need to learn it; he simply learned the lines he needed to deliver. It was the start of a long career of being typecast as Dracula, or similar horror roles, until his death.[72] Lugosi became so synonymous with Dracula than when he died in 1956 he was buried wearing Dracula's high-collared opera cape.[73]

In the 1931 film version the count lives in a fading, opulent mansion, thus demonstrating his vast wealth and class as Eastern European aristocracy. Unlike Count Orlok, Lugosi's Dracula is 'part snake-charmer and part pick-up artist. Dracula can claim ownership of a woman's heart (and nether regions) with a single glance.'[74]

It is this Dracula that introduces a sexualised vampire, and comparisons have been made between the fangs breaking the skin and the act of sexual penetration.[75] Indeed, one of the most reproduced shots is of Dracula, high on bloodlust, leaning over Helen Chandler, playing Mina, as she slumbers in innocence. This high sexuality is something that is exaggerated more and more as time and the genre progresses.

Though as Auerbach states: 'Stoker's Dracula was too single minded to bother with seductive rituals. He was fundamentally a rapist, but one with no lust for death, injecting into his victims incessant, frightening life.'[76]

This suave, sexualised version of Dracula is a far cry from Stoker's character, who lives alone in his castle and carries out the household tasks himself: he picks up Jonathan Harker in his coach disguised as a hirsute driver, and at the castle Harker walks in on Dracula making the beds. Throughout Stoker's novel Dracula changes his appearance based on the role he is playing and it has been suggested that he does not have an actual form, which is why he has no reflection or shadow.[77] Prior to his trip to England he even steals a pair of Jonathan Harker's trousers, which does not fit with the image of Dracula created by Lugosi.

Another movie taken from the Bram Stoker original was Francis Ford-Coppolla's *Bram Stoker's Dracula* (1992) with Keanu Reeves playing Johnathan Harker and Gary Oldman as Count Dracula. It has been described as a 'dark version of Beauty and the Beast, a romance, even, with all of the blood and fangs.'[78] Oldman's Dracula is very distinctive, starting as handsome prince Vlad before ageing to look every one of his immortal years. He also wears a very distinctive swooped widow's peak hairstyle which was replicated in the spoof *Dracula: Dead and Loving it*. Coppola bought into the theory that Dracula was based on Vlad the Impaler (discussed in Chapter 7) and Mina was the reincarnation of Vlad's wife.

While Lugosi formed the famous characteristics, the most iconic Dracula came with Christopher Lee playing Terence Fisher's leading man in *Dracula* (1958). Lee was Dracula in seven films, six with Hammer Horror and one with Spanish filmmaker Jesús Franco in *Count Dracula* (1970). His final Dracula movie was *The Satanic Rites of Dracula* (1974).

Throughout Lee's time as Dracula he morphed from an 'inarticulate killing machine to a suave seducer.'[79] He also introduced more familiar tropes of the vampire genre, including that of being able to produce new vampires by biting them but not killing them,[80] as he does with Lucy Westernra. Lee 'synthesizes the perfect fusion of high culture and low, of dignified Gothic literature and the scuzzy heritage of splatter cinema that would go on to cannibalize it.'[81] His brand new, sparkling, Art deco-style home was also seen as a modern alternative to the large, mausoleum-type mansion of Lugosi's Dracula and would have been attractive to the kind of audience Hammer were trying to appeal to.[82]

With such a pedigree in vampire movie Lee described the fascination with the vampire: 'He offers the illusion of immortality [...] the subconscious wish we all have of limitless power [...] a man of tremendous brain and physical strength [...] he is either a reincarnation or he has never died. He is a superman image, with erotic appeal for women who find him totally alluring. In many ways he is everything people would like to be – the anti-hero, the heroic villain [...] For women there is the complete abandonment of the power of a man.'[83]

Whereas the zombie is the movie monster of the twenty-first century, the vampire was the movie monster of the late twentieth century.[84] The 1970s 'tested the full pliability of the Dracula figure,'[85] as the character was reworked to fit different agendas, including remaking the franchise as *Blacula* in 1972. This film was directed by William Crain and the story follows Dracula as he meets with Prince Mamuwalde (William Marshall) of the Abani nation to discuss ending the slave trade between Europe and Africa. Dracula endorses slavery, flirts with the prince's wife, kills the prince and brings him back as a vampire who he nicknames Blackula, imprisoning him in a coffin.[86] Cain is making a political statement with this film by setting it in the Los Angeles district of Watts, a predominantly African-American neighbourhood, and peppering the script with racism from the white characters.[87] This film was followed by a sequel, *Scream Blacula Scream*, the following year.

In 1973 Bill Gunn released the movie *Ganja and Hess* which was seen as an analogy for 'the black population's assimilation in a country that repeatedly insisted it had no place for them.'[88] The main character, Dr Hess Green (Duane Jones), is a wealthy man with a palatial home and a butler. His assistant, George (Bill Gunn), messes up a murder-suicide with a cursed knife and turns Hess into a vampire. Hess is addicted to blood and has little choice but to feed his desires, which are described as comparable to substance abuse and 'symptomatic of social causes, rather than existential ones.'[89]

The most successful black vampire can be seen in the *Blade* franchise which first came to the screens in 1998 with Wesley Snipes as the daywalker Eric Brooks, also known as Blade. He was a vampire-human hybrid, the middle man between a group of vampires and the human race. Blade is mistrusted by many throughout the trilogy due to being able to walk in both the daytime and the night-time. It is thought this may be a commentary on how mixed-race individuals – with one black and one Caucasian parent – are never truly accepted into either community.[90] However, Wesley Snipes, in an interview in 2018, denies this was the intention: 'Often they perceive, once you put African Americans or people of colour in the film, then you have to address the social dynamic that may exist in the real world. I don't always agree with that, I think there's a time and place for everything.'

In *Blade II* however, race became more of an issue and Snipes adds: 'It was [*Blade II* director] Guillermo del Toro's idea to add that into the movie. It just gave some other dimension to the dynamic of these mercenaries, if you can call them that, right? Being plunged into a predicament that they were all resistant to. One of the personalities was this guy who was kind of a, you could say, a supremacist. I don't even know if he's a white supremacist, because he was a vampire. But that really wasn't the intent, and it was ancillary to what we were trying to accomplish in terms of the entertainment.'[91]

Blade has to play the intermediary between the two sides and according to Bramesco: 'the films would be mournful if they weren't so hopped-up on a cocktail of speed and spiked blood.'[92]

In 1995 Wes Craven produced *A Vampire in Brooklyn* in which Eddie Murphy plays Maximillian, an ancient vampire who possesses powers such as shape-shifting and mind-control, which are used to comedic effect. His *raison d'etre* seems to be solely to cause chaos wherever he goes and as a character 'props up as many black stereotypes as he counters.'[93] The film was not a major box office success.

Continuing with this idea of not been accepted – a stranger in a strange land – takes the vampire to the Wild West where everyone was looking for their role in the new communities. William Beaudine's *Billy the Kid versus Dracula* (1966) is a prime example. Dracula, played by John Carradine, follows in the footsteps of Lugosi, arriving in a Wild West town looking for a bride. He chooses the fiancée of Billy the Kid. The movie was shot in eight days on a low budget and was paid for by Embassy Pictures.[94]

In 1987 Kathryn Bigelow produced *Near Dark* in which a band of varmints who are never referred to as vampires roam from town to town leaving a trail of blood behind them. The newest vampire to their ranks, Caleb (Adrian Pasdar), meets love interest Mae and decides he is unable to kill her. He reverts back to human form by having a blood transfusion, allowing them to continue their relationship as humans.

Quentin Tarantino also got into the Western vampire flick with *From Dusk till Dawn* (1996) in which a family is held up by two criminals in a Mexican strip club where all the patrons and dancers are vampires.

A vampire movie classic is *The Lost Boys* (1987) produced by Joel Schumacher and starring Corey Haim, Corey Feldman, Keifer Sutherland and Diane Keaton. A family moves to Santa Carla, the self-proclaimed murder capital of the world, following a divorce. The oldest son, Mike (Jason Patric), gets caught up with a young biker gang which he discovers – once he has been initiated into their gang by being tricked into drinking blood – are vampires. The story follows his evolution into a vampire and the efforts of his brother, Sam (Corey Haim), and the Frog brothers (Corey Feldman and Jamison Newlander) – who are inexperienced vampire hunters and comic book aficionados – to try to stop the gang. The vampire epidemic in Santa Carla is more widespread than David (Keifer Sutherland) and his gang and the closing line of the film is given to Sam and Mike's grandfather, who says: 'One thing about living in Santa Carla I could never stomach: all the damn vampires.' The film epitomised the cool, punk rock vampire and became the cult movie of a generation.

Comedy vampires have been a sub-category of the genre since *Abbott and Costello Meet Frankenstein* (1948), when Bela Lugosi once more took on the role of Dracula. The film was a success and saw a number of sequels in which Abbott and Costello met a number of other classical monsters (see Chapter 1). Rather than adopting the characteristics of the horror genre, the Abbott and Costello act was simply placed in horror-comedy setting.[95] Lugosi played Dracula in the traditional way, which was offset against the two comedians' slapstick routines. Dracula was 'something for the main attraction to play off.'[96]

Roman Polanski even got in one the act with the slapstick comedy, *The Fearless Vampire Killers* (1967), in which Polanski cast himself as Van Helsing's less than bright sidekick. Again, a serious and staid Dracula was a contrast with the comedic elements of the other characters.

A comedy starring Johnny Depp in 2012 was *Dark Shadows*. Barnabas Collins, an eighteenth-century aristocrat, breaks the heart of a local witch, Angelique Bouchard, who turns him into a vampire as revenge. She buries him in a sealed coffin from which he is accidently released by some construction workers centuries later. He returns to his ancestral home to discover that his descendants still live there, but they are somewhat dysfunctional. Not only does he have to deal with the cultural shock of the 1970s but Angelique is still alive and still focused on revenge.

The classic spoof was Mel Brooks' *Dracula: Dead and Loving It* (1995) starring Leslie Nielson as Dracula. Brooks calls on all the previous classics in his portrayal of the count by having him crave the suave, aristocratic sophistication of Lugosi but with Nielson's own slapstick humour. Dracula is seen wearing the coiffed widow's peak from Oldman's *Dracula*, as well as recreating some classic scenes, such as Lugosi at the top of the sweeping staircase (before Nielson slips and tumbles down). Brooks' Dracula can also turn himself into a bat, hypnotise people and make new vampires, though 'they all seem to be on the fritz, subverting the vampire's crucial collected air.'[97]

Vampires also featured in the first and only signed film *Deafula,* produced in 1975. This was directed by, written by and starred Peter Wolf and was scripted in American Sign Language with an additional voiceover. The basic plot follows a theology student, Steve Adams, who suspects he is a vampire as he comes of age. His mother had been seduced by Dracula when she was pregnant. Steve then decides to hunt down Dracula, while himself being hunted for a series of murders in his town.

Female Vampires

There are very few films that feature a female vampire as the lead rather than the love interest of a male vampire. However, this is something that is being addressed, especially in late twentieth century television shows like *True Blood*. The traditional trope is the male vampire and the female victim, and this is still, to a certain extent, the case. In the earliest literature the female vampires were pretty characterless and only wanted to drink blood: voraciously.[98]

Female vampires are generally much more sexualised than their male counterparts. In Stoker's *Dracula* they are seductresses who are trying to entice Harker. This traditional characterisation shows the females as being irresistible to men but also less powerful than male vampires who have more than just appearance and sexuality in their arsenal.

Female vampires have, nevertheless, tried to fight back against being cast as secondary to male vampires since 1936. The production of

Dracula's Daughter (1936) shows the lead, Countess Marya Zaleska, trying to break out of the shadow cast by her father, Dracula, played by Bela Lugosi (who was not in the sequel). She tries to rid herself of the vampire's curse but is represented as 'hysterical'. The promotional poster warned 'Save the Women of London from Dracula's Daughter,' which, with its lesbian undertones, was seen as a threat to man's power over women's bodies.[99]

Later films with a female lead are *Vamp* (1986) with Grace Jones, and *Queen of the Damned* (2002), based on the Anne Rice novel, with R&B singer Aaliyah in the role of Queen Akasha. *Vamp* starts with two college boys entering a sleazy bar and looking for a stripper, without realising the bar is run by vampires. Despite holding the leading title roles, neither actress dominates the film. Aaliyah is on screen for nineteen of the 101 minutes of the *Queen of the Damned*. Grace Jones has more screen time in *Vamp* but does not speak throughout the movie and has others speak for her.[100]

One female vampire who almost matches the suave sophistication of the male version was Miriam Blaylock (Catherine Deneuve) in *The Hunger* (1983). The vampire was born in ancient Egypt and was the daughter of Lamia, a child-devouring monster.[101] She is well-dressed and cool, dating John (David Bowie), one of her many lovers, which helps satiate her deep-set loneliness. They entice prey from New York nightclubs to return home with them, thus combining sex and death. Miriam, though, is completely removed from the people around her. She gets bored with her lovers and starts hunting for the next one, who in the movie is played by Susan Sarandon.

A recent offering of female vampires is the 2013 *Byzantium*, which portrays a mother and daughter, played by Gemma Arterton and Saoirse Ronan. Both women have a strong bond forged over centuries and which cannot be broken by a man's affections. Until, that is, the teenage daughter becomes infatuated with a local boy, Frank. She decides to eschew her vampiric tendencies and will only feed on the willing. However, mother and daughter's past catches up with them, with dangerous consequences.

Pornography

Since the first film in 1922 the persona of the vampire has evolved to the point where they are considered the sexiest ghoul in the supernatural world.

It is, therefore, not surprising that a number of vampire pornographic movies have been produced.

Spanish filmmaker Jesús Franco produced *Vampyros Lesbos* in 1971 and *Female Vampire* in 1975, and José Ramón made *Vampyres* in 1974, which presented the female vampires as male playthings. In 1976 Charles Matton directed *Spermula*, considered a French softcore fantasy film. The more recent pornographic movies are riding on the back of the mainstream vampire movies and are little more than x-rated parodies. Sammy Slater directed *This isn't the Twilight Saga: Breaking Dawn - the XXX Parody Part 1* (2010), and in 2012 *Buffy the Vampire Slayer XXX: A Parody* was directed by Lee Roy Myers.

With vampires being the sexy monsters they are, there are innumerable pornography movies; too many to discuss in any depth here.

International Vampires

Vampire movies are not just popular in the English-speaking world. Over the years there have been a number of international film releases. Naturally, Bollywood, the biggest film industry in the world, has produced vampire movies, though they were late to the party with their first release being *Bandh Darwaza* in 1990, directed by Shyam and Tulsi Ramsay. The vampire lead is Nevla (Anirudh Agarwal) who is a combination of the suave vampire and the original Nosferatu, with a distinctive widow's peak as well as red flashing eyes and a bulging vein in the forehead. He possesses traditional powers of persuasion but can also impregnate women the 'traditional' way.[102]

In Japan, Nobuo Nakagawa produced the film *Lady Vampire* (Onna Kyûketsuki) in 1959 in which the male vampire, Shiro Sofue (Shigeri Amachi), only turned monstrous in the light of the moon,[103] and so is a cross between a werewolf and Mr Hyde. Sofue is an acclaimed artist and when Tamio Oki (Takashi Wada) sees a portrait of her mother, painted by him, in an art gallery, she starts to ask questions as her mother had disappeared twenty years previously but in the portrait she looks no different.

A trilogy then followed, with *Fear of the Ghost House*, *Bloodsucking Doll*, and the final *Evil of Dracula*. The first is a cultural crossover between the vampire and traditional Japanese spirits that inhabit the home.

The final film was more in tune with Bram Stoker's *Dracula*, with a 'combination of woe and lust towards death.'[104] There is also a certain political element to the film as vampirism is seen as a plague brought to Japan by the Europeans.

In China there are comedy movies about the *Jiangshi*, who were the reanimated corpses of the Qing dynasty. As they could only move while hopping it lent itself to the comedy genre. The earliest Chinese vampire movie was in 1936 with Yeung Kung-Leung's *Midnight Vampire*.

In 1980 *Close Encounters of the Spooky Kind* was produced by Sammo Hung and combined slapstick comedy, horror and martial arts. Hung then worked on a further vampire movie in 1985 called *Mr. Vampire*, which follows a pattern for *jiangshi* movies where a Taoist monk awakens and finds he must dispatch this hopping creature from beyond the grave.[105]

The Filipino vampire offering is *Blood is the Colour of Night* or *The Blood Drinkers,* produced in 1964 and shot in a single colour. The director, Gerardo de León, uses a lot of atmospheric lighting which Bramesco claims is to disguise the budget sets.[106]

The 'first Iranian feminist vampire Western' was released in 2014 and was produced by Ana Lily Amirpour. *A Girl Walks Alone at Night* is set in the desert village of Bad Town. The female vampire (Sheila Vand) is not named, but spends her time listening to vinyl and killing villagers. Amirpour said: 'the seed for this film began with the feeling of being like a bat while wearing her chador; with this film, she weaponizes her heritage and womanhood with a cultural and pop-cultural specificity.'[107]

Matinee Vampires

There have been a number of vampire movies and television shows for children. These have been softened to make them child-friendly while maintaining all the traditional features. For example, *Sesame Street* has the loveable Count Von Count, modelled on Bela Lugosi's Dracula with a widow's peak and silk cloak, who has a preoccupation with counting.

Vampire animals are also a feature of children's animation. These inlcude *Count Duckula* and *Bunnicula the Vampire Rabbit*, both of whom are vegetarian. *Duckula* ran from 1988 to 1993 and had sixty-five episodes. All of Duckula's ancestors were 'vicious vampire ducks' but in the resurrection of 'Ducky-poos', as he is affectionately called by his Nanny, ketchup rather than blood was used in the ritual. He was not, therefore, a traditional blood-sucking vampire but a vegetarian. In addition to Nanny, Ducky-poos is looked after by the butler, Igor, who has worked for the family for generations and is horrified at how Duckula is more interested in fame as an entertainer than pursuing vampire activities.

Bunnicula started life as a book in 1979, written by Deborah Howe, in which the vampire rabbit sucks the life out of vegetables. Bunnicula was found at the cinema by the Monroe family when they were watching a Dracula film. This inspired the name they gave him, and why the family cat, Chester, believes he is a vampire rabbit. In 1982 an animated series was created, which varied from the book and gave Bunnicula vampiric powers such as being able to turn into vapour, and having his ears turn into bat wings, allowing him to fly. A further adaptation of the book into a television series aired on the Cartoon Network and Boomerang in 2016.

A true success in children's vampire movies is the *Hotel Transylvania* (2012) trilogy produced by Genndy Tartakovsky. The hotel is run by Dracula (voiced by Adam Sandler) who is grieving after his wife was killed by humans. He wants to protect his daughter, Mavis, from the same fate so tells her tales of how monstrous the humans are, as well as keeping her in the hotel surrounded by safe monsters such as Frankenstein, werewolves and the invisible man. This overprotective parent role is one unfamiliar to the vampire genre, but works well in this context. Whereas traditionally vampires lust for blood and sex, Mavis has the same hunger for life, adventure and, of course, love, and throughout the movie she is looking for that 'zing.'

In *The Simpsons* Halloween special, *Treehouse of Horror IV* (1993), Mr Burns is a vampire who invites the Simpsons to Pennsylvania to stay in his mansion. When Bart and Lisa go into the basement it is full of coffins, which Bart claims is no different to his grandfather's rest home. The vampires that come out of the coffins are green and zombie-like, whereas Mr Burns has the elaborate coiffure favoured by Dracula in Francis Ford Coppola's movie. Bart becomes a vampire, along with Millhouse and Ralph, and they are seen levitating outside Lisa's bedroom before Bart turns into a bat. All the vampires are shown with pointed canines and glowing red eyes. Lisa determines – presumably from *The Lost Boys* – that to turn Bart back to a human they need to kill the head vampire, Mr Burns. As in *The Lost Boys*, they are mistaken in their assumption of who the head vampire is, and they realise that Marge is, in fact, the head vampire, as she says, 'I do have a life outside this house.'

Conclusion

The vampire on screen and in literature has made the most dramatic transformation of all the reanimated corpses, starting out as a rat-like creature in *Nosferatu*, and then developing into suave, sophisticated sexual creatures in pretty much every other film since. From Bela Lugosi to William Erasmus Compton, played by Stephen Moyer, in *True Blood*. The vampire has passed through, 'the tyranny of patriarchy, the power of the corrupt aristocracy or the nouveau bourgeois capitalists; he represents decadent foreigners. Slavs or Jews; he is a homosexual, a social outcast, even a mother, and he is dangerously erotic.'[108]

Despite these transformations, however, they have remained true to the father of vampires, Bram Stoker, and have built on his character rather than rewriting it.

One particular aspect of vampires in the modern Western world which is particularly intriguing is the group of individuals who wish to believe in them and the lifestyle to such an extent that they live their lives as vampires.

Chapter 6

The Modern Vampire

Vampires have caught the imagination of many in a way that mummies and zombies have not. This has manifested itself in a vampire sub-culture across the Western world. This sub-culture is one that believes vampires are real, with some adopting a vampire lifestyle. According to *Harper's Index* (October 1992), 'Number of the world's 810 vampires who live in the United States, according to the Vampire Research Center: 550, Number who live in Romania: 3.'

Twentieth-Century Vampires

There have been various cases throughout the twentieth century of mass-murderers who have been given the title of 'vampire'. One such case was the Vampire of Düsseldorf, Peter Kürten (1883–1932), who was executed in 1932 for murdering at least nine people.

He claims to have started his killings at the age of nine when he pushed a friend into the water. When another friend jumped in to help, Kürten claims to have held both under until they drowned. He had a lifelong obsession with blood, and as a child killed animals, which later as an adult escalated into bestiality.

His first recorded murder was Christine Klein, a ten-year-old girl who was sexually assaulted and murdered in 1913.[1] His real blood-lust, however, took off between 1929 and 1930 with the murder of at least nine people. These were primarily young women and children whom he sexually assaulted, killed and then, as the newspapers reported, drank their blood. When arrested he admitted to seventy crimes, including nine murders and seven attempted murders. At his trial the jury took ninety minutes to find him guilty. He was executed by guillotine, stating that he hoped, 'after my head has been chopped off I will still be able to hear,

143

at least for a moment, the sound of my own blood gushing from the stump of my neck.'[2]

The Hanover Vampire was another German serial killer, Fritz Haarmann (1879–1925), who was executed in 1925. Between 1918 and 1924 he killed twenty-four young men and boys, aged between ten and twenty-two years old, by biting into or through their throats. He referred to this act as his 'love bite'. He also mutilated and dismembered their bodies, earning the additional moniker of the Butcher of Hanover. Their body parts were then rumoured to have been eaten by Haarmann or sold as horse meat. Although this was never confirmed he was known as a trader in black-market meat.[3] He was charged with twenty-seven murders but was only found guilty of twenty-four of them and was executed on 15 April 1925.

Highgate Vampire

While nicknaming serial killers 'vampire' is one form of realising the myth, there are also a number of so-called sightings recorded of real vampires. An infamous case is that of the Highgate Vampire, which hit the British headlines in 1970.

In the 1960s Highgate cemetery in North London was run-down, overgrown with ivy and susceptible to vandals pushing over monuments and exposing the bodies buried there. It was a far cry from the tourist haven it has become today. This dilapidated state caught the eye of Hammer Studios who set their film *Taste the Blood of Dracula* in the cemetery in 1969.[4] This firmly connected Highgate with vampires in the minds of some individuals.

The legend of the Highgate Vampire was initially reported in the *Hampstead and Highgate Express* on 27 February 1970. Seán Manchester, the president of the British Occult Society, had, however, been investigating the various 'sightings' in the cemetery which had been reported since 1967. The earliest was by two teenage girls, who were walking past the entrance on the way home from school when they claimed to see bodies rising from the graves within. One of the girls, Elizabeth Wojdyla, suffered nightmares of an evil man trying to get through her window. Manchester sprinkled her room with holy water and he reported seeing two puncture wounds on her neck.[5]

Elizabeth Wojdyla's experience in the cemetery was followed by three years of sightings of a woman in white, a man wearing a hat, a tall figure with red eyes and ghostly cyclists. One of the most publicly active witnesses was tobacconist David Farrant, who, in 1970, reported seeing something that looked like it had been dead for some time. His descriptions, however, changed over the following thirty years.[6] His first letter to the *Hampstead and Highgate Express*, on 6 February 1970, claimed he had seen ghost-like apparitions at the North Gate at the top of Swains Hill.

Manchester debunked the idea that a ghost was roaming Highgate cemetery, saying: '[it] is not merely the apparition of an earth-bound spirit, which is relatively harmless, but much worse – that of a vampyr or as it is more popularly known, a vampire.' He told the press that his Vampire Research Society had discovered that the King Vampire of the Undead, a nobleman from medieval Wallachia, near Turkey, was able to walk the streets again after practising black magic in Romania.[7] 'His followers eventually brought him to England in a coffin at the beginning of the 18th century and bought a house for him in the West End – his unholy resting place became Highgate Cemetery.'[8]

Manchester further claimed that while vampires had often centred on Highgate, a recent spate of grave desecration for Satanic practices had helped the vampire king to rise from the grave. He offered to dispatch the vampire: 'by the traditional and approved manner – drive a stake through its heart with one blow just after dawn between Friday and Saturday, chop off the head with a gravedigger's shovel, and bury what remains. This is what the clergy did centuries ago. But we'd be breaking the law today.'[9]

David Farrant returned to the same spot where he had first witnessed spirits in March 1970 and found a dead fox. He told the *Hampstead and Highgate Express* that other foxes had been found dead in the cemetery with no obvious cause of death. 'Much remains unexplained, but what I have recently learnt, all point to the vampire theory as being the most likely answer.' He met with Seán Manchester in the cemetery and said, 'these incidents are just more inexplicable events that seem to complement my theory about a vampire.'[10]

David Farrant was later arrested for trespassing in the cemetery after opening hours. His intention was to stalk the vampire and stake it through the heart. In a television reconstruction, *24 Hours*,

Farrant demonstrated how he did it with a home-made wooden cross, a stake and a rosary. In his police statement he claimed: 'he heard the vampire rises out of a grave and wanders about the cemetery on the look-out for human beings on whose blood it thrives.'[11] This case of vampire hunting was dismissed in 1970 by Judge Christopher Lea following Farrant's mitigation that he and his coven were conducting a séance in an attempt to make contact with the entity. He was later arrested for further excursions into the cemetery and was sent to prison for four years and eight months in June 1974 for crimes relating to Highgate Cemetery and for threatening people with black magic. He was tried at the Old Bailey in London.[12]

By 1997 the legend of the Highgate Vampire had resulted in the establishment of the Highgate Vampire Society, led by David Farrant, who at this point claimed to have seen a seven-foot vampire in the cemetery with red eyes, which vanished leaving 'a feeling of overwhelming evil.' He claims this was not a blood-sucking vampire but a 'malevolent spirit that somehow remained earthbound.' The society had as many as sixty members at the time from all over the world, including from USA, Australia and New Zealand.[13]

However, the rival Vampire Research Society, led by the Right Reverend Seán Manchester, slammed Farrant's group, claiming the vampire had been exorcised in 1974. Manchester was now a bishop of an unrecognised old Catholic church and claimed he exorcised the vampire himself. The first exorcism carried out by Manchester was in August 1970 and the tomb of Charles Fisher Wace, in the Circle of Lebanon, was identified as the tomb housing the vampire (see fig. 10). He opened the tomb after being led there by one of the vampire's victims, the sleepwalking Lusia, who bore two bite marks on her neck.[14] Lusia is reported to have been Jacqueline Cooper, an ex-lover and common-law wife of Manchester's, who was named in his divorce proceedings.[15]

Apparently Manchester discovered the mausoleum full of empty coffins, which he filled with garlic, but this initial attempt was apparently 'ineffective'. Later that year Manchester records how Lusia led him to another mausoleum, whereupon removing the lid of the coffin he found a vampire 'gorged and stinking with the life blood of others,' with 'glazed eyes [staring] horribly, almost mocking me.' He did not stake the vampire at this point but instead bricked it up with garlic-infused cement. In 1977 the vampire had been reawakened and haunted the basement of a nearby house where he was able to stake it, thus saving London from danger.[16]

In 1982 Manchester realised that Lusia, although a so-called victim of the vampire, was in fact a vampire herself and he took it upon himself to end the Highgate vampire line for good by visiting her grave. He was confronted by a large spider-like creature, which he staked. It then turned back into Lusia, who was forever returned to the grave.[17]

David Farrant is still hunting for the Highgate vampire and in 2005 he returned to Highgate after a reported sighting of a vampire-like figure. This was his first visit in more than thirty years. He told the *Hampshire and Highgate Express,* 'The sighting of a tall, black figure in April on Swains Lane makes me think the vampire is active again. On my visit I saw the bricked-up vault, which some occultists say is inhabited by the vampire.'[18] Following this visit he relaunched the Highgate Vampire Society which had disbanded in 2000.

In 2014, speaking to the *Ham and High*, Farrant's wife, Della, said: 'David never said in seriousness that the Swain's Lane entity was a vampire, but some local eccentrics began encouraging this rumour [...] They were helped along by *Ham and High* headlines such as "Does a Wampyr Walk in Highgate?"'[19]

Della's comments would be more convincing if all the information about Highgate Cemetery and the vampire investigations were not on Farrant's Highgate Vampire Society Webpage.[20]

Leading a Vampire Lifestyle

Vampirism does not however stop at occultists glimpsing them in cemeteries. It is also not something designated to the past – either distant or recent – for there is a subculture of people living a vampire lifestyle in modern society. Many have tried to explain the compulsion to lead this lifestyle, with Jeffrey Cohen in his *Monster Theory* claiming: 'The cultural fascination with the monster is born of the twin desire to name that which is difficult to apprehend and to domesticate (and therefore disempower) that which threatens.'[21] Living the life of a so-called 'monster' allows the individual 'to explore the localised collisions and collusions between the boundaries of different identities.'[22]

147

David Keyworth describes modern vampirism as: 'a multi-faceted, socio-religious movement with its own distinct collective community and network of participants who share a similar belief system and customary lifestyle that reflect their concept of the vampire.'[23]

However, following Bram Stoker's novel in the late nineteenth century the concept of vampires walking, breathing and feeding off the living became very popular and they were reported to drink both blood and energy. In 1892 an essay of the Hermitic Order of the Golden Dawn states:

> A few years ago, I noticed that invariably after a prolonged interview with a certain person, I felt exhausted. At first, I thought it only the natural result of a long conversation with a prosy, fidgety, old gentleman; but later it dawned upon me, that being a man of exhausted nervous vitality, he was really preying upon me. I don't suppose that he was at all externally conscious that he possessed a vampire organization, for he was a benevolent kind-hearted man, who would have shrunk in horror from such a suggestion. Nevertheless, he was, in his inner personality an intentional vampire, for he acknowledged that he was about to marry a young wife in order, if possible, to recuperate his exhausted system. The next time, therefore, that he was announced, I closed myself to him, before he was admitted. I imagined that I had formed myself a complete investiture of odic fluid, surrounding me on all sides, but not touching me, and impenetrable to any hostile currents. This magical process was immediately and permanently successful — I never had to repeat it.[24]

It is only natural that, at some point, people would stop being afraid of such vampires and start to relate to them. In modern America there are two sub-cultures of vampires: the Real Vampires, who feel the need to drink blood and feed from the energy of people, and Lifestyle Vampires, who dress in a particular way and follow cultural behaviour but do not drink blood as a physical need.[25]

The main difference between the two is that Lifestyle Vampires choose the life they lead, whereas Real Vampires believe they have little choice in their lifestyle and at no point are they free to leave. It is also possible to be a Real Vampire but not to live the lifestyle,[26] although some choose the lifestyle as well.

Many Real Vampires 'interpret subtle energy as a metaphysical phenomenon that transcends the laws of nature, others believe that vampirism is a natural phenomenon not currently understood by Western science.'[27]

One such community is the Atlanta Vampire Alliance, which was set up by and for Real Vampires. The members of the Alliance include both Real and Lifestyle Vampires as well as non-vampires, mundanes or muggles,[28] who act as 'donors'. They have no leader and therefore there are no rules by which they have to live.[29] They consider themselves more a group of like-minded people who co-exist.

The 'leader' of the Nashville Vampire Clan does claim there are regional differences between the vampire groups and there is a clear cultural hierarchy.[30] Suscitatio Enterprises defines Real Vampires on their website as:

> essentially a blood drinker or an energy feeder that may display various levels of psychic ability. The vampires that are the focus of this study are individuals who cannot adequately sustain their own physical, mental, or spiritual well-being without the taking of blood or vital life force energy from other sources; often human. Without feeding (whether by a regular or infrequent schedule) the vampire will become lethargic, sickly, and often go through physical suffering or discomfort. Vampires often display signs of empathy, sense emotions, perceive auras of other humans, and are generally psychically aware of the world around them.[31]

Real Vampires who drink blood to survive are also known as Sanguinarian vampires and they typically drink human rather than animal blood.[32] Sometimes these 'vampires' are referred to as having Renfield Syndrome, named after the character in Stoker's *Dracula* who ate live insects, craving their life force. Renfield Syndrome is seen as an obsession with drinking blood, with the earliest recognised case being in 1964. However, sexual pleasure associated with drinking blood has been recorded since 1892 by the Austrian forensic psychiatrist Richard von Krafft-Ebing.[33] He published a number of vampire-related case studies gleaned from his patients. For example, Case number 48 was a man who had a number of scars up and down his arms. These were reportedly caused by his wife during their lovemaking. 'He first had to make a cut in his arm [...] she would suck the wound and during the act become violently excited sexually.'[34]

A third subset of the vampire culture are the Psychic Vampires who are able to draw energy from other people. Those who participate in both psychic and physical aspects are known as hybrids.

One of the problems facing Real Vampires is that 'Vampirism is often confused with or represented as a mental illness, a "cult", or a role-playing game.'[35] Real Vampires try to distance themselves from role-playing vampires, especially since there have been a lot of high-profile media attention regarding their activities.

The widely reported case of seventeen-year-old Rod Ferrell, who was charged with murdering two people, is a prime example. At his trial he claimed he was a 500-year-old vampire, Vesago. At the trial it was discovered he had mental problems, suffered with drug abuse and had a history of sexual abuse.

Another role-playing vampire who blurred the lines was sixteen-year-old Salvatore Agron who murdered a number of people while dressed as Bela Lugosi. He was leader of a New York gang called The Vampires and they were behind a number of gang-related stabbings.[36]

A teenage vampire group in Murray, Kentucky, USA, met in 'The Vampire Hotel' as the press named it, to participate in vampire role playing where they drank each other's blood and killed puppies. Four of the group then travelled to Florida to murder a friend's parents before taking a trip in the parents' car to New Orleans.[37]

The role-playing vampire culture has been implicated in other murders, such as the murder of sixteen-year-old Roderick Ferrell's girlfriend's parents where a copy of Anne Rice's *Queen of the Damned* was found in Ferrell's car. The film *Queen of the Damned* was further implicated in a murder in Scotland. Twenty-two-year-old Allan Menzies was so caught up in the vampire world he killed his best friend, drank his blood and started to eat him.[38] In 1980, twenty-three-year-old James Riva claimed a vampire instructed him to kill his seventy-four-year-old grandmother. He drank her blood as it flowed from the wounds. He believed he was 700 years old and his grandmother's blood was going to sustain him, although in the end she was too old for it to work.[39]

Real Vampires and Role-Playing Vampires 'avoid each other partly for fear of being confused with role-players like Ferrell who lack the ability to distinguish reality from fantasy.'[40] However, the members of the Atlanta Vampire Alliance have no interest in being acknowledged publically or legally as a religion or cult, or even having their behaviour diagnosed as a medical condition.[41]

Whether this particular group of vampires is considered a religious cult or not, they are a distinct social group, which separates them (in the group) from the others (those outside the group). They are, therefore, are a distinct identity group, which Amy Gutman describes as: 'politically significant associations of people who are identified by or identify with one or more shared social markers. Gender, race, class, ethnicity, nationality, religion, disability, and sexual orientation are among the most obvious examples of shared social markers around which informal and formal identity groups form.'[42] She believes that identity groups get together sometimes based purely on social markers and it could be that vampires see their sanguination as a physical need, which is different from the majority of the population.

In the Bible Belt of America this fascination with vampire cults is seen as evidence of family values gone awry, and at Nashville International Airport they used the image of a bat flying through an open window as a warning against AIDS, with the words of Dracula stating: 'Stop living in the dark – get the facts about AIDS. When I learned about AIDS I changed my ways. If I can control myself so can you! Beware of Fly-By-Night Relationships.'[43] The vampire here represents not only questionable morals but the contagious nature of the vampire.

Vampirism as a lifestyle received recent publicity on the Netflix documentary *Dark Tourist*, which was presented by journalist David Farrier. The eight-part series was aired in July 2018, and covered different aspects of alternative, macabre tourism. In episode three Farrier travels to New Orleans where he spends time with two groups of vampires.

The first group Farrier meets are Lifestyle Vampires, who live the life of vampires but do not believe they need blood to survive. Most of these vampires visit the Fangsmith, and pay $150 to have caps put on their teeth in the form of sharp fangs. Farrier then meets couple, Logan and Daley and their donor. They have just had an elaborate vampire wedding, and the drinking of blood from their female donor was very much a sexual act. They prick her finger and then sensually drink from it.

The second group Farrier meets are Real Vampires, who feel they need to drink blood to survive. One of the vampires claimed that if he did not drink blood he was dull, lifeless, his eyes glaze over and he cannot focus: 'when blood hits my tongue there's a crackle of energy. It's like I'm finally come to life.'

These Real Vampires also do not drink blood from the neck, as the movies would have us believe. Instead they make a cut on the back of the donor, and then suck and lick the blood off them. Farrier comments at the end of the episode, 'vampirism has very little to do with actual blood and more to do with a group of outsiders finding a community.'

Others actually view vampirism as a religion and the Temple of the Vampire was founded in 1989 in the United States. It boasts on its website: 'We are elitist for good reason and do not recognise any others who make claims upon our heritage and authority.'[44]

The Temple of the Vampire believes the vampire is 'the next step in human evolution,' and helps members to gain control over 'wealth, health, personal power, and unlimited life extension.' However, it makes it clear that the Temple only advocates: 'those aspects of the Vampire mythos that include a love and respect for all life, physical immortality, individual elegance, proven wisdom, civilised behaviour, worldly success and personal happiness. The Temple rejects those aspects of the Vampire mythos that are negative including any that are anti-life, anti-social, deathist, crude, gory, self-defeating, or criminal.'[45]

This is a fascinating take on the vampire lifestyle and seems to contradict all of the myths and legends about vampires (discussed in the next chapter) which are wholly negative, with vampires terrorising the living and living off their blood. The Vampire Creed, by which members of the Temple live, states:

I am a Vampire.

I worship my ego and I worship my life, for I am the only God that is.

I am proud that I am a predatory animal and I honor my animal instincts.

I exalt my rational mind and hold no belief that is in defiance to reason.

I recognize the difference between the worlds of truth and fantasy.

I acknowledge the fact that survival is the highest law.

I acknowledge the fact that Powers of Darkness to be hidden natural laws

Through which I work my magic.

I know that my beliefs in Ritual are fantasy but the magic is real.

And I respect and acknowledge the results of my magic.

I realise there is no heaven and there is no hell

And I view death as the destroyer of life.

Therefore I will make the most of life here and now.

I am Vampire.

Bow down before me.[46]

There is a Vampire Bible as well as a number of other religious texts available and reading these is essential to be admitted to Graded Temple membership. Additionally there are regular conclaves held around the world, including Australia, Europe and the United States. Essentially the Temple of the Vampire is a 'secret society' and when someone subscribes to the temple they must promise to 'refrain from criminal activity, physical blood drinking, and discussing the Temple with the public.'[47]

Conclusion

It is fascinating that the vampire is the only one of the three forms of reanimated corpse that has intrigued the imagination to such an extent that a sub-section of society have chosen to live in this way. It is a phenomena that is not seen with mummies or zombies. There are also no 'reported sightings' in the west of reanimated mummies or zombies ambling through cemeteries. Could this difference be a result of the 'sexy' image of vampires, which has been propagated through movies and novels? If zombies had been presented early on in their moving image as Liv Moore from *iZombie* would there be a sub-culture of white-haired, pale individuals raiding their butchers for calf, pig or sheep brains? If Anne Rice's Reginald Ramsey had made it onto the big screen perhaps reanimated mummies would be seen as sexier and people would want to live that lifestyle instead. Perhaps if Nosferatu had remained the typical vampire, then perhaps these Lifestyle or Real Vampire sub-strata would not exist. However, perhaps we should consider that they are onto something, as Van Helsing said in the 1931 film rendition of Bram Stoker's *Dracula*: 'The Strength of the vampire is disbelief.'

Chapter 7

Uncovering the Vampire Myth

Introduction

Looking for the original vampire is a difficult task as 'there is no such creature as The Vampire, there are only vampires'.[1] This emphasises that there is no Vampire X who started the whole genre, but rather a series of folktales, superstitions and monsters from all over the world that have created the vampire as we understand it in the West. Vampires are adaptable, and change according to their time so when looking at folklore, 'each feeds on his age distinctively because he embodies that age,'[2] and therefore fills a need that has arisen at that time.

Inspiration for Bram Stoker's *Dracula*

Since the late nineteenth century the name Dracula has been synonymous with the 'vampire' and is often mistaken for a real person. This misidentification is based on the belief that the inspiration for Bram Stoker's *Dracula* was a fifteenth-century Romanian count, Vlad Tepes or Dracul (b.1431), more commonly known as Vlad the Impaler.

Vlad is well-known for being barbaric, and it is recorded that between 1459 and 1460 on a single day he impaled 10,000 people in Sibiu and 30,000 more in Brasov. While this was going on, he held a feast for those who had escaped death. One man was not able to eat amidst all the rotting, impaled corpses and when Vlad noticed this, he impaled this man higher than all the other corpses so that he could die above the smell.[3]

In another similar tale of barbarism two ambassadors failed to remove their hats in Vlad's presence so he commanded that their hats were nailed to their heads.[4] A contemporary German propaganda pamphlet added that Vlad dipped bread in the blood of his victims and ate it. It could be said he was more a hunter than a vampire.[5]

Whether Stoker knew all this history, however, is unlikely and it is thought that he had only borrowed the name of the count rather than his character.[6] There is also very little chance that Stoker visited the Transylvania region in Romania, though he had visited Whitby, where the second part of his novel was set, with his family in 1890.

Whitby had its own sinister history and there was talk of a wrecked Russian Schooner, the *Dmitri of Narva*, which had sunk off the coast in October 1885. The whole crew of the ship had perished and it was rumoured to have been carrying a consignment of coffins. It is easy to see where Stoker got his inspiration. [7]

The name Dracul is Romanian (Wallachian) for 'dragon' or 'devil', which sits well with the character that Stoker created, though whether he was aware of this is not certain. William Wilkinson in *An Account of the Principalities of Wallachia and Moldavia* (1820) states: 'The Wallachians […] used to give this as a surname to any person who rendered himself conspicuous either by courage, cruel actions or cunning.'[8]

When Vlad Tepes died in 1476 his severed head was sent to the Turkish sultan, but monks retrieved his body and took it to the island monastery of Snagov, where he was buried in the chapel near the altar. Centuries later, between 1931 and 1932, a Romanian archaeologist, Dinu Rosetti, opened the tomb and discovered it to be full of animal bones and pottery. A similar burial near the doors was also excavated and a coffin was found in it with a gold-embroidered purple pall. The coffin held a headless skeleton wearing silk brocade, with a crown in place of the skull. Many believe the body to be that of Vlad Dracul. It is thought the monks were uncomfortable having such a notorious man near the altar. His body was then subsequently removed to Bucharest History Museum, but went missing during the Second World War.[9]

The story of Vlad the Impaler is not the sole source of the modern vampire. Folklorist R.C. Maclagan wrote an article for *Folklore* journal in 1897 about how Dracula had made a pact with the devil: 'Here we find that the drac is the devil in person, who instructs certain persons to be magicians and medicine men in a college under the earth. Of these, one in eight received instruction during fourteen years, and on his return to earth he has the following power. By means of certain magical formulae he compels a dragon to ascend from the depths of a loch.

He then throws a golden bridle with which he has been provided over his head, and rides aloft among the clouds which he causes to freeze and thereby produces hail.'[10] Such power over the weather, including producing mist and fog, is something that the Western Dracula was able to do.

It is thought that the concept of Dracula being able to turn himself to a bat was influenced by sixteenth-century tales from the conquistadors who recorded bats so large they: 'assaulted men in the night in their sleep, and so bitten them with their venomous teeth, that they have been [...] compelled to flee to such places, as from ravenous harpies.'[11] There were also records of the *desmodos* bats (vampire bats) in South America, which at night land on the necks of livestock and suck their blood.[12]

Although Bram Stoker put Transylvania on the map as the place for vampires, the Communist Party in the 1980s banned all related tourism and any use of the word Dracula for commercial purposes. Once the Communist government fell, Dracula was back on the menu and in 2000 there were plans for a Dracula theme park where blood-flavoured shakes were to be sold to tourists.[13] It had been planned to be built in the historic region of Sighisoara, the birthplace of Vlad Tepes, with a fake Castle Dracula towering over the citadel, and a cable car to carry tourists from the historic city into the theme park. It was met with international outcry from the likes of UNESCO, Greenpeace and even the Prince of Wales,[14] and the project was abandoned in 2002 before it was built.

Dracula-based commercialism in Romania today is still limited to Bran Castle (see fig. 11) and the village of Sighisoare (see fig. 12). Here you can go through the vampire experience and buy vampire themed red wine (see fig. 13).

The similarity in name between Vlad Dracul and Dracula has led many people to believe that the vampire myth as it presented in the West originates in Eastern Europe. The history of the folkloric vampire, however, is far older than the fifteenth century and more widespread than Eastern Europe.

Ancient Greeks

Vampires have existed in folklore since the beginning of recorded history with the Babylonians and Assyrians fearing the *ekimmu*. The ancient Greeks believed in a number of undead creatures such as *Efialtae,*

Striges, Lamiae, Epopidae, Empoussai, Yello, and Mormo. Homer describes in the *Odyssey* that the dead liked to drink blood and this could be an early reference to vampirism: 'Next, Odysseus drew his sword and took his post at the pit of blood and did not allow the spirits to drink the blood before he had spoken to Tiresias.'[15]

The *lamiae* were creatures that were thought to ensnare young men in particular. They took the form of alluring, voluptuous young women, who had the unfortunate habit of removing their own eyes, making them terrifying to behold. They are thought to be the forerunner of the gorgon.[16] Goethe's *Bride of Corinth*, and Keats' *The Lamia* were based on this mythology.

The ancient Greeks also had a fear of *aoroi*, or the untimely dead, who were children, young adults or those who were unmarried. The 'modern' Greek vampires are known as *vrykolakas* and evolved over time into the Slavic word for werewolves. It was believed that after death werewolves became vampires, so the word was used interchangeably for vampire or werewolf.[17] In Greek folklore the *vrykolakas* were witnessed both in the daytime and at night and were seen in a group of five or six eating green beans.

Another case describes a *vrykolaka* of a Santorini shoemaker from the seventeenth century who returned to 'frequent his house, mend his children's shoes, draw water at the reservoir, and cut wood for the use of the family.'[18] Despite such benign behaviour the villagers were still perturbed by the presence.

The Greek influence of the vampire myths continued into the medieval period where they readily appear in novels, religious law, exorcisms and folk stories.

Ancient Romans

The closest the ancient Romans got to vampires was the *larvae*, which were spirits of the dead who haunted and hurt the living by appearing at night and causing them to have explicit dreams 'that generate nocturnal emissions', which they took back to their nests in order to create further monsters.[19] They appeared to the living as decaying corpses. The deceased became *larvae* following a violent death, guilt over some act or if they felt they were wronged.

The Romans also believed in, and feared, the Greek *lamiae, striges* and *mormos*. The *striges* were a combination of a witch and a vampire, who had the ability to transform into a crow and drink the blood of humans to survive. The *mormos* on the other hand were thought to be servants of the goddess of the witches, Hacate.[20] It was believed that they were able to change into a crow and then attack people in order to drink their blood.[21]

One account of a Roman vampire was written by Phlegon of Tralles about a young girl called Philinnion. She had died but refused to leave her lover, Machates, and went to his home on a number of occasions to spend the night with him. One evening her parents confronted her, upon which all the life flowed out of her and she collapsed to the floor dead. Her coffin was found to be empty other than a ring from Machates. Her body was cremated outside the boundaries of the city, thus stopping the nocturnal visits.[22]

The most famous vampire was the emperor Caligula. He was assassinated, and buried quickly in a shallow grave while only being partially cremated. His unsavoury lifestyle, violent death, lack of attention to burial rituals and the shallow grave are all characteristics that were thought to produce the restless dead.[23]

International Vampires

Vampire legends have spread far and wide. In China the 'vampire', known as the *Jiangshi* (*ch'ing shih*), are corpses from the Qing dynasty (1644–1912). These corpses are thought to spring into action after laying dormant for centuries, and feed off the human life-force known as *qi*. They can only survive by feeding on living humans. They are identified by their seventeenth-century clothes and walk with their arms outstretched. They have red eyes, talons and foul breath and they can only move by hopping. To stop a person from becoming a *Jiangshi* a form of ancestor worship must be adopted and in order to stop one it is essential to set fire to the body.[24]

On the South Pacific island of New Caledonia the dead are thought to return to the land of the living disguised as living people. They are identified as vampires by snoring at night or by the ability to disappear, leaving only the head visible.[25] The Americas can claim a number of vampires: the *lobishomen* in Brazil feed on small amounts of blood without killing their prey, while Mexico has a combined witch/vampire called *tlaciques.*

Captain Cook reported that in Polynesia they believed vampires, called *talamaur*, were the returned dead whose objective was to walk at night and eat the heart and entrails of those sleeping.[26] In Australia their vampire is also called the *talamaur*, but has different characteristics. They could suck any remaining life-force from the remains of a fresh corpse.[27] However, the *talamaur* could also choose to use their undead state to do good and were not always considered evil.

In Malaysia there are two forms of vampire. The first is a *langsuir*, which is a mother who died following a still birth. This form of vampire is cormorant-like, eats fish and sucks the blood of newborn babies. The stillborn child however becomes a *pontianak*, a bloodsucking vampire in the form of an owl.[28] To prevent the mothers from coming back as a vampire, glass beads must be placed in her mouth, a chicken egg in each armpit and needles stuck into each palm.[29]

Ghana has two forms of vampire: the *adze*, which is in the form of a firefly and lives off blood, and the *obayifo*, which targets children and damages crops.[30] In Armenia there is a vampire known as the *Dakhanavar* (or *Dashnavar*) who kills his victims by sucking blood from their feet. Two people sleeping together can fool the vampire by sleeping with their feet in each other's armpits.[31]

In India there are a number of shrines called *bhandara*, which are there to placate the *bhutas* or 'living beings'. These are spirits of the dead which have not left the mortal world. They can possess a living or a dead body in order to carry out any post-death tasks. Offerings of grain are made in the morning and the evening in order to placate them and there are even temples dedicated to the most important *bhutas.*[32]

The *pisachas*, or flesh-eaters, are also thought to be prevalent in India. These are the spirits of criminals, adulterers or the insane and they can enter the mouth of a living person and survive in their intestines. Another type of vampire are the *rakshashas* or destroyers. These are shape-shifters with fangs and can take the form of an owl, dog or cuckoo. Fire and mustard repels them.[33]

Sutherland also suggests that the goddess Kali from the Hindu pantheon is in fact a form of vampire as she drinks the blood of the demon Raktabija (whose name means blood-seed) who could reproduce himself from each drop of his own blood as it hits the ground.[34] Kali laps the blood up before it hits the ground to prevent them turning into demons. This myth is found in the eighth chapter of the *Devi Mahatmya*:

> From the stream of blood which fell on the earth from him when he received multiple wounds by the spears, darts and other weapons, hundreds of asuras came into being.
>
> And those asuras that were born from the blood of Raktabija pervaded the whole world; the devas got intensely alarmed at this.
>
> Seeing the devas dejected, Chandika laughed and said to Kali, "O Chamunda, open out your mouth wide; with this mouth quickly take in the drops of blood generated by the blow of my weapon and (also) the great asuras born of the drops of blood of Raktabija."[35]

Although there are only a few selected examples of vampire mythology here it seems most countries around the work world mythical, vampire-type creatures who are restless spirits or reanimated corpses terrorising the living, with their existence centred around blood.

Eastern European Folklore

Despite the ancient and widespread prevalence of vampire-like creatures, the folklore of Eastern Europe is perhaps the most relevant to locating the origins of the modern Western vampire. The most prevalent folklore is along the cultural borders of Eastern and Western Europe, where there was a clash between Catholicism and Orthodox Christianity.[36]

The sheer number of cases of vampires throughout Europe can be explained by blurred lines between numerous mythical and threatening beings. In Romania *strigoi* were vampires but *strigele* were witches. In Italy *strega* are either witches or vampires and share many of the same characteristics.[37] In Ukraine a vampire was thought to be the spawn of a witch and a werewolf or demon, and in Serbia a *vukodlak* could be a vampire or a werewolf.

However, the vampires depicted in the mythology of Eastern Europe are a far cry from the suave vampires of Western movies.

As Collins Jenkins wryly observes: 'They would not have been caught dead in the crypts of castles. English and Irish writers, in creating the literate vampire, had tidied them up a bit.'[38]

In seventeenth-century Europe 'vampires' were almost a common affliction. They were often thought to be to blame for epidemics, bad weather destroying crops, or famine.[39] People within the community suffering from diseases including rabies, anthrax, photosensitivity and psychological and physical disorders, as well as those who died a violent death or drowned were targeted as potential vampires.

These people were then used as scapegoats to explain a spate of violent deaths or an epidemic such as the plague. Even if they succumbed to such an epidemic they were viewed as the cause rather than a victim. Often the 'vampires' were marginalised from society and treated with suspicion, either because they were strangers, looked different from the others in the village, followed a different religion or in some way went against the norm of society.

There are a number of examples of reports of vampirism corresponding with outbreaks of disease. Between 1721 and 1728 in the Balkans, for example, there was an epidemic of vampirism which corresponded with outbreaks of rabies in dogs, wolves and other animals. It was thought the 'snarling, slobbering look' of a creature suffering from rabies was very similar to the widespread descriptions of vampires.[40]

One case from 1848 was of a Russian woman, Justina Yuschkov, who died during a cholera outbreak. When others in the village also started to perish it was suggested that Justina's body be exhumed in order to identify whether she was pregnant when she died. When the corpse was unearthed there was indeed a baby with her, and Justina's mouth was open, which was a recognised sign of vampirism. She was reburied with an ash stake driven into her flesh. The villagers hoped this would bring an end to the cholera outbreak.[41]

Similar superstitions travelled from Europe to the New World, such as the case of a Rhode Island couple and their seven children. In December 1883 the mother (Mary Eliza) died of tuberculosis, followed six months later by one of the children (Mary Olive). When the second child, Mercy Leanna, died in January 1892 the ground was too hard to bury her so she was laid in a mausoleum. A son, Edwin, who had been away returned and also fell ill with tuberculosis. Village gossip blamed his illness on the malice of one of his relatives. He was advised to exhume his mother and sisters, and, if the bodies were not decomposed, rip out the hearts and burn them. His mother and Mary Olive were exhumed, and their bodies had decomposed sufficiently, but the body of Mercy in the mausoleum had been preserved by the cold weather. Her liver and heart were removed and burnt, and Edwin mixed the ashes into a liquid and drank it. Unsurprisingly, he died four months later.[42]

In 1906 there was an outbreak of Typhus in Bosnia. The widow of the first man to die believed her husband had returned from the grave and drank her blood, thus causing her to become ill. The next fifteen typhus deaths were attributed to this 'vampire'. The villagers therefore wanted to exhume and cremate his body, but the practice had been banned in the area in 1878 leaving them defenceless against the threat.

Other cases of vampires were not the cause of epidemics but were the result of being 'infected' by another vampire. In 1723 a soldier, Arnold Paole, in the Serbian village of Medvegia believed he had been the victim of a vampire when he was in Kosovo. To try to break the curse he ate some dirt from the vampire's grave and smeared himself with the vampire's blood. A number of weeks later he died after falling off the back of a hay-cart, then returned as a vampire. He is reported to have killed four of his neighbours and turned them all into vampires. They had all complained prior to their deaths that he had been strangling them at night. His body was exhumed and staked through the heart before being burnt. The neighbours whom he had reportedly killed and turned into vampires were treated in the same manner.[43]

The regimental doctor, Johannes Flückinger, supervised the exhumation of the corpses and reported, 'There was an eight-day-old child which had lain in the grave for ninety days and was similarly in a condition of vampirism.' The case of Paole became an international sensation and was reported across Europe.[44]

The irony of consuming the body – as in the Rhode Island vampires – or blood – as in the case of Arnold Paulo – was conveniently ignored by these heavily superstitious and religious people. It was widely believed that eating the blood from the corpse of a vampire offered some protection against future attacks.

Such superstitions were not limited to the uneducated peasants, as Pierre Des Noyers, a scholar and secretary to Queen Marie-Louise of Poland, wrote in 1693 that following an exhumation of a vampire's grave: 'there proceeds from his body a great quantity of blood, which some mix up flour to make a bread of; and that bread eaten in the usual manner protects them.'[45]

Other so-called vampires killed relentlessly after death – although not by biting – with no clear reason for their condition. For example, a famous case of vampirism was reported by an Austrian official in 1725, in the village of Kisilova in Serbia. He told of a Serbian peasant called Petar Blagojevic (Peter Plogojowitz), who, following his death, was said to have killed nine villagers in eight days, as well as demanding shoes from his wife.[46] All the victims had complained of being strangled by the resurrected Plogojowitz.

His body was exhumed and the official, Imperial Provisor Frombald, recorded: 'The body, except for the nose, which was somewhat fallen away, was completely fresh […] I saw some fresh blood in his mouth.'[47] The body also appeared to have newly grown hair and nails, and to have new skin shedding the old. The blood in his mouth was thought to have belonged to his nine victims. He was staked through the heart and blood apparently gushed from his mouth and ears and there were 'wild signs' (a euphemism for an erection). The body was then burned and the killing spree through the village stopped. [48]

As recently as 1924 a Serbian newspaper reported on a widow who was visited by her dead husband who ran through the house scaring the family. These visits apparently continued nightly for a month until it was decided to exhume the man, impale him with a hawthorn stake and cremate him.

A story from Poland, written by Casus de Striges in 1674, describes a small community haunted by a man who had become a demon and drank human blood. The local priests demanded that he be exhumed, and the body placed in a prone (face down) position as it was believed this would prevent vampirism.

Conversely, in Bulgaria and Greece it was believed that a prone burial actually caused vampirism. The local villagers did as they were bid and turned the corpse of one such vampire over, but he rose once more from the grave and beat his own son to death. His grave was once more opened and he was decapitated, which halted the haunting and enabled the villagers to live in peace.

In the majority of these stories the vampires were clearly identified and their corpses could be exhumed and dealt with, thereby stopping the vampire activity. However, in some cases it may have been that they were not aware of who the vampire was or where they were buried.

A Walloon officer from Hungary wrote a letter in 1732, which described how to locate a vampire burial: 'They select a young lad who is innocent of girls, that is to say who has never performed the sexual act. He is placed upon a young stallion who has not yet mounted a mare, who has never stumbled and who must be pitch-black without a speck of white. They stud is ridden into the cemetery to and fro among the graves, and the grave over which the horse refuses to pass in spite of blows liberally administered to him, is where the vampire lies.'[49] Once the grave is identified then it is possible to exhume the body and deal with it accordingly.

British and Irish Myths

Such folkloric superstitions were not limited to the European mainland. In the British Isles there were also medieval superstitions surrounding vampires. One of the first to record a belief in vampires was William of Newburgh. He was a historian and canon at Newburgh Abbey, near the Yorkshire moors, and records an event in his *Chronicles* (1196 CE) in which a man rose from his grave in Buckinghamshire and attacked his wife, brothers and animals: 'On the following night, however having entered the bed where his wife was reposing, he not only terrified her on awaking, but nearly crushed her by the insupportable weight of his body.'[50] His wanderings escalated and he was recorded as walking during the day as well as at night. The Bishop of Lincoln was consulted for advice on how to handle this supernatural phenomena. He advised that the man was exhumed and a letter of absolution was laid on his chest.[51] His wanderings throughout the village ceased.

William of Newburgh also recorded that in Anantis Castle (possibly in Dumfriesshire, Scotland) villagers were 'beaten black and blue by this vagrant monster'. When they exhumed the corpse the villagers dealt with it and, 'laid open its side by repeated blows of the blunted spade, and thrusting in his hand, dragged out the accursed heart.'[52] This particular vampire was not sucking the blood of the living, and it is thought vampires at this time drank the blood from the neighbouring graves, and reserved beatings only for the living.[53]

However, by the seventeenth century the belief that vampires sucked the life-blood from their victims developed. Pierre Des Noyers, writing in 1693, describes how the vampire 'sucks their blood so much as to weaken and attenuate them, and at last cause their death.'[54]

It is thought that Bram Stoker may have been influenced by myths from his native Ireland. One such tale is focused on Slaughtaverty in County Derry. The local chieftain, Abhartach, a cruel and unpopular man, unsurprisingly rose from his grave the day after he was buried. He was once more killed and buried, but yet again he returned to seek fresh blood. A druid advised that he should be dispatched with a yew sword and buried with his head at the foot of the grave. Mountain Ash was planted on top of the grave and a large stone was also placed there to prevent any further activity.[55]

In Scotland there was the myth of the *baobhan-sith*, a female vampire who attracts men using her sexual charms. She is represented wearing green, which was the colour of the forest, but during the medieval period this was the colour commonly worn by prostitutes.

Vampire Burials

All of the vampire myths refer to exhuming the graves and staking the body or removing the head. Some of this is supported in the archaeology of cemeteries. Such adapted burial practices throughout Europe are referred to 'vampire burials' or 'deviant burials', as they differ from traditional burials of the time.

When examining such atypical burials they need to be studied in context: what is unusual in one cemetery may be the norm in another. The most common forms of deviant burials were prone burials (face down), decapitated bodies, limb removal, bodies covered in stones, or bodies held down with metal spikes or wooden stakes, objects in the mouth (coins, stone, clay), contrary position and orientation of the grave in comparison to others in the cemetery, or partial cremation. In fact, anything that is not the traditional supine, extended burials are considered 'deviant' by archaeologists.

It was not until 1950 that the first atypical burial was termed 'vampire'. It described a medieval burial of a man on his side covered with large stones. Between the tenth and the thirteenth centuries more than twenty graves with stones weighing down a body at the chest, legs and feet were discovered. Some textual evidence suggests that being stoned to death was reserved for traitors and therefore stone burials may have contained an element of shame. Sometimes a burial involved a combination of two of these deviancies; e.g., decapitation and stone placement.

For example, a burial from Złota Pińczowska, Poland, contained a man buried on his side with a knife impaled in his spine, and a woman from Stary Zamek, also in Poland, was pinned face down with wooden stakes. Such vampire burials in Eastern Europe reached a peak between the ninth and twelfth century CE, although evidence shows there were deviant burials of this type from all time periods, each led by different superstitions or social customs.

Decapitations, for example, are common in burials of executed criminals, and those denied a typical churchyard burial (suicides and the unbaptised). Some decapitations happened post-death, and the corpse may also have been weighed down with rocks or pinned into the grave with spikes or nails. Until 1823 CE in England a suicide was not allowed to be buried in consecrated ground and was buried instead at a crossroads with a stake through their heart. After this date a law prevented the staking of suicide victims and eventually they were permitted in consecrated cemeteries.

Such atypical burials have taken place throughout the world, from the Palaeolithic period to the twentieth century CE, showing these are not a religious or regional phenomena. In Cyprus, at the site of Khirokitia Neolithic (4500–3800 BCE), bodies were discovered in pit graves with large, heavy millstones placed either on the head or body to prevent the deceased from rising from the grave. It is possible they were ritually sacrificed and placed here as foundation rituals for a structure.

At Poundbury in Dorset the prone burial of a six-year-old child was discovered with the coffin covered in heavy roof tiles in order to prevent them from returning. It is quite likely that the child had been profoundly deaf. This is not the only example of a deviant burial where the deceased appears to have been disabled in one way or another. Another British burial, in Guilden Morden, southwest of Cambridge, dating from the Roman period, is of a disabled woman whose head was removed and placed at her feet. The archaeologist, T.C. Lethbridge, states that this was, 'to ensure that her spirit – perhaps bad tempered owing to her infirmity – should not walk and haunt her relatives.'[56] While rather presumptuous about the woman's demeanour, such treatment after death could have been due to a lack of understanding about disability. Such a lack of understanding leads to fear.

On the Greek Island of Lesbos, near Mytilene, a deviant medieval burial was discovered in a crypt. The body was thought to have been Muslim rather than Christian, and this may have set him apart from the rest of the community. The body had been pinned into the grave using iron spikes hammered through the neck, pelvis and ankle. The body itself showed a number of pathologies, which would have resulted in facial deformities, thus further setting him apart from society and which may have been the reason for the atypical burial practices.

In Turkey two bodies displaying some form of disability were also given a similar burial. However, one was Muslim and the other Christian, indicating that religion was not the reason for their separation from society. A similar discovery was found in Southwell in Nottinghamshire, in 1959, with a skeleton dated from 550–700 CE. The skeleton was pinned down with metal spikes through the heart, shoulders and ankles.

Even in the cemetery of the town of Griswold, Connecticut, which was in use between 1757 and 1840, evidence of vampire burials has been discovered. One coffin was marked out in tacks with the initials JB-55, and the body itself had been desecrated after burial. It had been decapitated and the skull was placed on the chest, and the femurs were used to create a typical skull and crossbones motif. It also seems that five years after burial the body had been exhumed and the heart removed, which was a typical means of preventing the nocturnal wanderings of a vampire.

The male body showed signs of various ailments including arthritis in the left knee and a number of fractures on the collarbone that were healed but not set properly, and were likely inflicted by blunt trauma. This is thought to be evidence that he was a labourer or farmer; someone who was no stranger to manual labour. Evidence also indicated he suffered from primary pulmonary tuberculosis, which would have caused him to cough and produce bloody sputum from his lungs. He would have probably also walked with a limp and this may have made him a figure of suspicion, especially if following his death other people in the village died from tuberculosis. Excavation of the cemetery suggests this is the case. [57]

DNA taken when the body was discovered in 1990 has recently been studied with more up-to-date techniques. Y-chromosomal DNA profiling and surname prediction was applied to the burial, and using genealogical data archaeologists were able to discover a great deal about this unfortunate man.

He seems to have been a farmer called John Barber, and using death notices it has been identified that in 1826 his son, Nicholas Barber, died aged twelve. A coffin had been discovered near to JB-55 identified as NB-13 supporting this evidence.[58]

There are no records as to why John Barber was identified as a vampire, but often epidemics of disease, such as tuberculosis often resulted in superstitious scapegoating.

Not all deviant burials, though, are of people with disabilities or illnesses, indicating that it was not always something physical that set these people apart from the wider community. Perhaps it was a behaviour, a tic, or some difference in the soft tissues which marginalised them in society. However, each deviant burial needs to be assessed individually, placing it in context socially, politically and culturally in order to be able to ascertain what was 'different' about them.

One of the most recent discoveries of a 'vampire' burial was in Bulgaria in October 2014.[59] The excavation took place in the ruins of an ancient Thracian city, Perperikon, near the Greek border. More than one hundred deviant burials have been discovered in the region. At Perperikon the 2014 discovery was of a medieval male aged between forty and fifty, with a metal stake, which was part of a plough, through his chest pinning the body down. The left leg below the knee had also been removed and was buried in the grave with the body. The grave dates to the early thirteenth century and was similar to discoveries at the Bulgarian town of Sozopol in 2012–13 of two skeletons with iron rods impaled through their chests.[60] These were nicknamed by the media 'the twin vampires of Sozopol'.

Poland also has its fair share of atypical burials, with a number in the region of Kuyavia, dating between the tenth and thirteenth centuries. In this region prior to Christianity cremations were the common means of disposing of the dead. Once Christianity was introduced in the later tenth century bodies were buried in the supine (face up) position, oriented from west to east, and may have contained some grave goods. It is thought that these atypical burials were a result of the clash of traditional superstitious beliefs and Christianity. As they were no longer cremating the dead, their superstitions concerning the dead returning and causing harm to the living grew stronger.

It could even be said that 'without Christianity, the vampire would have died'.[61] Without this new religion, with its specific rituals, practices and beliefs, natural superstitions would not have developed and been maintained over such a long period. Witches and any other supernatural beings were seen to be 'perverted parodies of Christianity.'[62]

Fourteenth-century execution sites in Poland have archival evidence indicating that people believed to be revenants were disinterred from the traditional cemeteries and reburied at the sites of gallows. If these bodies were still believed to be haunting an area they were exhumed once more to be cremated and the ashes were scattered in the river. Although most deviant burials in the region are called 'vampire' burials, the textual evidence from Silesia and Lusatia in Central Europe suggest that 'vampires' were in fact cremated and not buried. Therefore burials including prone (face-down) burials or limb removal need to be reinterpreted, perhaps as a judicial punishment or for some social misdemeanour such as suicide.

A prolific site of vampire burials is a seventeenth- and eighteenth-century cemetery in Drawsko County, Poland. It was originally thought that six deviant burials were of immigrants who were viewed as different. However, radiogenic strontium isotope ratios from the first molars show they were in fact from the local community. Therefore there must be some other aspect of these individuals that separated them from the rest of the community. Cholera seems likely. Each of the bodies was staked down with sickles around their neck, pinning them to the floor of the grave, so they would be decapitated should they attempt to rise. Alternatively, a stone was placed in the mouth or under the jaw so they could not feast on the dead. This prevented the jaw from opening (it was believed a cadaver with an open mouth is likely to rise from the dead).

Burials in the southern Polish town of Giliwice made the news in 2013,[63] when it transpired there were four decapitated skeletons with their heads buried between their legs. They were also not buried with any grave goods, making dating more complex, but it is estimated they were from the sixteenth century.

Many of the Polish atypical burials are devoid of burial goods and those buried in a prone position were often not placed in coffins, though some were provided with the dignity of a shroud. Some of the combinations, however, are puzzling. For example, a young woman from Gwiazdowo was buried face down but with numerous expensive grave goods, including a lead Slavic head ornament, an iron knife in a leather scabbard, and rings for her fingers in bronze and silver. She was clearly wealthy, but buried in a deviant way. The reason why is not clear.

A 'vampire' burial has also been discovered in Italy by a project working on the mass plague pits in Nuovo Lazzaretto, Venice, which date to the sixteenth and seventeenth centuries. This is despite Constantino Grimaldo writing in 1750 that vampires only existed 'where beer, this unhealthy drink, is widespread,'[64] and not where the locals drank wine. Venice was affected by the plague in 1576, which infected more than 90,000 of its residents.[65] Anyone who was infected was exiled on *lazarettos* (quarantine ships), and when these were full large galleons were used and moored in the lagoon in order to try to stop the spread of the infection. This was unsuccessful and Rocco Benedetti wrote in the sixteenth century: 'Workers collected the dead and threw them in the graves all day without a break. Often the dying ones and the ones too sick to move or talk were taken for dead and thrown on the piled corpses.'[66]

The Lazzaretto Nuovo cemetery is located near a fifteenth-century wall designed to create a barrier against the spread of such epidemics. The cemetery included burials from the plague outbreak in 1576 and then another from 1630–1631, which killed a further 40,000 people.[67]

The excavation in 2006 was carried out by the La Spezia Archaeological Group under the directorship of Dr Matteo Borrini. One of the burials (ID6) from this earlier stratigraphy was a woman buried in the supine position with a large brick pushed into her mouth. Bricks do not feature as part of the grave fill, and there was no misalignment of the jaw so it is assumed the brick was inserted into her mouth intentionally after death.

The woman in ID6 was likely to have been a Roman Catholic as rosary beads were discovered in the grave fill. She was just 5ft tall and was probably aged between sixty-one and seventy-one.[68] The archaeology shows that her grave was disturbed, perhaps weeks or months after her death while another was being dug, and they saw she had 'chewed' a hole in her shroud.

It was at this secondary point that the brick was inserted. It is also likely that her body was not in advanced stages of decomposition, adding to their superstitions that she was a vampire. It is, however, interesting to note that whoever inserted the brick was not so superstitious that they were too afraid to handle the body despite the danger of infection with the plague.

171

The theory of the 'chewing dead' was recorded in a work called *De Mastication Mortuorum* in 1679 by Phillip Rohr. Here he claims that 'corpses eat only during the time of plague', which was the result of the devil using corpses to spread the plague through the act of chewing.[69]

The phenomena of a hole 'chewed' in the shroud can be caused by the shroud being wound too tightly around the corpse. With ID6 it was wound so tightly that her left clavicle had been pushed upwards. The shroud slipped into the cavity created at the front and gases from the corpse's mouth made the shroud wet in that area; it therefore rotted at a different rate to the rest of the dry shroud.[70] According to superstition, in order to prevent the further spread of the disease the corpse's mouth had to have a stone placed in it to prevent it from chewing. And in eastern Germany in the nineteenth century it was believed that the dead would become a vampire should any clothing or the shroud come into contact with the mouth, so they attempted to prevent this from happening prior to burial.

A similar treatment of the dead was discovered in a grave in Kilteasheen, in County Roscommon, Ireland. There were two men, one middle aged and the other in his twenties, who were buried with their mouths filled with rocks. One of them had his head facing up and had a large black stone in his mouth, the other was facing the side and his jaw had nearly been dislocated with the violence of the large stone wedged into his mouth. They are dated to the eighth century, which may be too early for vampiric beliefs, but they could have been carriers of an illness.

So, while all burials with stakes or nails holding the body in the grave is termed by the common media as 'vampire', there is rarely accompanying evidence to suggest these were the superstitious beliefs behind the atypical burial practice. The idea that such ritualistic practices indicate the deceased were believed to be vampires is rarely questioned, however.

There is, in fact, little evidence that medieval western Slavs believed in the idea of 'vampires' or revenants at all. It is better to look for the level of deviant practices in a grave before jumping to conclusions. For example, a decapitated body is likely to have more ritualistic meaning behind it than a burial in a remote part of the cemetery. Also, the stones placed around the heads could be an adaptation of a Christian ritual of the body facing in a particular direction. The stones may have kept the head in position enabling them to be resurrected.

It is possible that stones may have been used to weigh down a body and prevent it from being robbed rather than to prevent it from leaving of its own undead volition. This happened in nineteenth-century Britain when body snatchers were prolific due to the difficulty of medical schools getting bodies for their students. (The most (in)famous body snatchers were Burke and Hare, in 1828 in Edinburgh, who decided that it was easier to create fresh corpses rather than continue digging up old ones. In total they murdered sixteen people.[71])

Often contemporary superstitious beliefs are used to explain such variance in burial methods, though Wojtucki suggests it is important to look for reasons other than a belief in vampires[72] for the unusual treatment after death. For example, at the site of Drawsko[73] it was decided that the deviant burials may have been used for cholera victims, to set them apart from the rest of the community. It was thought the villagers believed anyone who was not baptised died as the result of violence, or an epidemic, or was from another locality, and was in danger of returning.

Deviant burials in remote areas of a cemetery, or in the exact centre of the cemetery, may have carried out as a means of blessing the new burial ground and creating a sanctified space. It is even suggested that the deceased may have been ritualistically sacrificed for this purpose, or at times of social disaster when the gods need to be appeased.

While in many places a prone burial was seen as a means of preventing a corpse from becoming a vampire, some have suggested they could have been due simply to carelessness at the funeral with the body being dropped unceremoniously into the pit. Some have even suggested that the undertaker may have been drunk. This is often the explanation for such 'untidy' burials, but as such prone burials were common, and often followed a similar pattern, such carelessness is unlikely to account for all of them. If the deceased had been marginalised in the community, or was a criminal, such carelessness could have been borne out of contempt, though this is likely to be the exception rather than the norm.

Furthermore, prone burials may not necessarily have been due to the fear of the dead returning, but instead to a fear of the evil eye, which was believed to induce death. Often during a funeral the deceased was carried face down so as not to inflict the evil eye upon the mourners. There could also be a moralistic association with prone burials, with the position being a symbol of shame, and atonement for sins carried out in life.

Many prone burials were also interred on the margins of cemeteries and indicate a separation from society in one form or another.

While the idea of 'vampire burial' seems to explain why people were buried in such ways, there are so many variants to the burial forms that the term is almost meaningless, not to mention the fact that not all of the communities who practised these 'vampire burials' actually believed in the vampire myth.

Modern Science Explains All

To modern eyes such beliefs of the dead raising from the grave and tormenting the villagers may seem superstitious, but it must be considered that their beliefs were based on what they witnessed with decaying bodies but did not fully understand. For example, one reason a body was identified as a vampire was due to the lack of rigor mortis in the corpse, though rigor mortis happens very soon after death and then disappears some forty hours later. Bodies were often buried quickly after death, sometimes before rigor mortis had subsided. Therefore there would be a change in position as rigor mortis released its grip on the corpse, which could be viewed as the body moving.[74]

Rates of decomposition also vary depending on a number of reasons. For example, bodies exposed to the air or summer heat decompose much quicker than those in the winter. Additionally, those who are buried deeper in the ground decompose slower than those buried near the surface where they are exposed to air, insects, moisture and bacteria. These variables are unlikely to have been taken into consideration when identifying a 'vampire.'

In the seventeenth century, when a corpse was exhumed they may have witnessed what appeared to be blood on its lips, as well as the corpse appearing larger than they did in life. This may appear as if the corpse had just eaten and was sleeping off a meal of blood. There may have also been a change in skin colour, or an enlargement of the genitals in both men and women.

However, these phenomena are easily explained by forensic science and the study of decaying bodies. A gas build-up in the bowels, mostly methane, can expand the chest, giving a bloated appearance, as well as pushing blood from the lungs to the mouth.[75]

Alternatively, the decomposition of the internal organs can create a fluid known as 'purge fluid' which can then flow freely from the nose and mouth.

This gas build-up can also explain a cadaver emerging from the grave, especially if it was not buried particularly deep. The gas makes the corpse more buoyant and may have resulted in bodies being weighed down with bricks and rocks to keep them in the grave.[76]

The long-held myth that human hair and nails continue growing after death led many people to be accused of vampirism, causing panic in communities from the twelfth to the nineteenth centuries. Nails and hair give the appearance of continued growth but it is actually due to the skin retracting as it decomposes.

Some seventeenth-century scholars did try to take a scientific approach, but it was clear they still held a belief in the possibility of vampires. The 1628 study *De Masticatione Mortuorum*, written by the German scholar Michael Ranft, tried to explain away the various phenomena attributed to vampires. He explained the chewing sound coming from graves was likely to be caused by rats, and the appearance of freshly grown hair and nails was a result of natural decay causing the skin to shrink. He explained the swelling of the body as a normal post-mortem phenomena, so that when staked the escaping sound was like a groan. He also explained that many vampires looked 'fresh' because they were recently deceased.[77]

Despite Ranft's scientific and logical questioning he held some superstitions, such as the belief that the thoughts of a pregnant woman could damage her unborn child. He also assumed that such evil thoughts would remain following death and therefore would arise as vapour from a decaying body. This enabled people like Plogojowitz (see above) to continue his vendettas after death.[78]

Dom Augustin Calmet (1672–1757), the abbé of Senones in Lorraine, wrote the *Treatise on the Vampires of Hungary and Surrounding Regions* in 1746, in which he attempted to scientifically disprove the vampire phenomenon. He concluded, 'the stories told of these apparitions, and all the distress caused by these supposed vampires are totally without solid proof.'[79]

In 1755, following a number of reports and a renewed epidemic of vampirism in Silesia, the queen of Austria-Hungary, Maria Thérèse, believed this was due to 'the dark, disturbed imagination of the common people.'[80]

She commissioned her physician, Gerard van Swieten, to investigate the reports and put an end to the speculation. He reported: 'Gravediggers assured me that it was common for about one of every thirty corpses to be desiccated without putrefaction.' He furthermore stated that the villagers' hysteria was due to ignorance and the Orthodox Church. The queen then issued a decree preventing exhumations without specialist permission.[81]

Even Pope Benedict XIV became involved in the discussion and stated the real problem was 'those priests who give credit to such stories, in order to encourage simple folk to pay them for exorcisms or masses.'[82]

Preventing Vampirism

There are a lot of case studies showing the devastation caused by the return of the dead as a vampire, and evidence of keeping vampires in their graves, but there was little recorded on how to prevent someone becoming a vampire in the first place.

Paul Barber describes four ways in which a person can become a vampire:

1) Predisposition – when an evil life is followed by an evil death. This can be someone who is an alcoholic or 'deceitful and treacherous barmaids and other dishonourable people.'[83] Oftentimes such people were those who had been excommunicated.

2) Predestination – a child born out of wedlock, seventh child in a family, those conceived during a festival when the parents should have been abstaining, or children born with a red caul or teeth.

3) A violent event such as a vampire bite or a violent death.

4) Where burial rituals have not been carried out.[84]

The key preventative action was to carry out the correct burial rights on the deceased. There was a great deal of superstition associated with religion, and Catholics in particular were terrified of not having the correct confession and absolution following death. They believe in a forty-day purgatory period, by the end of which the soul should have finished the journey and the physical body would be in a state of decomposition.

In some places the pastor even opened the grave at the end of the forty days to check on the progress of the decomposition. If everything was going according to plan the bones were moved to a charnel house or reburied. If the body was not decomposing as it should this was seen as a sign of vampirism and steps were needed to ensure the permanent death of the creature.[85] It was assumed that any signs of vampire characteristics were due to the correct rituals not being carried out properly. 'Even if they had lived an exemplary Christian life, a lapse right at the last could sentence them to eternal damnation.'[86] However, the rituals were sometimes so complicated that it would be possible to look back on any burial and find something amiss.[87]

Even up until quite recently it was considered traditional in Britain to open the windows and doors following a death so the spirit could exit the house. Sometimes animals were kept outside until the funeral to prevent the spirit from entering the animal.[88] Additionally, too many tears from the grieving family would prevent the spirit from leaving.

This concern about the correct burial rituals was also held by the Jewish faith, although they did not have such a prolific folklore regarding vampires. Vampires were known as *estrie*, a cross between a monster and a witch who took the form of a woman and drank the blood of children.[89] Careful preparation of the body for burial prevented predisposed people from becoming vampires. This would include putting soil into the mouth of the corpse.[90]

In the Jewish tradition death is the means of atonement for the sins of the deceased and the surviving family. It was important to prepare the corpse for this, and for their resurrection in the messianic era.[91] In the sixteenth and seventeenth centuries, when there were a number of Jewish exiles from Spain and Portugal arriving into Eastern Europe, a new body of texts was written to consolidate a number of cultural burial practices into a single set of rituals.[92]

However, this large movement of Jewish people was often met with suspicion by the resident Christian population, and Weinstock believes that much of the traditional vampire mythology is rooted in anti-Semitism. For example, by the fourteenth century, Christians believed that Jews used Christian blood to make their unleavened bread and wine for the Passover Feast. In 1329, at Savoy, it was said they: 'Compound out of the entrails of murdered Christian children a salve of food called aharance (haroseth), which they eat every Passover in place of a sacrifice.'[93]

The Jews were subsequently exiled from Spain because of the belief that they drank Christian blood. This suspicion was still held in 1882 when a semi-official journal from the Vatican, *La-Cruila Cattolica*, stated: 'Every practicing Hebrew worthy of that name is obliged even now, in conscience, to use in food, drink, in circumcision, and in various other rites of his religious and civil life the fresh or dried blood of a Christian child.'[94] This propaganda was revisited in the 1930s by the Nazis who claimed Jewish rabbis were sucking the blood of German children.

There are very few cases of vampires in Jewish folklore, but one surviving tale from the sixteenth century is similar to those of Eastern Europe discussed above. It was penned by the Egyptian rabbi David ben Solomon Ibn Abi Zimra and warns about not carrying out two specific rituals correctly: that of a quick burial and that of not leaving the body unprotected prior to burial. Traditionally, the body should be guarded, and the guard should recite psalms until the time of the burial in order to protect it from demons and rats.

The tale is of an old woman who had died and her body lay undiscovered for three days: 'The residents of her village considered her stingy towards the poor and she was suspected of causing [bad things to occur] all her life. She had sons, daughters, sons-in-law, and daughters-in-law but she did not live with any of them. She [rather] lived alone, although her children provided for her [...] She died while her sons were away on business, and her death remained unknown for three days.'[95] During this time she had been possessed by a vampire-like demon and she appeared to the neighbours, after which they died. 'After they had buried her, every night she would visit those who were ill [...] she would call to them or hit them.'[96]

Two hundred died following a visit within a forty-day period.[97] As would be expected they exhumed her and discovered she had 'half swallowed her burial hat,' and 'blood was flowing from her mouth and eyes.'[98] She was then cremated, which goes against Jewish tradition, but explains the desperation of the people to rid themselves of this epidemic.

In the Jewish tradition it was believed that when a person dies their corpse becomes contaminated and can transmit this to anyone who touches it. It was, therefore, essential for the body to be buried as quickly as possible. The Egyptian rabbi explained that they (vampires) work more at night than during the day, and therefore the dead must be guarded at all times to prevent them being possessed.

It could also be said that the moral of this story was that the children of the old woman were responsible for her vampirism, as they should have checked on her regularly especially when her sons were away.[99] This idea of a social recluse being used as a scapegoat for an epidemic or plague in the village is one that is repeated throughout Eastern European vampire stories.

Could Vampires be Real?

There has always been a debate about whether vampires are creatures of legend or reality, in a way never questioned when discussing zombies or reanimated mummies. From the discussion above it is possible to identify where all the characteristics of vampires were observed, and then exacerbated by religion and superstition. However, even in the modern 'enlightened' age, this discussion persists.

In the late 1920s Reverend Montague Summers wrote two books on vampires: *The Vampire: His Kith and Kin* (1928) and *The Vampire in Europe* (1929). These books did little to dispel the myth of vampirism and instead insisted they were creatures that still roamed the earth and that attacks were being covered up by the authorities.[100] In other words, an early conspiracy theory.

Other authorities approached the problem logically. Dom Augustin Calmet (1672–1757) questioned the logistics of the vampire theories:

> How a body covered with four or five feet of earth, having no room to move about and disengage itself, wrapped up in lime, covered with pitch, can make its way out, and come back upon the earth, and there occasion such effects as are related of it; and how after that it returns to its former state, and re-enters underground, where it is found sound, whole and full of blood, and in the same condition as a living body. This is the question. Will it be said that these bodies evaporate through the ground without opening it, like the water and vapours which enter into the earth or proceed from it, with sensibly deranging its particles?[101]

Calmet clearly did not believe in the possibility of vampirism. However, discussions still abound as to the feasibility of vampires, especially with the need of human blood to survive.

Studies have been carried out and the conclusion is that, should vampires feed as often as they do in movies, the human race would be extinct in two-and-a-half years. A conservative assumption was made that vampires feed on one human per month and have done since 1600 CE (which was chosen as an arbitrary date when the first records of vampires were made). Using the US census website the global population in 1600 CE was 536,870,911, plus one mythological vampire. Every month the vampire population would increase and the human race would decrease.

So, assuming that on 1 January 1600 CE there were 536,870,911 people and one vampire, a monthly breakdown would look something like this:

    1 Feb 1600   – 536,870,910 + two vampires
    1 March   – 536,870, 908 + four vampires (two feeding
                   creates two new)
    1 April 1   – 536,870, 904 + eight vampires

This is known as geometric progression with ratio two. By the thirtieth month the human population would be zero meaning that in two-and-a-half years of vampirism the entire human population would be dead and the only way to survive would be for the population to at least double every month. By simple deduction, however, if the human race is extinct within this time years then shortly afterwards the vampire population would also be extinct due to lack of food.

The calculations have not taken into account deaths by natural causes or indeed births during those thirty months which could perhaps prolong the human race for another month. Another omission is the secondary death of vampires – as during this period it is inevitable that some vampires would expire[102] – though staking, holy water, garlic or going out in the sun.

Additionally the rather low ratio of one meal per month is suggested, whereas in the movies and literature, vampires have a tendency to feed considerably more often than that.[103]

Such deduction is known as *reduction ad absurdum* as the existence of vampires contradicts human existence. As humans exist then it must be true that vampires do not exist.[104] This calculation could also be applied to the zombie phenomenon. As Dino Sejdinović said: 'Their argument has a hole in it, large enough that you can drive a stake through it.'[105]

The main assumption is that one meal for a vampire would reduce the human race by one, but this assumes that every human who is bitten by and fed on by a vampire dies. This is not necessarily the case, as evidenced by numerous examples from the vampire world. In *True Blood* there were a number of human donors who were bitten regularly by vampires, but they did not turn and did not die. Additionally, in the 'modern' vampire culture (see previous chapter) there is a sub-group of muggle donors who supply blood but do not die.

However, despite logic, science and mathematical calculations indicating that vampires are not real this does not prevent people from still believing in them.

References

Alcott L.M. and Messina L., *Little Vampire Women* (Harper Collins, London, 2010).

Anderson W., 'Tetrodotoxin and the Zombi Phenomenon (Letter to the Editor)' in *Journal of Ethonopharmacology* 23, 12–6 (1988).

Anonymous, 'Books and Arts: Invasion of the Living Dead: Zombie Films' in *The Economist* (17 December 2009).

Auerbach N., *Our Vampires, Ourselves* (University of Chicago Press, Chicago, 1995).

Bailey B., *Burke and Hare: The Year of the Ghoul* (Mainstream Publishing (Edinburgh) Ltd., Edinburgh, 2002).

Bak J. (ed),) *Post/Modern Dracula: From Victorian Themes to Postmodern Praxis* (Cambridge Scholars Publishing, Cambridge, 2007).

Bane T., *Encyclopaedia of Vampire Mythology* (McFarland and Co. Jefferson, 2017).

Bartlett W. & Idriceanu F., *Legends of Blood: The Vampire in History and Myth* (Sutton Publishing, Stroud, 2005).

Bishop K., 'Raising the Dead' in *Journal of Popular Film and Television* (33.4. 196–205, 2006).

Blake M., 'Archaeologists Unearth "Vampire Graves" Containing Decapitated Skeletons with Skulls Placed Between their Legs on Polish Building Site,' (2018) in https://www.dailymail.co.uk/sciencetech/article-2361883/Archeologists-Poland-unearth-vampire-graves-containing-decapitated-skeletons-heads-placed-legs.html.

Bradman T. & Chatterton M., *Magnificent Mummies* (Henemann and Mammoth, London, 1997).

Bramesco C., *Vampire Movies* (William Collins, New York, 2019).

Brier B., *Egyptian Mummies: Unravelling the Secrets of a Sacred Art* (Michael O'Mara, New York, 1996).

References

Brier B., *Egyptomania: Our Three Thousand Year Obsession with the Land of the Pharaohs* (Palgrave Macmillan, New York, 2013).

Brosnan J., 'Terror from Tomb' *in Hammer's Hall of Horror* (22: 42–45, 1978).

Browne T., *Hydriotaphia, ch. V.* (1658) http://penelope.uchicago.edu/hydrionoframes/hydrion.html

Browne T., *Fragment on Mummies* (1683) http://penelope.uchicago.edu/misctracts/mummies.html

Brunas M., Brunas J., & Weaver T., (2011) *Universal Horrors: Studio's Classic Films. 1931–1946* (McFarland and Co., Jefferson, North Carolina, 2011).

Carter H. & White P., 'The Tomb of the Bird' in *Pearson's Magazine* 56, (November 1923).

Chatfield T., 'Escape the Marauding Zombies … and Burn Calories at the Same Time', In *The Guardian* (2012) https://www.theguardian.com/technology/2012/mar/25/mobile-app-zombies-fitness

Christian J., *The Judgement of the Mummy* (Simon & Schuster, London, 2010).

Cohen J., *Monster Theory* (University Of Minnesota Press, Minneapolis, 1996).

Collins A. & Ogilvie-Herald C., *Tutankhamun: The Exodus Conspiracy* (Virgin, London, (2002).

Collins Jenkins M., *Vampire Forensics: Uncovering the Origins of an Enduring Legend* (National Geographic, Washington, 2010).

Collins P., 'The Real Vampire Hunters' in *New Scientist Features No 759* (2011). Barber P., *Vampires, Burial and Death* (New Haven and London, 1988, 29–30).

Cook D., 'The Cultural Life of the Living Dead,' in *Contexts* 12 (no. 4. 54–56, 2013).

Daley, J., 'New England "Vampire" Was Likely a Farmer Named John,' in *Smithsonian Magazine* (5 August 2019). www.smithsonianmag.com/smart-news/new-englands-mystery-vampire-was-likely-farmer-named-john-180972815/

David R., & Tapp E., *Evidence Embalmed: Modern Medicine and the Mummies of Ancient Egypt* (Manchester University Press, Manchester, 1984).

Davis E.W., 'The Ethnobiology of the Haitian Zombi' in *Journal of Ethnopharmacology* 9 (1983).

Davis W., *The Serpent and The Rainbow* (Touchstone, New York, 1985).

Day J., *The Mummy's Curse: Mummymania in the English-Speaking World* (Routledge, London, 2006).

Day J., 'The Rape of the Mummy: Women, Horror Fiction and the Westernisation of the Curse,' in www.Academia.edu (2008).

Day M., & Alexander H., 'Vampire Grave Found in Bulgaria,' in https://www.telegraph.co.uk/news/worldnews/europe/bulgaria/11153923/Vampire-grave-found-in-Bulgaria.html (2014)

Deary T., *True Horror Stories* (Chivers Press, Bath, 1993).

Dendle P., *The Zombie Movie Encyclopaedia* (McFarland & Company Inc., Jefferson, 2001).

Drezner D., 'Night of the Living Wonks' in *Foreign Policy* 180 (2010, 34–38).

Drezner D., *Theories of International Politics and Zombies* (Princeton University Press, Oxford, 2011).

Eaton Simpson G., *Religious Cults of the Caribbean: Trinidad, Jamaica and Taiti* (Institute of Caribbean Studies, University of Puerto Rico, 1980).

Edwards C., 'Blown Away: Tutankhamun's "cursed" trumpet that causes "deadly conflict" has arrived in the UK'. https://www.thesun.co.uk/tech/10260538/tutankhamuns-cursed-trumpet-uk/.

Edwards R., & Brooks M., *Hollywood Wants to Kill You* (Atlantis Books London, 2019).

Efthimious C., & Gandhi S., 'Cinema Fiction vs Physics Reality: Ghosts, Vampires and Zombies,' in *Sceptical Inquirer* (Vol. 31, No. 4, 2007).

El Mahdy C., *Tutankhamun: The Life and Death of a Boy King* (Headline, London, 1999).

Epstein S., & Robinson S., 'The Soul, Evil Spirits, and The Undead: Vampires, Death, and Burial' in *Jewish Folklore and Law in Preternature: Critical and Historical Studies on the Preternatural* (Vol 1, No 2., 2012, 232–251).

Finnis A., 'Zombie chic: Indonesian province's bizarre annual ritual of digging up its dead to give them a wash, groom and dress them in new clothes' https://www.dailymail.co.uk/news/article-2745169/Zombie-chic-Indonesian-village-Toraja-s-bizarre-annual-ritual-Ceremony-Cleaning-Corpses-MaiNene.html.

Forbes D.C., *Tombs, Treasures, Mummies: Seven Great Discoveries of Egyptian Archaeology.* KMT *Communications* (Sebastapol, 1998).

References

Frater Resurgam V.H, 'Thoughts on the Imagination,' in *Flying Roll No. V.* (1892).

Frayling C., *The Face of Tutankhamun* (Faber and Faber, London, 1992).

Gardela L., & Kajkowski K., 'Vampires, Criminals or Slaves? Reinterpreting "Deviant Burials" in Early Medieval Poland,' in *World Archaeology* (Vol 45, No. 5, 2013, 780–796).

Gautier T., *The Mummy's Foot* (J.B. Lippencott, Philadelphia, 1882).

Geschiere P., *The Modernity of Witchcraft: Politics and the Occult in Postcolonial Africa* (University Press of Virginia, Charlottesville, 1997).

Glut D., *Classic Movie Monsters* (Scarecrow Press, Metuchen & London, 1978).

Goddu T., 'Vampire Gothic,' in *American Literary History* (Vol 11, No 1, 1999, 125–141).

Grady F., 'Vampire Culture' in Cohen J.J. (ed) *Monster Theory* (University of Minnesota Press, London, 1996).

Grant B.K., *Invasion of the Body Snatchers* (British Film Institute, London, 2010).

Gregoricka L.A., Betsinger T.K., Scott A.B., Polcyn M., 'Apotropaic Practices and the Undead: A Biogeochemical Assessment of Deviant Burials in Post-Medieval Poland,' *PLoS ONE 9* (2014, 1–24).

Gutman A., *Identity in Democracy* (Princeton University Press, Princeton, 2003).

Hallab M., *Vampire God: The Allure of the Undead in Western Culture* (Suny P., Albany, 2009).

Hawass Z., 'Finding the Tomb of the Pharaoh's Vizier in the Valley of the Mummies' on www.egyptvoyager.com/drhawass_ findingthetomb-2.html (1999, accessed 2007 (no longer active)).

Hawass Z., *Curse of the Pharaohs; My Adventures with Mummies* (National Geographic Society, Washington, 2004).

Hawass Z., *Mountains of the Pharaohs* (Cairo University Press, Cairo, 2006).

Hay M., *Europe and the Jews* (Beacon Press, Boston, 1961).

Herodotus (ed Trans. A. de Sélincourt), *The Histories* (Penguin, London, 1972).

Hollinger V., 'Vampire and/as the Alien' in *Journal of the Fantastic in the Arts* (Vol 5, No. 3 (19), 1993, 5–17).

Holte J.C., 'A Century of Draculas' in *Journal of the Fantastic in the Arts* (Vol 10, No. 2 (38) 1999, 109–114).

Hoving T., *Tutankhamun: The Untold Story* (Touchstone, New York, 1978).

Howard R., 'Pigeons From Hell' in Penzler O. (ed) *Zombies: A Compendium of the Living Dead* (Corvus Press, London, 1951, 615–32).

Hsu J., 'Lenin's Body Improves with Age,' in https://www.scientificamerican.com/article/lenin-s-body-improves-with-age1/ (2015).

Hunter D., *Papermaking: The History and Technique of an Ancient Craft* (Dover Publications, London, 1978).

Hunter I., *British Trash Cinema* (British Film Institute, London, 2013).

Ikram S., & Dodson A., *The Mummy in Ancient Egypt; Equipping the Dead for Eternity* (Thames and Hudson, London, 1998).

Jackson S., & Livingstone I., *The Curse of the Mummy* (Icon Books Ltd, London, 1995).

James T.G.H., *Howard Carter; the Path to Tutankhamun* (Kegan Paul International, London, 1991).

Kemp B., & Zink A., 'Life in Ancient Egypt; Akhenaten, the Amarna Period, and Tutankhamun.' In *RCC Perspectives, No. 3, Sickness, Hunger, War, and Religion: Multidisciplinary Perspectives* (2012, 9–24).

Keyworth D., 'The Socio-Religious Beliefs and Nature of the Contemporary Vampire Subculture,' in *Journal of Contemporary Religion* (17:3, 2002, 355–370).

Khan S., 'Egypt Sarcophagus: Thousands Sign Up to Drink Red Liquid from 2000-year-old Mysterious Box Found in Alexandria,' in *The Independent* (2018) https://www.independent.co.uk/news/science/black-sarcophagus-egypt-blood-red-liquid-drink-petition-curse-alexandria-a8458036.html

Lallanilla M., 'Why Egyptian Statue Moves on its Own,' in www.livescience.com (2013)

Laycock J., 'Real Vampires as an Identity Group: Analyzing Causes and Effects of an Introspective Survey by the Vampire Community,' in *Nova Religio: The Journal of Alternative and Emergent Religions* (Vol. 14, No. 1, August 2010, 4–23).

Lee C., *The Grand Piano Came by Camel: Arthur C. Mace – The Neglected Egyptologist* (Mainstream Publishing, Edinburgh, 1992).

Lessing T., Berg K., et al, *Monsters of Weimar: The Stories of Fritz Haarmann and Peter Kurten* (Nemesis Publications Ltd, London, 1993).

References

Levine E., 'Buffy and the "New Girl Order"; Defining Feminism and Femininity,' In *Undead TV: Essays on Buffy the Vampire Slayer* (Duke Up, Durham, 2007).

Littlewood R., & Douyon C., 'Clinical Finding in Three Cases of Zombification,' in *The Lancet* (Vol 350, 1997, 1094–1096).

Luckhurst R., *The Mummy's Curse: The True History of a Dark Fantasy* (Oxford University Press, Oxford, 2012).

Lumley B., *Khai of Ancient Khem* (Grafton, London, 1980).

Lupton C., '"Mummymania" for the Masses – is Egyptology Cursed by the Mummy's Curse?' In Macdonald S., & Rice M. (eds), *Consuming Ancient Egypt* (UCL Press, London, 2003).

Marx K. (Trans. Ben Fowkes), *Capital; A critique of political Economy, Vol 1.* (Penguin Books, London, 1976).

McAlister E., *Rara! Vodou, Power and Performance in Haiti and its Diaspora* (University of California Press, London, 2002).

McAlister E., 'Slaves, Cannibals, and Infected Hyper-Whites: The race and Religion of Zombies,' in *Anthropological Quarterly* (Vol 85, No. 2, 2012, 457–86).

McClusky T., 'While Zombies Walked,' in Penzler O. (ed), *Zombies: A Compendium of the Living Dead* (Corvus Press, London, 1939, 299–315).

McCouat P., 'The Life and Death of Mummy Brown,' in *Art in Society* (2013) http://www.artinsociety.com/the-life-and-death-of-mummy-brown.html

Mellow G., 'Pinch of Pigment: Mummy Brown,' in *Scientific American* (2014) https://blogs.scientificamerican.com/symbiartic/pinch-of-pigment-mummy-brown/.

Melrose R., *Magic in Britain: A History of Medieval and Earlier Practices* (McFarland & Company, Jefferson, 2018).

Métraux A., *Voodoo in Haiti* (Shocken Books, New York, 1972).

Moreman C., 'Dharma of the Living Dead: A Meditation on the Meaning of the Hollywood Zombie' in *Studies in Religions* (39 (2), 2010, 263–281).

Morrissette J.,'Zombies, International Relations, and the Production of Danger: Critical Security Studies versus the Living Dead,' in *Studies in Popular Culture* (36:2, 2014, 1–27).

Muir B., *Dr Dale's Zombie Dictionary: The A-Z guide to Staying Alive* (Allison and Busby Limited, London, 2010).

Mukherjea A., 'My Vampire Boyfriend: Post-Feminism, "Perfect" Masculinity, and the Contemporary Appeal of Paranormal Romance,' in *Studies in Popular Culture* (Vol 33, No. 2, 2011, 1–20).

Nelson M., 'The Mummy's Curse: Historical Cohort Study,' in *BMJ* (325:1482, 2002).

Niehaus I., 'Witches and Zombies of the South African Lowveld: Discourse, Accusations and Subjective Reality,' In *The Journal of the Royal Anthropological Institute* (Vol 11, No 2., 2005, 191–210).

Peake B., 'The Zombies of Toronto,' in *Anthropology Now* (Vol 2, No. 3, 2010, 65–73).

Penzler, O., 'Introduction' in Penzler O. (Ed), *Zombies: A Compendium of the Living Dead* (Corvus Press, London, 2011, xi-xii).

Perez Z., 'The Ma'nene Death Ritual: An Indonesian Tradition Where People Dig Up And Hang Out With Their Dead' (2018) in https:// culturacolectiva.com/history/manene-death-ritual-indonesia

Peters E., *The Curse of the Pharaohs* (Robinson Publishing, London, 1981).

Pettigrew T.J., *A History of Egyptian Mummies* (Longman, London, 1834).

Pettit H., 'Khamun out: Mystery box from Tutankhamun's "cursed tomb" opened for first time ever on camera' (2019) in https://www. thesun.co.uk/tech/9942648/king-tutankhamnuns-cursed-tomb-box-opened-curse/

Pielak C., & Cohen A., 'Yes, But In A Zombie Apocalypse …' in *Modern Language Studies* (Vol 43, No 2, 2014, 44–57).

Prag A., & Neave R., *Making Faces: Using Forensic and Archaeological Evidence* (British Museum Press, London, 1997).

Pringle H., *The Mummy Congress* (Fourth Estate, London, 2001).

Pulliam J., 'Our Zombies, Ourselves: Exiting the Foucauldian Universe in George A. Romero's "Land of the Dead",' in *Journal of the Fantastic in the Arts* (Vol 20, No 1, 2009, 42–56).

Reeves N., *The Complete Tutankhamun* (Thames and Hudson, London, 1995).

Rice A., *Queen of the Damned* (Ballantine, New York, 1989).

Richards J., *The Parliament of Blood* (Faber and Faber, London, 2008).

Rider Haggard H., *She* (Longman's, Green and Co., London, 1886).

Russell J., *Book of the Dead: The Complete History of Zombie Cinema* (Titan Books, London, 2014).

References

Seabrook W.B., 'Dead Men Working in the Cane Fields,' in Penzler O. (Ed) *Zombies: A Compendium of the Living Dead* (Corvus Press, London, 1929, 3–12).

Sejdinović D., 'Mathematics of the Human-Vampire Conflict,' in *Math Horizons* (November 2008, 14–15).

Shelley M., *Frankenstein* (Sever, Francis & Company, London, 1869).

Strudwick N., *Texts from the Pyramid Age* (Society of biblical literature, Atlanta, 2005).

Sugg R., 'Corpse Medicine: Mummies, Cannibals and Vampires' in *The Lancet* (Vol 371, Iss 9630, 2008).

Sugg R., *Mummies, Cannibals and Vampire: The History of Corpse Medicine from the Renaissance to the Victorians* (Routledge, London, 2009).

Sutherland J., *Who is Dracula's Father?* (Icon, London, 2017).

Taylor J., *Unwrapping a Mummy* (British Museum Press, London, 1995).

Turlington S., *Do You Do Voodoo: The Real Religion Behind Zombies and Voodoo Dolls* (South Street Press, Reading, 1999).

Tyldesley J., *Tutankhamun's Curse* (Profile Books, London, 2013).

Vandenberg P., *The Forgotten Pharaoh. The Discovery of Tutankhamun* (Hodder and Stoughton, London, 1975).

Viegas J., 'Curse of the Mummies: Unearthing Ancient Corpses,' (1999, www.toxicmold.org/documents/0407.pdf).

Weigall A., 'The Malevolence of Ancient Egyptian Spirits,' in Frayling C., *The Face of Tutankhamun.* (Faber and Faber, London, 1992).

Weinstock J., 'Circumcising Dracula,' in *Journal of the Fantastic in the Arts* (Vol 12, No 1, 2001, 90–102).

Wright L., 'Post-Vampire: The Policies of Drinking Humans and Animals in "Buffy the Vampire Slayer", "Twilight" and "True Blood",' in *Journal of the Fantastic in the Arts* (Vol 25, No 2/3 (91), 2014, 347–365).

Wynne B., *Behind the Mask of Tutankhamun* (Souvenir Press, London, 1972).

Yaden, J., 'Days Gone Sold More Physical Copies Than Any Other Game in April in the UK,' PlayStation LifeStyle (2019) https://www.playstationlifestyle.net/2019/05/03/days-gone-sales-top-the-uk-charts-for-the-month-of-april/

Yasumoto T., & Kao C., 'Tetrodotoxin and the Haitian Zombie (Letter to the Editor),' in *Toxicon* (Vol 24, No 8, 1986, 747–749).

Notes

Introduction

1. Quoted in Dendle 2001, 12.

Chapter 1 – Mummies in the West

1. Dendle 2001, 14.
2. Lee 1992, 47.
3. Ikram & Dodson 1998, 64.
4. Ikram & Dodson 1998, 65.
5. Sugg 2009, 32.
6. Pringle 2001.
7. Ikram & Dodson 1998, 64.
8. Pettigrew 1834, 7.
9. Pettigrew 1834, 8.
10. Pettigrew 1834, 8.
11. Sugg 2008.
12. Ikram & Dodson 1998, 65.
13. 378.
14. Collins Jenkins 2010, 177.
15. Ikram & Dodson 1998, 65.
16. Sugg 2009, 32.
17. Pettigrew 1834, 10.
18. McCouat 2013.
19. McCouat 2013.
20. Original quote in a *Time Out* article quoted in http://www.cultofweird.com, accessed 9 September 2019.
21. McCouat, 2013.
22. Mellow 2014.
23. McCouat 2013.
24. Hunter 1978, 96.
25. Browne 1658.
26. Browne 1683.

27. Ikram & Dodson 1998, 69.
28. Pettigrew 1834, 103.
29. Ikram & Dodson 1998, 71, Pettigew 1834, xvi.
30. David & Tapp 1984.
31. Prag & Neave 1997, 49.
32. Day 2006, 135.
33. Luckhurst 2012, 63.
34. Weigall 1923, 253.
35. http://scottish-places.info/features/featurefirst9974.html Accessed 12 September 2019.
36. http://www.summum.org/again.shtml Accessed 20 October 2019.
37. Edwards 1923.
38. Day 2006, 31.
39. Shelly 1869, 45.
40. Lupton 2003, 24–5.
41. Day 2008, 3.
42. Day 2006, 47.
43. Day 2006, 47.
44. El Mahdy 1999, 130.
45. Lupton 2003, 27.
46. Brier 1996, 302.
47. 1882, 245.
48. Brier 1996, 317.
49. Haggard 1886, 208.
50. By Christian Jacq.
51. 465.
52. 2008, 510.
53. 2008, 515.
54. 1981.
55. 20.
56. 100.
57. 176.
58. Lumley 1980, 116.
59. Series 4, 2006.
60. 1993, 185–98.
61. 2008, 27–8.
62. 2008, 241.
63. 1995.
64. Section 277.
65. Section 359.
66. Day 2006, 67.

67. Brosnan 1978, 45.
68. Day 2006, 73.
69. Day 2006, 69.
70. 2006, 242–3.
71. 12.
72. 24.
73. Day 2006, 177.
74. Brier 2013, 179.
75. Brier 1996, 308.
76. Brier 2013, 179.
77. Day 2006, 89.
78. Brier 1996, 309.
79. Lupton 2003, 37.
80. Brier 1996, 299.
81. Day 2006, 83.
82. Glut 1978, 165.
83. Brier 1996, 313, & Ikram & Dodson 1998, 123.
84. Richards 2008, 374.
85. Brier 1996, 314.
86. Brier 1996, 314.
87. Day 2006, 87.
88. https://www.hollywoodreporter.com/news/alex-kurtzman-star-trek-discovery-adapting-james-comeys-tell-all-1174518 Accessed 4 September 2019.
89. http://collider.com/alex-kurtzman-the-mummy-dark-universe/#images Accessed 4 September 2019.
90. Brier 2013, 183.
91. https://www.tvguide.com/movies/the-awakening/review/101583/ Accessed 18 November 2019.
92. Glut 1978, 170.
93. Day 2006, 93.
94. LeBorg cited by Brunas el al. 1990, 434.
95. Brosnan 1978, 43.
96. Brunas et al 1990, 232.
97. Day 2006, 93.
98. Day 2006, 66.
99. Day 2006, 92.
100. Day 2006, 9.
101. Brier 2013, 180.
102. 1997, reference.
103. https://www.poemhunter.com/poem/mummy-boy/ Accessed 20 October 2019.
104. 2003, 23 episodes directed by R. La Duca.

105. Day 2006, 126.
106. 1997 by T. Bradman and M. Chatterton.
107. Mummy's Curse, Series 2, episode 5 was released on November 1 1984.
108. Day 2006, 121.
109. 2002.
110. Brier 2013, 158.
111. Brier 2013, 158.
112. http://www.themummies.com/ Accessed 20 October 2019.
113. https://herecomethemummies.com/ Accessed 20 October 2019.
114. 1997.
115. October 2007, Memories of the Tutankhamun Exhibition at the British Museum, 1972. In *The Telegraph* https://www.telegraph.co.uk/culture/3668643/Memories-of-the-Tutankhamun-Exhibition-at-the-British-Museum-1972.html Accessed 17 December 17 2019.
116. Hawass 2004, 40.
117. El Mahdy 1999, 131.
118. https://discover.ticketmaster.co.uk/special-events/tutankhamun-44306/ Accessed 18 November 2019.
119. Pettit 2019.
120. Edwards 2019.
121. James 1991, 389.
122. Vandenberg 1975, 197.
123. Vandenberg 1975, 197.
124. Day 2006, 45.
125. Day 2006, 49.
126. Weigall 1923, 236.
127. https://www.britishmuseum.org/research/collection_online/collection_object_details.aspx?objectId=117233&partId=1 Accessed 21 October 2019.
128. Weigall 1923, 236.
129. https://www.britishmuseum.org/research/collection_online/collection_object_details.aspx?objectId=117233&partId=1 Accessed 21 October 2019.
130. Day 2006, 34.
131. Lallanilla 2013.
132. Lallanilla 2013.
133. https://egyptmanchester.wordpress.com/2013/02/25/the-mystery-of-the-spinning-statuette/ Accessed 17 December 2019.
134. https://www.bbc.co.uk/news/av/uk-25034950/mystery-of-moving-egyptian-statue-is-solved Accessed 17 December 2019.
135. Weigall 1923, 233–4.
136. Shah 2018.
137. Khan 2018.

138. Day 2006, 169.
139. Day 2006, 116.
140. Day 2006, 171.
141. Kemp & Zink 2012, 22.
142. 1991 cited in Day 2006, 111.

Chapter 2 – Unwrapping the Mummy Myth

1. https://www.ucl.ac.uk/culture/projects/fake-news Accessed 7 August 2019.
2. https://www.ucl.ac.uk/culture/projects/fake-news Accessed 7 August 2019.
3. https://www.ucl.ac.uk/bentham-project/who-was-jeremy-bentham/auto-icon Accessed 7 August 2019.
4. https://www.theguardian.com/world/2016/may/09/lenin-lab-team-keeping-first-soviet-leader-embalmed-moscow Accessed 8 August 2019.
5. Hsu 2015.
6. Hsu 2015.
7. Finnis 2014.
8. Perez 2018.
9. Netflix documentary *Dark Tourist*, Episode 6. Aired in July 2018.
10. Perez 2018. Accessed 21 September 2019.
11. Herodotus 1972 ed, 160–2.
12. Mummification is described in dozens of books but good records are given in Taylor 1995 and Ikram & Dodson 1998.
13. Vandenberg 1975, 20.
14. Hawass 2004, 41.
15. Tyldesley 2013, 216.
16. Tyldesley 2013, 224.
17. El Mahdy 1999, 130.
18. Forbes 1998, 549.
19. Forbes 1998, 549.
20. Vandenberg 1975, 20.
21. http://www.griffith.ox.ac.uk/discoveringtut/ Accessed 1 November 2019.
22. Ikram & Dodson 1998, 72.
23. Hawass 2006, 170–1.
24. Hawass 2006, 171.
25. Hawass in Day 2006, 17.
26. Strudwick 2005, 217–18.
27. Weigall 1923, 233.
28. Vandenberg 1975, 22.
29. Reeves 1995, 62–3.
30. Weigall 1923, 243.
31. Vandenberg 1975, 26.

32. https://www.healthline.com/health/septicemia#symptoms Accessed 18 November 2019.
33. Hawass 2004, 38.
34. Vandenberg 1975, 27.
35. Collins & Ogilvie-Herald 2002, 88.
36. Tyldesley 2013, 227.
37. Collins & Ogilvie-Herald 2002, 89.
38. Carter & White 1923, 433–7.
39. Weigall 1923, 232.
40. 1932, 232.
41. Lupton 2003, 32.
42. Collins & Ogilvie-Herald 2002, 80.
43. Collins & Ogilvie-Herald 2002, 83.
44. Wynne 1972, 104.
45. Collins & Ogilvie-Herald 2002, 83.
46. Collins & Ogilvie-Herald 2002, 81.
47. Unpublished article quoted in James 1992, 371, Nelson 2002, 1484 & Reeves 1995, 62–3.
48. Collins & Ogilvie-Herald 2002, 91.
49. Vandenberg 1980, 158.
50. Collins & Ogilvie-Herald 2002, 85.
51. Vandenberg 1975, 50.
52. Vandenberg 1975, 53.
53. Vandenberg 1975, 58.
54. Vandenberg 1975, 46.
55. 1975, 64–7.
56. Figure taken from Kings Fund statistics.
57. Reeves 1995, 63.
58. Hoving 1978, 228.
59. Vandenberg 1975, 27.
60. Forbes 1998, 549.
61. Vandenberg 1975, 26 & Reeves 1995, 62–3.
62. Reeves 1995, 62–3.
63. Tyldesley 2013: 233.
64. Vandenberg 1975, 28.
65. Tyldesley 2013, 234.
66. Reeves 1995, 62–3.
67. Reeves 1995, 62–3.
68. Reeves 1995, 62–3.
69. Hoving 1978, 229.
70. Nelson 2002, 1482.

71. Tyldesley 2013, 240.
72. El Mahdy 1999, 130.
73. Collins & Ogilvie-Herald 2002, 92.
74. New York Morning Post, April 1923.
75. Gotthard Kramer from the University of Leipzig carried out a studied on 40 mummies.
76. Vandenberg 1975, 169–70.
77. Viegas 1999, 2.
78. Collins & Ogilvie-Herald 2002, 93.
79. Hoving 1978, 221.
80. Collins & Ogilvie-Herald 2002, 95–6.
81. Hawass 1999, 2.
82. Hawass 2004, 89.
83. Ikram & Dodson 1998, 73.
84. Vandenberg 1975, 187.
85. Vandenberg 1975, 190.
86. Hawass 2004, 121.
87. Hawass 2004, 20.
88. Hawass 2004, 72.
89. Hawaas 2004, 75.

Chapter 3 – Zombies in the Modern West

1. Collins Jenkins 2010, 10.
2. https://www.dictionary.com/browse/zombie Accessed 19 February 2019.
3. Penzler 2011, 3.
4. Seabrook 1929 in Penzler 2011, 5.
5. Seabrook 1929 in Penzler 2011, 6.
6. Penzler 2011, xi.
7. McClusky in Penzler 2011, 301.
8. McClusky in Penzler 2011, 301.
9. Howard 1951, 627.
10. https://www.boxofficemojo.com/release/rl2154530305/?landingModalImage Url=https%3A%2F%2Fm.media-amazon.com%2Fimages%2FG%2F01% 2FIMDbPro%2Fimages%2Fhome%2FwelcomeToBomojov2._ CB1571421611_.png Accessed 17 December 2019.
11. Drezner 2011, 45.
12. Drezner 2011, 50.
13. Drezner 2011, 68–9.
14. Morrissette 2014, 20.
15. 2010, 53.
16. Pulliam 2009, 50.

17. DC Comics. New York.
18. 2019 Here's the real reason why Netflix cancelled Santa Clarita Diet. Accessed 26 June 2019.
19. February 2019 https://1428elm.com/2019/01/05/karl-schaefer-interview-z-nation/ Accessed 3 March 2019.
20. Dendle 2001, 7.
21. Drezner 2011, 2.
22. Katy Harshberger of St Martin's Press Quoted in Drezner 2011, 3.
23. Drezner 2010, 36.
24. 2014, 353.
25. Dendle 2001, 2.
26. Dendle 2001, 11.
27. Dendle 2001, 4.
28. Quoted in Drezner 2011, 6.
29. 2010, 19.
30. Drezner 2011, 71.
31. Grant 2010, 24.
32. George Romero's *Night of the Living Dead* (1968).
33. Stephen King's Cell (2006).
34. The T-virus in the *Resident Evil* series and Solanum virus in Max Brooks's *World War Z* (2006), in *I am Legend* (2007) it was a result of trying to cure cancer and the Aids virus in *Zombie '90: Extreme Pestilence* in Dendle 2001, 12.
35. *I was a Teenage Zombie* and *My Boyfriend's Back,* Dendle 2001, 12.
36. Moreman 2010, 271.
37. Drezner 2011, 27.
38. Hunter 2013, 66.
39. Hunter 2013, 67.
40. Moreman 2010, 272.
41. Edwards & Brooks 2019, 29.
42. Muir 2010, 245.
43. Muir 2010, 10.
44. Drezner 2011, 4.
45. Anonymous 2009.
46. Morrissette 2014, 15.
47. Bishop 2006, 201
48. Dendle 2001, 9.
49. https://www.empireonline.com/movies/reviews/cockneys-vs-zombies-review/ Accessed 24 November 2019.
50. https://www.imdb.com/title/tt6433880/videoplayer/vi870563097?ref_=vi_nxt_ap Accessed 24 November 2019.
51. https://www.youtube.com/watch?v=hnYddpsP67U Accessed 24 November 2019.

52. Russell 2014, 300.
53. Drezner 2011, 23.
54. Dendle 2001, 11.
55. Moreman 2010, 265.
56. Quoted in Moreman 2010, 269.
57. Drezner 2011, 5.
58. Drezner 2011, 30.
59. Anonymous, 2009.
60. Grant 2010, 26.
61. Drezner 2011, 23.
62. Quoted in Drezner 2011, 28.
63. Dendle 2001, 4.
64. Peter Jackson's *Dead Alive* (2002), Romero's *Dawn of the Dead* (1978), *Survival of the Dead* (2010) and the television series *The Walking Dead* (Series 2).
65. Pielak & Cohen 2014, 45.
66. 2010, 145.
67. Russell 2014, 349–50.
68. https://beta.theglobeandmail.com/arts/film/zombie-film-les-affames-echoes-quebecs-culturalfears/article36676802/. Accesses 17 December 2019.
69. Russell 2014, 306.
70. Russell 2014, 306.
71. Russell 2014, 302.
72. Russell 2014, 294.
73. Russell 2014, 294.
74. https://www.amazon.co.uk/Plaid-Hat-Games-PH1000-Crossroads/dp/B00HFKITJC/ref=sr_1_1?ie=UTF8&qid=1529257711&sr=8-1&keywords=dead+of+winter+board+game Accessed 17 June 2019.
75. https://www.popularmechanics.com/culture/gaming/g28723252/zombie-games/?slide=1 Accessed 24 November 2019.
76. https://www.popularmechanics.com/culture/gaming/g28723252/zombie-games/?slide=3 Accessed 24 November 2019.
77. Yaden 2019.
78. https://www.ea.com/en-gb/games/plants-vs-zombies/plants-vs-zombies-battle-for-neighborville Accessed 24 November 2019.
79. Peake 2010, 66.
80. https://www.ukrunningevents.co.uk/inflatable-5k-zombie-run-peterborough Accessed 10 February 2019.
81. Chatfield 2012.
82. https://play.google.com/store/apps/details?id=com.sixtostart.zombiesrunclient&hl=en_GB Accessed 23 February 2019.

83. Chatfield 2012.
84. https://play.google.com/store/apps/details?id=com.sixtostart. zombies5ktraining&hl=en_GB Accessed 23 February 2019.
85. http://zombieexperiences.co.uk/ Accessed 10 February 2019.
86. http://zombieexperiences.co.uk/zombie-for-a-day/ Accessed 10 February 2019.
87. https://www.zombieuprising.co.uk/ Accessed 10 February 2019.
88. https://www.zombiepaintball.co.uk/ Accessed 10 February 2019.
89. Cook 2013, 55.
90. https://www.theguardian.com/world/2013/feb/12/zombie-apocalypse-newsflash-montana-tv Accessed 21 December 2019.
91. http://zombiesurance.com/insurance-plans/ Accessed 5 May 2019.
92. Drezner 2010, 37.
93. Pielak & Cohen 2014, 45.
94. https://www.cdc.gov/cpr/zombie/index.htm Accessed 17 December 2019.
95. Cook 2013, 54.
96. Drezner 2010, 37.

Chapter 4 – Identifying Zombie X

1. McAlister 2012, 459.
2. Collins Jenkins 2010, 241.
3. Collins Jenkins 2010 242.
4. Davis 1985, 41.
5. Moreman 2010, 266.
6. Moreman 2010, 268.
7. Dendle 2001, 13.
8. Turlington 1999, 2.
9. Métraux 1972, 323.
10. Turlington 1999, 17.
11. Turlington 1999, 23.
12. Métraux 1972, 332.
13. Métraux 1972, 326.
14. McAlister 2002, 3.
15. Moreman 2010, 266.
16. McAlister 2002, 107.
17. Moreman, 2010, 264.
18. Efthimious & Gandhi 2007, 7.
19. Moreman 2010, 267.
20. Moreman 2010, 268.
21. Métraux 1972, 283.
22. Littlewood & Douyon 1997, 1094.

23. Littlewood & Douyon 1997, 1094.
24. Métraux 1972, 282.
25. Métraux A. 1972, 283.
26. Littlewood & Douyon 1997, 1094.
27. Métraux 1972, 281.
28. Littlewood & Douyon 1997, 1096.
29. Moreman 2010, 267.
30. Littlewood & Douyon 1997, 1096.
31. Métraux 1972, 275.
32. Métraux 1972, 327.
33. Métraux 1972, 280.
34. Métraux 1972, 279.
35. Niehaus 2005, 199.
36. Niehaus 2005, 192.
37. Geschiere 1997, 193.
38. Niehaus 2005, 195–6.
39. Niehaus 2005, 201.
40. Niehaus 2005, 202–3.
41. Niehaus 2005, 195.
42. Niehaus 2005, 198.
43. Littlewood & Douyon 1997, 1095.
44. Efthimiou &Gandhi 2007, 8.
45. Littlewood & Douyon 1997, 1095.
46. Littlewood & Douyon 1997, 1096.
47. In his 1983 article Davis identifies him using the pseudonym Louis Ozias and yet in *Serpent and the Rainbow* he is identified as Clairius Narcisse.
48. Davis 1983, 88 & Davis 1985, 108.
49. Davis 1985, 116.
50. Davis 1983, 94.
51. Davis 1985, 62.
52. Davis 1983, 88.
53. Littlewood & Douyon 1997, 1096.
54. Littlewood & Douyon 1997, 1094.
55. Turlington 1999, 44–5.
56. Davis 1985, 26.
57. Littlewood & Douyon 1997, 1094.
58. McAlister 2002, 103.
59. Turlington 1999, 40–1.
60. Turlington 1999, 48.
61. McAlister 2012, 462.
62. MsAlister 2012, 463.

63. McAlister 2012, 463.
64. Métraux 1972, 282.
65. Davis 1983, 100.
66. Davis 1983, 101.
67. Anderson 1988, 121.
68. Moreman 2010, 267.
69. Yasumoto & Kao 1986, 747.
70. Davis 1985, 37.
71. Davis 1985, 39.
72. Davis 1985, 40.
73. Efthimiou & Gandhi 2007, 8.
74. Davis 1983, 96.
75. Anderson 1988, 123.
76. Efthimiou & Gandhi 2007, 9.
77. Efthimiou & Gandhi 2007,9
78. Anderson 1988, 124 & Davis 1985.
79. Davis 1985, 216.
80. This book was also made into a movie of the same title, directed by Wes Craven in 1987.
81. Davis 1985, 93–6.
82. Davis 1985, 100.
83. Yasumoto & Kao 1986, 747–8 & Littlewood & Douyon 1997, 1094.
84. Davis 1983, 89.
85. Davis 1983, 89.
86. Davis 1985, 115.
87. Davis 1983, 97.
88. Anderson 1988, 121.
89. Littlewood & Douyon 1997, 1094.
90. Métraux 1972, 282.
91. Yasumoto & Kao 1986, 748.
92. Anderson 1988, 122.
93. Yasumoto & Kao 1986, 748.
94. Anderson 1988, 123.
95. Anderson 1988, 122.
96. Anderson 1988, 121.
97. Littlewood & Douyon 1997, 1096.
98. Moreman 2010, 267.
99. Davis 1983, 95.
100. Davis 1983, 95. This is also retold in more detail in Davis 1985, 124.
101. Anderson 1988, 122.
102. Davis 1983, 98.

103. Davis 1985, 127.
104. Davis 1985, 128.
105. Anderson 1988, 123.
106. Yasumoto & Kao 1986, 747.
107. Yasumoto & Kao 1986, 748.
108. Yasumoto & Kao 1986, 747.
109. Davis 1985, 99.
110. Davis 1985, 126.
111. Davis 1983, 96.
112. Davis 1983, 96.
113. Davis 1985, 123.
114. Davis 1983, 85.
115. Hurston 1981, 206 quoted in Davis 1983, 86.
116. Davis 1983, 93.
117. Davis 1983, 87.
118. Drezner 2011, 15.
119. Davis 1985, 139–40.
120. Davis 1985, 223
121. McAlister 2002, 3.
122. McAlister 2002, 98.
123. McAlister 2002, 110.
124. McAlister 2002, 105.
125. McAlister 2002, 100.
126. McAlister 2002, 100.
127. McAlister 2002, 105.
128. McAlister 2002, 104.
129. McAlister 2002, 106.
130. Moreman 2010, 263.
131. Moreman 2010, 265.

Chapter 5 – Vampires in Western Media

1. Bartlett and Idriceanu 2005, 1.
2. Quoted in Auerbach 1995, 102.
3. Collins Jenkins 2010, 10.
4. Collins Jenkins 2010, 162.
5. Auerbach 1995, 5.
6. Quoted in Collins Jenkins 2010, 38.
7. Collins Jenkins 2010, 48.
8. Collins Jenkins 2010, 93.
9. Collins Jenkins 2010, 69.
10. Bartlett & Idriceanu 2005, 31.
11. Bartlett & Idriceanu 2005, 31.

12. Collins Jenkins 2010, 83.
13. Bartlett & Idriceanu 2005, 33.
14. Bartlett & Idriceanu 2005, 40.
15. Sutherland 2017, 17.
16. Collins Jenkins 2010, 9.
17. Moreman 2010, 270.
18. Grady 1996, 226.
19. Grady 1996, 228–9.
20. Collins Jenkins 2010, 13.
21. Grady 1996, 227.
22. Grady 1996, 233.
23. 22.
24. 1989, 302.
25. Bramesco 2019, 179.
26. Bartlett & Idriceanu 2005, 44.
27. Weinstock 2001, 91.
28. Bartlett & Idriceanu 2005, 187.
29. Bartlett & Idriceanu 2005, 172.
30. Bartlett & Idriceanu 2005, 140.
31. Bramesco 2019, 184.
32. Bramesco 2019, 184.
33. Bramesco 2019, 187.
34. Wright 2014, 353.
35. Mukjerjea 2011, 11.
36. Wright 2014, 354.
37. Drezner 2010, 36.
38. Mukherjea 2011, 7.
39. Bramesco 2019, 175.
40. "Review: 'Abraham Lincoln' a murky, joyless hunt in *The Kansas City Star*. https://www.playstationlifestyle.net/2019/05/03/days-gone-sales-top-the-uk-charts-for-the-month-of-april/ Accessed 12 December 2019.
41. 285.
42. Collins Jenkins 2010, 13.
43. Hollinger 1993, 8–9.
44. 2014, 358.
45. Levine 2007, 174.
46. Bartlett & Idriceanu 2005, 46.
47. https://in.ign.com/what-we-do-in-the-shadows-tv-series/133640/preview/10-things-you-need-to-know-about-fxs-what-we-do-in-the-shadows-tv-show Accessed 10 December 2019.
48. Sutherland 2017, 56.
49. Weinstock 2001, 95.

50. Sutherland 2017, 56.
51. Sutherland 2017, 59.
52. Collins Jenkins 2010, 51.
53. Bramesco 2019, 17.
54. Sutherland 2017, 57.
55. Quoted in Bramesco 2019, 19.
56. Bramesco 2019, 22.
57. Sutherland 2017, 55.
58. Collins Jenkins 2010, 14.
59. Bramesco 2019, 25.
60. Bremsco 2019, 28.
61. Bremsco 2019, 29.
62. Collins Jenkins 2010, 52.
63. Auerbach 1995, 113.
64. Collins Jenkins 2010, 53.
65. Auerbach 1995, 117.
66. 2008, 340.
67. Bremsco 2019, 39.
68. Bremsco 2019, 42.
69. Bartlett & Iriceanu 2005, 147.
70. Auerbach 1995, 109–10.
71. Collins Jenkins 2010, 53.
72. Bartlett & Idriceanu 2005, 41.
73. Collins Jenkins 2010, 54.
74. Bremsco 2019, 40.
75. Bremsco, 2019, 40.
76 1995, 114.
77. Sutherland 2017, 22.
78. Holte 1999, 113.
79. Holte 1999, 111.
80. Bramesco 2019 46.
81. Bramesco 2019, 47.
82. Auerbach 1995, 123.
83. Bartlett & Idriceanu 2005, 169.
84. Holte 1999, 111.
85. Bramesco 2019, 47.
86. Bramesco 2019, 97.
87. Bramesco 2019, 98.
88. Bramesco 2019, 101.
89. Bramesco 2019, 102.
90. Bramesco 2019, 104.

91. https://slate.com/culture/2018/02/wesley-snipes-on-blade-black-panther-and-black-culture-in-hollywood.html Accessed 9 March 2019.
92. Bramesco 2019, 106.
93. Bramesco 2019, 107.
94. Bramesco 2019, 138.
95. Bramesco 2019, 57.
96. Bramesco 2019, 58.
97. Bramesco, 2019, 63.
98. Auerbach 1995, 107.
99. Bramesco 2019, 117.
100. Bramesco 2019, 115.
101. Collins Jenkins 2010, 13.
102. Bramesco 2019, 205.
103. Bramesco 2019, 207.
104. Bramesco, 2019, 207.
105. Bramesco 2019, 209.
106 2019, 211.
107. Bramesco 2019, 199.
108. Hallab 2009, 2.

Chapter 6 – The Modern Vampire

1. https://www.biography.com/crime-figure/peter-kurten Accessed 9 June 2019.
2. Quoted in Bartlett & Iriceanu 2005, 59.
3. Lessing et al. 1993, 47.
4. Collins Jenkins 2010, 24.
5. Collins Jenkins, 2010, 24.
6. http://highgatevampire.blogspot.com/2008/12/why-do-foxes-die.html Accessed 20 March 2019.
7. Ham and High, February 27 1970.
8. Mr Manchester quoted in Ham and High February 27 1970.
9. Ham and High, February 27 1970.
10. Hampstead and Highgate Express, Friday March 6 1970.
11. The *Daily Express*, 19 August 1970.
12. http://highgatevampire.blogspot.com/2008/12/why-do-foxes-die.html Accessed 20 March 2019.
13. Camden New Journal, September 10 1998, 19.
14. Collins Jenkins 2010, 2010.
15. http://dawwih.blogspot.com/2012/01/interesting-find.html and https://www.theparacast.com/darkmatters/borisdocument.pdf 7. Accessed 20 March 2019.
16. Quoted in Collins Jenkins 2010, 26.
17. Collins Jenkins 2010, 27.

18. Written by Marc Mullen, Ham and High, September 2 2005.
19. https://www.hamhigh.co.uk/news/heritage/infamous-highgate-ghosts-paranormal-investigator-s-book-explores-village-s-haunted-history-1-3838191 Accessed 17 December 2019.
20. http://www.davidfarrant.org/the-highgate-vampire/ Accessed 8 November 2019.
21. Cohen, 1996, viii.
22. Goddu 1999, 128.
23. Keyworth 2002, 256.
24. Frater Resurgam 1892.
25. Laycock 2010, 4.
26. Laycock 2010, 7.
27. Laycock 2010, 9.
28. Laycock 2010, 18.
29. Laycock 2010, 8.
30. Goddu 1999, 126.
31. http://www.suscitatio.com/research/definitions.html Accessed 26 March 2019.
32. Laycock 2010, 6.
33. Sutherland 2017, 184.
34. Richard Von Krafft-Ebing quoted in Collins Jenkins 2010, 29.
35. Laycock 2010, 7.
36. Collins Jenkins 2010: 28.
37. Goddu 1999, 125.
38. Collins Jenkins 2010, 28.
39. Collins Jenkins 2010, 33.
40. Laycock 2010, 12.
41. Laycock 2010, 16.
42. Gutman 2003, 9.
43. Bak 2007, xxiii note 3 & Goddu, 1999, 125.
44. http://templeofthevampire.com/history Accessed 9 December 2019.
45. http://templeofthevampire.com/mission Accessed 9 December 2019.
46. http://templeofthevampire.com/creed Accessed 9 December 2019.
47. http://templeofthevampire.com/join-us/membership Accessed 9 December 2019.

Chapter 7 – Uncovering the Vampire Myth

1. Auerbach 1995, 5.
2. Auerbach 1995, 1.
3. Collins Jenkins 2010, 61.
4. Collins Jenkins 2010, 58.
5. Auerbach 1995, 133.

Notes

6. Collins Jenkins 2010, 59.
7. Sutherland 2017, 76.
8. Sutherland 2017, 7–8.
9. Collins Jenkins 2010, 64.
10. Sutherland 2017, 11.
11. Pietro Martyre Anghiera writing in 1510 quoted in Collins Jenkins 2010, 55.
12. Collins Jenkins 2010, 56.
13. Sutherland 2017, 73.
14. 2002 https://www.independent.co.uk/news/world/europe/dracula-land-theme-park-bites-the-dust-182065.html Accessed 7 May 2019.
15. Book 11.
16. Bartlett & Idriceanu 2005, 5.
17. Collins Jenkins 2010, 200.
18. Collins Jenkins 2010, 206.
19. Bane 2017, 92.
20. Bartlett & Idriceanu 2005, 5.
21. Bane 2017, 129.
22. Bartlett & Idriceanu 2005, 7.
23. Bartlett & Idriceanu 2005,181.
24. Collins Jenkins 2010, 234.
25. Collins Jenkins 2010, 238
26. Collins Jenkins 2010, 239.
27. Bartlett & Idriceanu 2005, 4.
28. Collins Jenkins 2010, 230–31.
29. Bane 2017, 91.
30. Bartlett & Idriceanu 2005, 4.
31. Bartlett & Idriceanu 2005,188.
32. Collins Jenkins 2010, 224.
33. Collins Jenkins 2010, 222.
34. Sutherland 2017, 89.
35. http://astro121.com/index.php/durga-saptashati-in-english/durga-saptashati-chapter-8 Accessed 8 December 2019.
36. Bartlett & Iriceanu 2005, 153.
37. Collins Jenkins 2010, 169.
38. Collins Jenkins 2010, 97.
39. Bartlett and Iriceanu 2005, 139.
40. Collins Jenkins 2010, 15.
41. Bartlett and Idriceanu 2005, 23.
42. Collins Jenkins 2010, 126.
43. Collins Jenkins 2010, 104–6.

44. Collins 2011 2 and Collins Jenkins 2010, 112.
45. Collins 2011, 1.
46. Collins 2011, 2.
47. Collins 2011, 2.
48. Collins Jenkins 2010, 107.
49. Quoted in Bartlett and Idriceanu 2005, 18.
50. Collins Jenkins 2010, 179.
51. Collins Jenkins 2010, 181.
52. Collins 2011, 1.
53. Collins 2011, 1.
54. Collins 2011, 1.
55. Bartlett & Idriceanu 2005, 2.
56. Melrose 2018, 27.
57. Collins Jenkins 2010, 125–7.
58. Daley 2019.
59. Day & Alexander 2014.
60. https://www.bbc.co.uk/news/world-europe-18334106 Accessed 8 December 2019
61. Bartlett and Idriceanu 2005, 167.
62. Bartlett and Idriceanu 2005, 179.
63. Blake 2013.
64. Collins Jenkins 2010, 112.
65. Collins Jenkins 2010, 136.
66. Collins Jenkins 2010, 137.
67. Collins Jenkins 2010, 138.
68. Collins Jenkins 2010, 145.
69. Collins Jenkins 2010, 141.
70. Collins Jenkins 2010, 154.
71. Bailey 2002.
72. Gardela & Kajkowski 2013, 780–796.
73. http://www.slavia.org/fieldschool.php?go=drawsko_vampires Accessed 8 December 2019.
74. Collins Jenkins 2010, 150.
75. Collins 2011.
76. Collins Jenkins 2010, 153.
77. Collins 2011, 2.
78. Collins 2011, 2.
79. Quoted in Bartlett and Iriceano 2005, 20.
80. Bartlett & Idriceanu 2005, 25.
81. Collins 2011, 2.
82. Bartlett & Idiceanu 2005, 24.
83. Barber 1988, 29–30.

84. 1988.
85. Collins Jenkins 2010, 167.
86. Bartlett & Idriceanu 2005, 184.
87. Bartlett & Idriceanu 2005, 26.
88. Bartlett & Idriceanu 2005, 184.
89. Epstein and Robinson 2012, 237.
90. Bartlett & Idriceanu 2005, 186.
91. Epstein and Robinson 2012, 232.
92. Epstein and Robinson 2012, 233.
93. Weinstock 2001, 93.
94. Hay 1961, 311–12.
95. Epstein and Robinson 2012, 241–2.
96. Epstein and Robinson 2012, 241–2.
97. Epstein and Robinson 2012, 234.
98. Epstein and Robinson 2012, 242.
99. Epstein and Robinson 2012, 244.
100. Collins Jenkins 2010, 22.
101. Quoted in Collins Jenkins 2010, 115.
102. Sejdinović 2008, 14.
103. Sejdinović 2008,14.
104. Efthimiou & Gandi 2007, 5–7
105. Sejdinović 2008, 14.

Index